New Developments in Self Psychology Practice

New Developments in Self Psychology Practice

Peter Buirski and Amanda Kottler

JASON ARONSON
Lanham • Boulder • New York • Toronto • Plymouth, UK

Published in the United States of America
by Jason Aronson
An imprint of Rowman & Littlefield Publishers, Inc.

A wholly owned subsidiary of
The Rowman & Littlefield Publishing Group, Inc.
4501 Forbes Boulevard, Suite 200, Lanham, Maryland 20706
www.rowmanlittlefield.com

Estover Road
Plymouth PL6 7PY
United Kingdom

British Library Cataloguing in Publication Information Available

Library of Congress Cataloging-in-Publication Data

Buirski, Peter.
New developments in self psychology practice / Peter Buirski and Amanda Kottler.
p. ; cm.
Includes bibliographical references.
ISBN-13: 978-0-7657-0435-1 (cloth : alk. paper)
ISBN-10: 0-7657-0435-8 (cloth : alk. paper)
ISBN-13: 978-0-7657-0436-8 (pbk. : alk. paper)
ISBN-10: 0-7657-0436-6 (pbk. : alk. paper)
1. Self psychology. I. Kottler, Amanda. II. Title.
[DNLM: 1. Self Psychology. 2. Psychoanalysis—methods. 3. Psychoanalytic Therapy—methods. WM 460.5.E3 B932n 2007]

RC489.S43B77 2007
616.89'17—dc22 2007016799

Printed in the United States of America

∞™ The paper used in this publication meets the minimum requirements of American National Standard for Information Sciences—Permanence of Paper for Printed Library Materials, ANSI/NISO Z39.48-1992.

Contents

Acknowledgments

We would like to express our appreciation and gratitude to the contributing authors, whose gracious participation has made this book possible. Most of the contributors wrote original papers for this volume. Some papers had already been written but the authors generously agreed to share them with us. The chapters are of uniformly high quality and this volume derives its strength from the knowledge, experience, and clinical expertise of these original thinkers.

Peter Buirski would like to thank Tracie Kruse, who has been a benevolent enabler and who, in countless ways, helped me keep focused and on task. Having grown up in South Africa, I am attuned to the accent, which drew me to Amanda and the other South African participants at an International Conference on the Psychology of the Self. From there, my relationship and participation with the Cape Town Psychoanalytic Self Psychology Group grew. I'm grateful to the group for the opportunities they have provided for the sharing of ideas and for their friendship. I also want to express my deep appreciation to my wife, Cathy Krown Buirski, whose encouragement, clinical wisdom, and selfobject relatedness continue to enrich my life and work.

Amanda Kottler would like to acknowledge her patients, past and present, from whom she has learned a great deal, and Mireille Landman for being there in so many ways for so long. Thanks also to all those who have shared her discovery of, and passion for self psychology, particularly Ellen Lewinberg, Doris Brothers, Sally Swartz, Cathy Aaron, and Noleen Seris, for their willing participation in many fruitful hours discussing contemporary self psychology. Also, for planting the seed for this volume, thanks to the lively and energetic Cape Town Psychoanalytic Self Psychology Group for asking the question some years back, Where is self psychology now?, and to those who attempted to answer this question: Howard Bacal, Martin Gossman, Alan Kindler, Frank Lachman, Joe Lichtenberg, Paul Ornstein, Estelle Shane, Dennis Shelby, Max Suchorov, Judy Teicholz, Marian Tolpin, and Ernest Wolf. Thanks to Peter, who ran with and implemented the idea of the book, and to Penny Murdock, who supportively and lovingly shared the frustrations and joys of bringing it to fruition. And finally, this book is in memory of Ann Levett.

Introduction

Peter Buirski and Amanda Kottler

We should always be a little ashamed of the way we were five years ago.

—McGuire in Malin, 2004, p. 287

It has been thirty-six years since the publication of Kohut's monumental book, *The Analysis of the Self*, in 1971, and in this period the world inhabited by self psychology has been experiencing important theoretical and clinical developments. We decided that the time is right for a volume that draws on many of these developments. Over these years, self psychology, as Kohut first conceived it, has undergone quite an evolution. In fact, where other theories of mind can tend to stagnate and resist innovations that transcend the founding figure, Kohut's self psychology continues to grow in depth, complexity, and richness. One of the great strengths of the self psychology movement has been the openness of succeeding generations to push the theoretical envelope, to entertain, examine, and integrate new understandings and perspectives.

One measure of the progressive, forward-looking nature of the self psychology movement can be seen in the name chosen for the volume that summarizes the work of the annual conference and the developments in the field: *Progress in Self Psychology*. Looking back, it is fascinating to note that in his preface to the first volume of *Progress in Self Psychology*, Goldberg made some prophetic observations about self psychology's future. These included thoughts that self psychology "may never be invited into the house of orthodox psychoanalysis," that "no one wants an arrogant newcomer to take over" and that self psychology might perhaps always be "branded as an intruder" because "it does not know it's proper place" (Goldberg, 1985, p.

ix). At that time, he predicted three possible fates for self psychology, that is, either continued isolation as alien, gradual assimilation into main body of psychoanalysis, or domination of all analysis.

In the twenty-two years that have followed, while some may wonder whether the uniqueness of Kohut's revolutionary vision might be absorbed within the larger world of relational psychoanalysis, self psychology has most certainly not continued in isolation as an alien perspective. Nor has it been gradually assimilated into or dominated other psychoanalytic theories. It has had a vibrant and exciting evolution that has significantly influenced and expanded the range of psychoanalytic thinking.

In the course of its history, self psychology has gone through a number of shifts, while still keeping as a central core of the theory the developmental importance of selfobject relatedness and the primacy of subjective experience. In this process Goldberg's (1985) comment that "keeping the invader at bay changes the invaded" (p. ix) has proved to be astute and predictive. Self psychology has most certainly been significant in changing the "invaded."

These changes have not been without struggle. In 1995, ten years after Goldberg made his predictions, the eighteenth annual self psychology conference was entitled "Cross Currents in Self Psychology," signaling tension in the field over the multiple foci that today constitute what would be broadly referred to as contemporary self psychology. The nineteenth conference in 1996, entitled "Reconceptualizing the Clinical Exchange," attempted to directly address these tensions in panel IV, entitled "Integration: Is it possible? Is it desirable?," chaired by Alan Kindler. The panelists were Paul Ornstein, from a "classical" perspective, Bob Stolorow, from an intersubjective systems perspective, and Joe Lichtenberg, through the lenses of what he, Frank Lachman, and Jim Fossaghe were developing as motivational systems theory.

In 1997, at the twentieth annual conference held in Chicago, there was a heated discussion following a case presentation by Alan Kindler in the final panel that elicited references to the plurality of new theoretical and clinical perspectives. Kindler (1997) reports that James Fisch, the chair "began the proceedings by evoking a . . . metaphor of a house." He insisted that the three discussants (Fosshage, Ornstein, and Stolorow) "have lots in common . . . must get along fine together . . . [and] share the same toys." He added that there was "no need for fighting" (p. 1). Taking up the idea of the self psychology house, a struggle began as to who would occupy the central wing and in fact, how many wings were needed. At the time, there were three occupants: 1) classical/traditional (Ornstein); 2) intersubjectivity (Stolorow); and 3) motivational theory (Lichtenberg). Ornstein challenged the other two occupants to show that either "could offer a richer analytic experience without the aid of the concept of the selfobject transferences" (in

Kindler, 1997, p. 2). He added that if he were to occupy the same house, he would want to be in the central wing with "adequate sound proofing" as he felt his neighbors were too noisy. He also added, perhaps preempting the shift that has clearly taken place in this area, that he struggled with the "rather bland, non-specific notion of 'attachment needs'" (Kindler, 1997, p. 1). Stolorow drew attention to what he described as "the multidimensional (intersubjectivity theory) versus the unidimensional (selfobject theory) perspectives" (Kindler, 1997, p. 2) and said at the time that "intersubjectivity and motivational systems theory reside at a higher level of abstraction than does selfobject theory" (Kindler, 1997, p. 2). In her discussion, Tolpin said that she "could never live with any of the panelists, and would insist on a house of her own" (Kindler, 1997, p. 2) while developing the idea of the forward edge.

By the next conference, in San Diego in 1998, (the twenty-first) entitled "Self Psychology: Integrating and Evolving," the house had expanded. The same three residents occupied their same wings, with the same theories, but more residents had moved in. There were now wings for optimal responsiveness (which has become known as specificity theory), articulated by Howard Bacal, and for dynamic dyadic systems approach, put forward by Morton Shane and Estelle Shane.

As of the publication of this book, the self psychology house has been able to accommodate many diverse perspectives as reflected in the multiplicity of theoretical voices welcomed at the annual conference. Among the new voices are relational self psychology, nonlinear dynamic systems /complexity/chaos, evolutionary/biology, developmental systems theory, attachment theory, and the views of the Boston Change Process Study Group, as well as the contributions of cognitive neuroscience. As Coburn (2006) has observed, "Contemporary self psychology, as a perspective is increasingly distributed across a variety of creative, innovative points of view. . . . At this point, it cannot be found exactly anywhere. This is healthy evolution" (p. 3). One significant indicator of the multiplicity of voices heard spoken in the self psychology house is the transformation of the annual book series, *Progress in Self Psychology*, into a quarterly scholarly journal, the *International Journal of Psychoanalytic Self Psychology*. As Coburn (2006), the journal editor, has observed in his introduction to the new journal,

> Perhaps something we have all picked up from postmodernism, or vice versa, is an appreciation for abandoning the search for a grand narrative in favor of knowing that each of our voices does count in some way toward not what is right exactly, but toward helping shape what emerges next in our intellectual community. Our field seems to have become less an "irritable reaching after fact and reason" (Keats, 1817, p. 492) a grasping for a grand narrative and more an engagement in a lively conversation. I think that's progress in self psychology. (p. 2)

This present volume is concerned with giving a hearing to the multiplicity of voices speaking under the expanded canopy of self psychology. With this in mind, we have divided this volume into four parts, each using many of the furnishings that have been used in the older "wings" of the house, but also making use of and expanding on recent contributions to the broad domain of self psychology.

The first section concerns the assimilation of new theoretical contributions into the world of contemporary self psychology. Here we have included a comprehensive article by William Coburn on complexity theory. According to Coburn, psychoanalytic complexity emphasizes the complexity of human experiencing, stresses the role of context in constructing emotional experience, and by focusing on the patterning of emotional experiencing, offers fresh perspectives on human development. Shelley Doctors, looking at working with adults, adolescents, and couples, contributes a wide-ranging chapter that draws on the research and insights of attachment theory to enrich both the theory and clinical practice of self psychology. Concluding this section is a chapter by Dorienne Sorter and Jaqueline Gotthold focusing on the concept of "implicit relational knowing" and its contribution to enriching clinical understanding and practice. They offer important thoughts about how analysts working with both children and adults from a self psychological framework can integrate the insights and understandings of the Boston Change Process Study Group. These contributions are being assimilated into the self psychology lexicon and are enriching many of the wings in the self psychology house.

The second section is concerned with the applications of contemporary self psychological thinking to the treatment of children. Working with children has not thus far received the same attention as that of adults in the self psychology literature and the two chapters included here redress that deficit. Rosalind Kindler goes a long way toward correcting the neglect of child treatment from the perspective of self psychology. Her chapter provides rich clinical examples that illustrate the therapeutic effectiveness of self psychological relatedness in working with children. In her chapter, Amy Joelson applies the concept of self- and interactive regulation, which grew out of infant research but has more commonly been applied to adult treatment (Beebe & Lachmann, 2002) to child treatment. In an especially interesting case illustration, Joelson describes how she engaged the child and her mother in an examination of the regulatory process.

The third section examines the application of contemporary self psychological thinking to various therapeutic modalities that have often been neglected in the literature. Carla Leone has written an extensive examination of the application of contemporary self psychological and intersubjective systems thinking to family treatment. Her innovative work contributes new insights and understandings to the challenges presented when multiple subjectivities are all interacting together. Similarly, Arthur Gray addresses the contemporary self psychological approach to group treatment, another subject not well covered in the literature. Like working with families, the multiple subjectivities interacting in groups present challenges to the group therapist and the theory. The topic of the self psychological approach to the supervisory process is discussed by Judith Teicholz. She labels her approach "radical" because her model of supervision has strong parallels to self psychological treatment, in that it views the subjective experience of the supervisee as central to the process. Each of the chapters in this section includes generous and engaging clinical material.

The final section considers the contributions of contemporary self psychology to the ongoing therapeutic process. Shame has been written about extensively by Kohut, as well as Morrison and others. Here, Andrew Morrison expands on his self psychological understanding of the role of shame in instigating secrets. He makes interesting use of the characters in Philip Roth's novel *The Human Stain* to bring his points to life. Ellen Shumsky and Donna Orange address the topic of enactments, raising important questions about the utility of the concept and its applications in treatment. Max Sucharov uses a dialogic approach to examine traumatic experiences in which the survivor is left frozen in a nondialogic space without the capacity to generate meaning. With reference to the writings of Kafka and Kohut, Sucharov draws attention to the role of the analyst as a dialogic other in the effort to help the survivor make sense of a world that exists outside the boundaries of ordinary discourse. Amanda Kottler draws on postmodern ideas and Kohut's underdeveloped concept of twinship to examine the subject of difference within both the therapeutic dyad and the therapeutic community. Finally, Philip Ringstrom introduces the notion of improvisation into the therapeutic process. Improvisation is spontaneous, unplanned, playful, and provocative and can open up the therapeutic process to multiple fresh possibilities.

The chapters in this volume overflow with clinical wisdom and theoretical understandings. We hope that you, like Alan Kindler in 1996, can "move around [the self psychology] house with ease, visiting with each tenant, trying out their theories for relative comfort and suitability" (Kindler, 1997, p. 1). In doing so, we hope that you will find reading the book evocative and informative.

REFERENCES

Beebe, B., & Lachmann, F. (2002). *Infant research and adult treatment: Co-constructing interactions.* Hillsdale, NJ: Analytic Press.

Coburn, W. (2006). Introduction: self psychology after Kohut—One theory or too many? *International Journal of Psychoanalytic Self Psychology, 1,* 1–4.

Goldberg, A. (1985). Preface. *Progress in self psychology: Volume 1.* Hillsdale, NJ: Analytic Press.
Kindler, R. (1997). A biased view: Report on the final panel of the twentieth self psychology conference. www.selfpsychology.org/1997conf/RKindlerReport.htm.
Kohut, H. (1971). *Analysis of the self.* New York: International Universities Press.
Malin, A. (2004). Personal reflections: Fifty years of psychoanalysis. *Progress in self psychology: Transformations in self psychology, vol. 20.* Hillsdale, NJ: Analytic Press.

I

THEORETICAL CONTRIBUTIONS

1

Psychoanalytic Complexity: Pouring New Wine Directly into One's Mouth[1]

William J. Coburn, PhD, PsyD[2]

> All things (including those that come at last to triumph mightily) are at their beginnings so small and faint in outline that one cannot easily convince oneself that from them will grow matters of great moment.
>
> —Matteo Ricci et al. (1622)

> Ceaselessly the philosopher finds himself obliged to reinspect and redefine the most well-grounded notions, to create new ones, with new words to designate them, to undertake a true reform . . .
>
> —Merleau-Ponty (1968)

> How wonderful life is while you're in the world.
>
> —Bernie Taupin (1969)

Often new lenses are disconcerting when you first try them on. The world seems too blurry, too clear, too distorted, or perhaps too frightening. For many of us, trying on a complexity theory lens, clinically or otherwise, is no exception. For me, it has been exciting, mind-altering, sometimes perplexing, sometimes unnerving. But, on balance, I have found this burgeoning perspective, particularly as applied to psychoanalytic psychotherapy, remarkably useful clinically, if profoundly challenging to our usual and familiar ideas about development, transference, countertransference, defense, trauma, and therapeutic action. In this chapter, I will share with you a perspective that is relatively new to our field, one variously and sometimes imprecisely described as nonlinear dynamic systems theory, catastrophe theory, chaos theory, complex adaptive systems theory, self-organized systems theory, and so forth.[3] I prefer the designation of *complexity theory*, for reasons that will become evident. Sometimes I think of it as *perplexity theory.* I will also propose a few specific inferences and advantages I draw from such an all-encompassing framework, one that could not possibly be fully elaborated within the confines of a single chapter, or even a book for that matter.

This chapter does not aim to plunge the reader into the roiling and complex waters of complexity theory as it is understood by molecular biologists or astrophysicists, but instead stands as an invitation to psychotherapists and psychoanalysts to consider more seriously the richness and utility of a multidisciplinary sensibility that has revolutionized our assumptions about the emergence and transformation of emotional life.[4] At its base, I believe the therapeutic advantage of a psychoanalytic complexity sensibility emerges certainly not in technical prescriptions or developmental expectations but through the therapist's essential attitude and presuppositions about the patient and the therapeutic relationship. This chapter hopes to illustrate some of these attitudes and how they might determine a therapeutic outcome.

Psychoanalytic complexity provides us a richer paradigm of experiential worlds and the means by which we can convey a deeper respect for the complexity of human experiencing. Second, it helps us understand more deeply the highly contextualized nature of emotional experience and the meanings we attribute to it. And third, it revolutionizes concepts of human development, so-called psychopathology, and the process of change. In many respects, it is the logical extension of, and arguably the conceptual suprastructure for, psychoanalytic paradigms such as intersubjective systems theory (Stolorow, Atwood, & Orange, 2002), specificity theory (Bacal, 2006), and other more radical contextualist perspectives—those that center on an appreciation of the role of context in understanding experience and meaning and of the unpredictability and fluidity of emotional development. And, not surprisingly, complexity theory directly opposes the philosophical and practical assumptions of many, more traditional approaches in psychotherapy and psychoanalysis today.[5] It has increasingly infiltrated many of our more familiar paradigms, including self psychology. At its postmodern foundation lies a profound alteration in our more customary worldviews, one that invariably challenges our essential and perhaps more comfortable presumptions about truth, reality, the therapeutic relationship, and, more broadly, the origins of emotional experience and emotional meaning. Psychoanalytic complexity is concerned with the emergence and patterning of emotional experience from the self-organization and cooperation of many parts, with the conditions necessary to produce adaptive change, and with the process of making meaning out of apparent randomness. Henri Atlan (1984), in the field of biophysics, comments that "randomness is a kind of order, if it can be made meaningful; the task of making meaning out of randomness is what self-organization is all about" (p. 110).

THEORY PREFERENCE AND THE INCOMMENSURABILITY OF PARADIGMS

Before I address in detail what, exactly, complexity theory is, including its theoretical and clinical value, I wish to discuss briefly the issue of theory preference and the problem of the incommensurability of paradigms (Kuhn, 1962). When new ideas emerge on the horizon, they often, though not always, are couched in a deferential language. We witnessed this when Heinz Kohut began the psychoanalytic odyssey that would become self psychology. His seminal 1959 paper reflected not just the nascence of his revolutionary ideas about empathy, the primacy of lived experience, and the relationship between mode of observation and theory, but also a deep respect for the work of Sigmund Freud and the accompanying qualifiers that Kohut and colleagues were not exactly saying anything new. Later he comments that he was pouring "new wine into old bottles" (1984, p. 114), redefining the meanings and implications of a variety of traditional concepts (e.g., defense and resistance), while often maintaining familiar psychoanalytic terminology. He would refer to the foundational compatibility of his perspective with that of his *in absentia* mentor through invoking (and stretching the meaning of) the principle of complementarity (drawing from Bohr and Mottelson [1957])—meaning, for Kohut, that apparently disparate ideas can live together, can complement one another, in useful ways.

It wasn't until later in his career, the late 1970s, that Kohut more explicitly distanced himself from this view by asserting that his psychology of the self was *more* essential, *more* foundational, to the science of a pure psychology. Self psychology could account for a broader range of human experiencing and its developmental vicissitudes. Freudian theory became increasingly subsumed under this new perspective, or it was, in instances, opposed and rejected outright. The evolution of Kohut's understanding of the Oedipal experience and its vicissitudes reflects a clear instance of this. This is all to highlight that the paradigm of complexity theory, as rigorously as we might desire its integration into and synthesis of more familiar ideas, stands as ultimately incommensurable with the more traditional perspectives that adhere to objectivist, positivistic assumptions about truth and reality (including psychic reality).

Kohut and colleagues (1984) asserted that the "elimination of [psychoanalytic] terms, then, is crucial only when they contribute to the perpetuation of substantive conceptual errors" (p. 115). Psychoanalytic complexity does not argue for the elimination of self psychological or in general psychoanalytic terms, but rather, first and foremost, fosters an insistence on distinguishing between those that refer to lived, subjective experience, on the one hand, and those that refer to theoretical explanation, on the other hand. This distinction obviates the invariable confusion that arises when the language of experience (phenomenology) and the language of theory (explanation) are conflated. The use of the term "self" provides a glaring example: viewed through a psychoanalytic complexity theory lens, it denotes a *dimension of experience* and *not* a theoretical explanation for such an experience. This is consonant with intersubjective systems theory.

Psychoanalytic complexity does sport an unusual and impressive array of terms that are organized around theoretical explanation, not phenomenological description. A complex system, for instance, is not one in which one *feels* complex or chaotic, or *experiences* the world as chaotic, though indeed we sometimes do. Rather, it is one that is loosely guided by principles of self-organization, nonlinearity, emergence, unpredictability, and transformation. Psychoanalytic complexity does not describe or prescribe how self and other should *feel* but instead aims at understanding and explaining the emergence and vicissitudes of our experiences and the meanings we attribute to them. Thus, psychoanalytic complexity does not necessarily call for the elimination of our familiar languages and terminology; rather, it helps determine whether a specific term (e.g., selfobject) references a *dimension of experience* or a *theoretical construct*; it necessitates a greater specification of meaning of the terms we do choose to use.

We can no longer think of our world, including our experiential world, as containing disparate, unrelated parts. Not only is the whole greater than the sum of its parts, as systems theorists are wont to say, but the parts—*all* the parts, *without exception*—are inextricably intertwined and ceaselessly embedded in a larger context. Psychoanalytic complexity reflects a worldview fundamentally incompatible with presumptions we may have had about separateness of self and other, the individuality of personal minds, the solid, static nature of truth, human emotional development as epigenetic and teleological, the rule-based and design-based nature of the universe, and so forth.

PSYCHOANALYTIC COMPLEXITY AND THE RESPONSIBILITY FOR INDIVIDUAL EXPERIENCE

Complexity theory is relentlessly multidisciplinary and interdisciplinary. No one invented it. One of its essential tenets, that of self-organization, is demonstrated in its very nature—how it developed and continues to be elaborated by highly innovative thinkers from a variety of disciplines such as mathematics (Poincaré, et al., 1900; Thom, 1974), physics (Bak, 1996), biology (Waddington, 1966; Kauffman, 1995), and meteorology (Lorenz, 1993), just to name a few. In psychology, psychotherapy, and psychoanalysis, an increasing number of theorists are finding complexity theory compelling and useful (Galatzer-Levy, 1978; Sashin and Callahan, 1990; Moran, 1991; Spruiell, 1993; Thelen & Smith, 1994; Stolorow, 1997; Shane, Shane, & Gales, 1997; Palombo, 1999; Miller, 1999; Lichtenberg, Lachmann, & Fosshage, 1992; Varela, Thompson, & Rosch, 1991; Scharff, 2000; Beebe and Lachmann, 2001; Trop, Burke, & Trop, 2002; Charles, 2002; Magid, 2002; Bacal and Herzog, 2003; Ghent, 2002; Harris, 2005; Shane & Coburn, 2002; Seligman, 2005; Thelen, 2005; Weisel-Barth, 2006; Pickles, 2006; Sucharov, 2002; Sander, 2002; Coburn, 2002; Piers, 2005; Bonn, 2006; Steinberg, 2006; Orange, 2006; DuBois, 2005); each seems to have his or her own take on it. And it is, to paraphrase Kauffman (1995), its own shortest description. It cannot be reduced down to something simpler than its surface appearance. And its surface appearance, to be sure, is not exactly simple, but certainly elegant, provocative, and unsettling.

And such is the case with experiential worlds; they are their own shortest description and are relentlessly irreducible. They are not reducible to self and object representations, or selfobject experiences. In fact, complexity theory eschews the notion of intrapsychic representation (not to be confused with the action of consciously representing something via symbol),[6] as well as the notion that emotional experience and meaning emanate from an inside, intrapsychic space concerned with the management of representations of an *objective, external* world. Orange (2001), from an intersubjective systems perspective, makes this vital distinction when she delineates the implications of Cartesian (and ultimately, clinical) assumptions about the potential source of emotional experience as necessarily lying either *inside* of one's psyche, and hence subject to the distorting effects of one's subjectivity, or *outside* in the real world, the ultimate and true arbiter of truth and reality. She rightly states, "this dichotomy is particularly dangerous in clinical work. Patients and analysts can become endlessly entangled in trying to determine where a particular reality lies, inside or outside, or where responsibility for a reaction, for a life pattern, or for some interpersonal disaster lies" (p. 291). Instead of experiencing the "outside world" and then "internalizing" it, "representing" it, and arranging it in some manner for future adaptational use, sources of emotional experience instead are more usefully pictured as *distributed* throughout multiple relational systems. In that sense, in the *explanatory* sense, no one authors or owns their emotional experience. In the phenomenological sense—that is, how we actually experience things—we may very well feel that we are the authors and owners of our experiential worlds, though not necessarily (see Atwood, Orange, & Stolorow, 2002). To paraphrase Merleau-Ponty (1968), we can no longer say, this is mine and this is yours.

An advantage of psychoanalytic complexity, to extend Orange's perspective, is not just the purging of the inside/outside dichotomy in trying to account for the sources of emotional experience and their corresponding meanings, but also the elimination of the assumption that such experience and meaning can be attributed solely to one's history, to one's current (*inside*) mental state, or to one's immediate (*outside* world) environment. This false trifurcation, another clinical quagmire in which we are drawn into the hunt for the "true and real" sources of an individual's experience (i.e., Is it your history or your present, is it me or is it you, that accounts for your experience?), dissolves when we realize that at no moment can the source of an individual's experiential world be relegated to any one of the three, and, furthermore, at no point can we ever draw an actual line (*explanatorily* speaking) between any of the three (i.e., this comes from your past, this comes from now, this comes from your environment, etc.). From a psychoanalytic complexity perspective, that would be akin to holding a single bird responsible for the flight trajectory of the entire flock. And locating the lines of demarcation between each of the three would be tantamount to claiming to know simultaneously the position and momentum of a subatomic particle at a given moment in time.[7] Working with this explanatory assumption has profound clinical implications, which I address below.

COMPLEXITY AND COMPLEX ADAPTIVE SYSTEMS

Descriptively, complexity theory and the concept of complexity can be approached from a variety of angles, can be talked about in different ways. Indeed, each author who has written about it seems to highlight one or a few specific aspects of the idea in the course of applying it to psychotherapy and psychoanalysis, and there are many facets from which to choose. Some highlight the importance of initial conditions, some the property of self-organization, some focus on the concept of self-criticality (or a particular system's propensity toward hovering around the "tipping point"), some underscore the dynamism, fluidity, and unpredictability of a system, others the role of perturbation in altering the trajectory of a system, and still others the characteristic of emergence and the idea that nonlinear systems are not rule-driven or design-driven. There are many other descriptive aspects of the theory that theorists draw on as useful metaphors for understanding human experiencing and therapeutic action.

Briefly, let's look at the nature of a *complex adaptive system* with which the characteristic *complexity* is often associated. Previously I described the essential characteristics of such a system (2002). Complex systems comprise a large number of elements; this is a necessary but not sufficient condition of a complex system. The elements must interact in a dynamic fashion; this interaction does not have to be physical, but often simply involves a transference of information from one component to another. Such interactions need to be *rich*, that is, any constituent in the system influences and is influenced by many others. Interactions are *nonlinear*: "Nonlinearity . . . guarantees that small causes can have large results, and vice versa" (p. 4). Nonlinear interactions often have a short range. For example, one person has an immediate effect upon another when in close physical proximity; one neuron directly impacts its immediate neighbor only. But such interactions also have a wide-ranging influence on components more distally located. Furthermore, elements in a complex system share the quality of *recurrency*, that is, the "effect of any activity can feed back onto itself, sometimes directly, sometimes after a number of intervening stages" (p. 4).

Complex systems are thought to be *open*, in the sense described by Thelen and Smith (1994); this means that they are capable of interacting with their environment. As Cilliers (1998) states, "Instead of being a characteristic of the [complex] system itself, the scope of the system is usually determined by the purpose of the *description* of the system, and is thus often influenced by the position of the observer" (p. 4). *Framing* is involved as a way of defining specific systems as a system, subsystem, or suprasystem; any element potentially can be considered a system in its own right, as can any system be understood as an element, depending upon the perspective of the observer. Framing does not apply to a closed system, which is necessarily "framed" or concretely delimited by its own boundaries. Complex, open systems, as mentioned earlier, function under conditions far from equilibrium; in the context of human life, "equilibrium is another word for death" (p. 4). Moreover, a complex system has a history: Cilliers (1998) states, "Not only do they evolve through time, but their past is co-responsible for their present behaviour" (p. 4). This reveals the limitations of, for example, naïve constructivist or "here and now" perspectives in which psychological phenomena arising between two people are believed to have been "constructed" in the moment, quite apart and somehow insulated from both individual's relational histories.

Finally, the nature of a complex system is such that "[e]ach element in the system is ignorant of the behaviour of the system as a whole, it responds only to information that is available to it locally. . . . If each element 'knew' what was happening to the system as a whole, all of the complexity would have to be present *in that element*" (Cilliers, 1998, p. 4–5). For Cilliers, the notion of each element "knowing" the status of the system as a whole constitutes either a "physical impossibility" or a leap to metaphysical descriptions (Coburn, 2002).[8]

Given this cursory view of complex adaptive systems, let's turn to the concept of complexity. Complexity has been defined in a variety of ways—two that are particularly interesting to me. Generally it refers to a quality or characteristic of a gathering of constituents (e.g., biological cells, people, governments) that are related in some way (a system). It is assumed tha such a system—an *open* system—is capable of 1) absorbing and using an influx of energy, 2) behaving autocatalytically (self-generative and self-transformative), and 3) adapting to its environment to insure its survival and increased efficiency. There are many other characteristics of an open system (as discussed above), but given these essentials, complexity refers to the relative state of an open system such that it is more or less poised for and capable of change. This is what complexity theorists mean by "poised on the edge of chaos," "self-criticality," or "the tipping point." Thus complexity can be understood as the state of a system in which there is enough fluidity and randomness (or "chaos") to allow for innovation, novelty, and change, on the one hand, and in which there is enough order and apparent structure to allow for the sustaining and continuance of those changes that do occur, on the other hand. Understood in this way, a system can be said to be *more complex* the more centrally it is poised between the two ends of this spectrum, between order and chaos. A system that is less complex may have too much order, such that transformation is exceedingly slow and/or negligible, or it may exhibit too much randomness, such that change is too rapid, wild, and/or not sustainable. This is one way to talk about complexity.

Keep in mind also that when we speak of people and complex systems in the context of psychotherapy and psychoanalysis, it is tempting to slide into thinking of an individual person as *the* complex system under investigation and as that which we aim to change. Yes, an individual person can be thought of as a complex system, but in the dynamic, contextualist world of human relationships, in which each individual is understood as a coadaptive, mutually and reciprocally organizing component of a larger complex adaptive system, it is essential that we think of the system under investigation as, *at the least,* the therapeutic dyad. Previously I commented that "people alone do not change, systems change—and on multiple levels . . . apparent change is reiterated or *distributed* throughout all systems and their respective constituents, just as those constituents *support* or *are responsible* for those changes in the first place" (2002). This is only an initial, skeletal view, given that each individual belonging to a specific dyad has enumerable other relational connections, past, present, and future, and that these vast, interconnected experiential worlds, so many we can never know them, are what is responsible ultimately for the emergence of an individual's emotional experience. To extend Martin Buber's assertion that without the Thou, there is no I, we might say that without the greater relational system, there is no self.

The second definition of complexity, one that I am especially drawn to, refers to the property of *incompressibility*—a term originating in mathematics and information theory (see Chaitin, 1990). Mathematicians and information theorists are often interested in the degree to which a series of numbers, concepts, or processes can be reduced down or *compressed* for ease of representation. This can be accomplished with algorithms, using "algorithmic compression" (Taylor, 2001), a series of logical statements (e.g., a computer program) that aims to describe (and perhaps give directions about) something in a shorter space than that which the thing occupies. A concrete example is the compression of a hundred numbers (say, the number 8) into a convenient three number packet (i.e., the number 800). This is easier than writing out the number 8 one hundred times. A high degree of compressibility means a low degree of complexity, and vice versa. A string of a hundred randomly chosen numbers has an extremely high degree of incompressibility; it cannot be reduced down to an algorithmic statement (such as "multiply 8 times 100") that is shorter than itself. In fact, if we think in terms of *representing* something, we would say that it (the string of a hundred randomly chosen numbers) is its own shortest description; it can only be *represented* by itself. And such is the case with human beings, their experiential worlds, and their corresponding evolving emotional meanings. Extending this definition of complexity (i.e., as incompressibility) to human experiencing and the meaning-making process has enormous implications for how we understand (and treat, in both senses of the term) people. In this light, and given that we humans comprise complex systems, we can no longer understand our experiential worlds as compressible or *representable*, for instance, as drives or drive derivatives, a set of object relations, a configuration of neurobiological connections, a self structure with missing parts, or any other form of abbreviation of what is human. (The notion of diagnostically categorizing as a means of saying something substantial or meaningful about a person is anathema to a complexity theory sensibility.) The Freudian caricature of compressibility would be the reduction of an individual to the vicissitudes of his Oedipus complex.

As complex adaptive systems in our own right, however, each human being (and the larger system of which we are all a part) is quite capable of identifying, compressing, and storing important information about emotional experience (one of the hallmarks of a complex adaptive system, as distinct from an ocean wave or a weather pattern). Metaphorically we can think of this type of compression of emotional knowledge as the "implicit relational knowing" to which Stern, et al. (1998) and others refer, but keep in mind this type of knowing does not, of course, originate in a relational vacuum and likewise never emerges in one. Implicit relational knowing is always a product and property of past, present, and imagined future relating with others (Loewald, 1972; Stern, 2004) and can be understood as distributed throughout larger interpenetrating relational systems. In this sense, relational expectancies are "compressed," metaphorically speaking, more as relational *potentialities* that are *completed* and brought to life as a product and property of context. An aspect of the relational context (e.g., the analyst), here, is not understood simply as a provocateur of an individual-mind template but as a system constituent that *completes* a potentiality.[9] You can't hold one individual responsible for the sometimes-excruciating repetitiveness of relational expectancies and patterns that emerge in the context of a dyad.

Experiential worlds have a high degree of complexity, or incompressibility, not in that they are completely random or chaotic—that would suggest no identifiable shape, sense, or meaning to be had—but in the sense that they can be envisioned as potentially represented, or witnessed, through the medium of the felt experience of the analysis and therapy process itself, as it unfolds, *over time.* In other words, we might say that experiential worlds are algorithmically "described," *over time,* via their gradual unfolding and investigating in the context of the therapeutic relationship. They cannot be captured in one statement, or one picture, but must be understood as an unfolding, emerging, and relentlessly evolving landscape that is insistently and continually shaped by one's history, one's current state, and one's environment—the lines between which, as I stated before, are forever indeterminate. In this sense, our lived lives, *over time,* are their own shortest description. Therapeutic action, in part, arises from the explicit, articulated appreciation of this assumption. This is consonant with Orange's invocation of the concept of fallibilism (1995), which, for me, underscores the necessity of not only holding our theories lightly but also holding lightly the emergent and accrued *truths and realities* that coalesce within the analytic dyad from one day to the next, or from one year to the next. And thus, experiential worlds are changing as they are emerging, and emerging as they are changing. As complexity theorists are wont to say, "the rules of the game change as a result of the play."

COMPLEXITY AND CLINICAL WORK

The work of complexity is perhaps no more profoundly evident than in witnessing the unexpected, abrupt, sometimes startling shifts in human experiencing and relating that flow from the psychoanalytic relationship. This was certainly the case with Jack, who had been struggling with an excruciatingly impoverished self-esteem and propensity toward social withdrawal and isolation. His mother had forgotten him in his outdoor crib during a rainstorm in the Colorado Mountains when he was quite young, and it wasn't until he was substantially soaked that his mother, inside and well into mahjong and martinis, realized her negligence and retrieved him. He was either forgettable or grotesque. Two and half years into a three-times-per-week analytic therapy, something hit both of us like a lightning bolt, though I think I was more startled than he was. Jack, then forty-five years of age and divorced for a little longer than I had known him, had been contemplating Internet dating and the likelihood of a future relationship (or the lack thereof). As much as he yearned for closeness and intimacy, he knew that his potential female companion would discover fairly quickly upon meeting him, or seeing a picture of him, his true beast-like nature. He would refer to himself as a creature somehow akin to Frankenstein's monster. These references of his of course conjured for me the sense of loneliness, isolation, rage, self-hatred, and longing of the monster that Mary Shelley so beautifully portrayed in her novel, and Jack would occasionally perk up from his otherwise rather depressed and subdued affect—an ambiance that often left us both feeling doomed—when I made these references. Yes, he would say, that's *just* how a woman would experience me if I showed her what I look like. Despite my intermittent interpretations that perhaps there was something of how he felt about himself (monster-like, unapproachable, repellant) that had infiltrated and colored how he experienced his physical appearance, he remained irrevocably ensconced in this conviction. Through his eyes, he actually looked like a monster of sorts, not so hideous that people would shriek and run away, but awful enough that he would remain either gross and unwanted, or, at best, quite forgettable in the eyes and minds of others. Rarely would he look in the mirror. Photos generally had been out of the question.

These dimensions of his self experience intensified when he finally dared to have his picture taken by a colleague who said he knew something about photography. He had reached an impasse at the Internet dating threshold when he discovered that he really did need to post a photograph—something predictably he was loathe to do, given his beast-like nature. He was tormented as he anxiously awaited his colleague's digital photos of him. Not surprisingly, Jack hated the photos immediately, and I silently assumed that that was the end of his dating attempts. There is nothing quite like having a painful emotional conviction confirmed. What emerged, though, much to the surprise of both of us, was his exclamation that he thought *he* could have taken *much* better photos and that, in fact, he had rushed to purchase his own camera, took his own photographs of himself, and promptly posted them on his Internet dating website, all within the span of a day! He was quite proud not only of his accomplishment but also of how he appeared in the photos. Where was the monster I had been treating for two and a half years?

There are many ways of speculating about and understanding what had emerged here, but doubtless the forgettable though now memorable Jack, in concert with his sometimes pessimistic and frustrated analyst, had undergone a transformation in their combined experiential worlds. This was the therapeutic equivalent of the Belousov-Zhabotinsky reaction in chemistry—the sudden and unexpected emergence of strikingly discernable patterns and color in an otherwise clear, stable, and predictable chemical solution—in which the appearance of predictability and linearity collapses, revealing the actual fluidity and unpredictability of a soft-assembled attractor state.[10] It was also a striking illustration of the *autocatalytic* behavior of a complex adaptive system, in that the relational system itself, comprised of Jack, myself, and a variety of other essential people (past, present, and imagined future) in his life, self-organized in a manner that produced its own agent of change. In that sense, it would be impossible to claim what, exactly, that agent is, given the multitude of variables at play. In molecular biology, we might be able to identify, in retrospect, the specific catalyst implicated in the transformation of cell structure, but it is not so easily identifiable when considering the medium of emotional experience.

An especially illuminating instance of this occurred early on in treatment. Heretofore I had experienced Jack as affectively constricted, highly measured, and self-consciously methodical in his choice of words: he was playing to an audience about to castigate him for the slightest sign of emotional life or creativity. He had his ducks in line, a complete, predesigned card catalog of responses to any questions aimed at encouraging reflection or experimentation. I was the unforgiving job interviewer for whom he had better supply the right answers, lest I forget him or find him monstrous: the vaguer the inquiry, the more anxious he got.

During one particularly anxious exchange—anxious for both of us—in which he was speaking about his having little sense of space in his life in which to be creative vis-à-vis his interest in painting and building things, I had asked him if he had ideas about having come to feel so constricted and prohibited. As he reached for one of his standard-issue, card catalog responses, I noticed he hesitated, his eyes momentarily glancing at the floor, as if he were stumped in an otherwise fast-paced game of Jeopardy with millions at stake. Despite the anxiety, however, I also ever-so-briefly noticed a gentle, soft, and enlivened expression wash over his face. I felt I had had a nanosecond glimpse into an alive, accessible, and creative Jack, the Jack, it seemed, I had been waiting around for, though I didn't realize I had been waiting for anything at all really. As he quickly recovered from his shameful stumble, not having located the particular card he was searching for but having found another, I quickly interrupted him and asked if he had just noticed something. He said, uh, no, not really; what did I mean? I shared with him my nanosecond experience, describing him as particularly accessible, alive, unsure, and perplexed. He smiled with recognition, saying that that was exactly how he never allowed himself to be. He then began to hyperventilate and sob, rather violently actually, occasionally glancing at me through his tears. As he bolted from his chair, apparently preparing for a lightening-speed exit, I said that perhaps it might be worth our while to consider staying. As he sat back down, I said that I thought we had hit upon something quite meaningful, something that perhaps he was after, and maybe we could speak about it. He seemed moved by this, his eyes widening. What followed was an intense and elaborate exchange about the terror and shame he felt at the emergence of such a sudden reaction—one that he couldn't possibly understand. No card catalog for this. I told him that I thought that I may have acknowledged something special about him—a moment of Jack with no prefabricated responses, no filter to stave off my inevitable attack or abandonment, a moment of real life and emotional presence—and that this perhaps was quite moving for him, and subsequently quite terrifying as well. He agreed. I think this was pivotal in sending our relationship off into new directions, a trajectory shift in our system in which we were now coadapting to each other in different ways. This shift was punctuated by, or perhaps reflected in, our final exchange as he walked out the door: Jack said, "Gosh, I'm sorry about all that—I feel like I should apologize"—to which I quipped, "That's all right; I'll let it go, but just this once." When he smirked at me, I again witnessed a sense of surprise and aliveness wash across his face. In the brief span of that momentary exchange, we witnessed the rapidly alternating and competing attractor states[11] that increasingly emerged over the course of treatment and that came to characterize our relationship.[12]

A complexity perspective might suggest here that I had provided a *perturbation*, with its expectable anxiety, to an otherwise *repetitive system*, momentarily transforming it into a *transformative system* (Lachmann, 2000). However, it is important to underscore that we cannot claim, exactly, what the perturbation was. Who, really, is perturbing whom in the psychotherapeutic system? The perturbation here was an emergent property of the system, as I believe it always is, not something I *did to* Jack that can account for therapeutic action in this instance. Jack was perturbing the system as much as I was, via his brief, unexpected, and enlivening "stumble." His brief and sudden doorknob slide into shame and apology was as perturbing to me and to our system as my rejoinder to him was to him and to our system.

Here are instances of using psychoanalytic complexity to understand and describe more richly and usefully the appearance of change, its sense of emergence and unpredictability, the system's autocatalytic tendencies, the benefit of living near "the tipping point," the acknowledgment that the responsibility for emotional experience and emotional meaning are distributed throughout the system's constituents, but in what manner can we say that the theory gets *applied* in clinical work?[13] What might that look like? How, really, is this theory useful?

First, a psychoanalytic complexity perspective doubtless embraces the relatively tried and true assumptions about therapeutic action in psychoanalysis. This would include the investigation, understanding, and articulation of the patient's intersubjectively derived organizing themes that contour the patient's experiential world; the patient and analyst's self/other configurations that are brought to light, engaged, and experientially lived out in the context of the therapeutic relationship; the patient's selfobject needs and the inevitable disruption and repair cycles that permeate the therapeutic relationships; and the patient/analyst implicit (nonsymbolized and non–verbal symbolized) relating that may never come to light but that often determines the ultimate trajectory of their combined experiential worlds. Choose any part of the elephant you want. But second, its mutative effects largely rest in the attitude(s) it imbues in and/or requires of the analyst, and in the attitude(s) at which the therapeutic dyad ultimately arrives.

From one standpoint, one could certainly argue for a simple *disconfirmation theory*, that what "transformed" Jack generally was my disconfirming his relational expectancies, indeed my not finding in Jack the shame-ridden, forgettable monster he felt himself to be. Or, alternatively, one could argue for an *integration theory*, that what was mutative for Jack was our combined willingness to bring to life, in the context of our relationship, a host of previously sequestered and/or dissociated self-other configurations, on both our parts. One could also argue (if one must) a simple *insight theory* alone, such that our investigation and understanding of the origins of his experience led him to grasp how he came to experience himself and the world in the way that he did. And one could argue a *deficit theory*, that Jack's deficits in his self structure were essentially repaired, or *filled in*, as a result of an attuned, selfobject presence capable of withstanding the inevitable negative reactions to disillusionment and disruption in the course of treatment. Or not.

Instead, I believe what proved useful, at least in this particular treatment, were the systemically derived attitudes about emotional experience and emotional meaning at which Jack and I arrived during the course of our relationship. Over time, we began to be able to identify what it was like to live in a system that was too ordered or too random. We learned, through investigation and experimentation, that Jack's emotional experience was an emergent property of our combined histories, our combined current emotional states, and our combined relational environments, that it was dynamic and didn't emanate from an isolated, subjective mental apparatus (nor from simply being left out in the rain).

Fundamentally, I think psychoanalytic complexity is useful in how it alters our essential assumptions about and attitudes toward people, which, in turn, transforms how we interact and relate with others (with our patients). It conveys a human sensibility that says, essentially, you are not responsible for your emotional experience, even though ultimately you might want to *take* responsibility—at times, *must* take responsibility—for it. It says that you did not create yourself, though you may wish to have—and *can* have—a say in what you think, feel, and do next. It proclaims that your emotional development continues on a nonlinear path, such that who or how you will become is unpredictable, potentially fluid, and emergent as a function of numerous other components of a larger coadaptive, complex system. It also says that you are not a category into which you may be assigned for defining, labeling, treating, and conforming. And it asserts that people *can* change, and we can never really know a priori what might bring about that change, or if change ultimately will ever take place.

More broadly, therapeutic action can be conceptualized as the process of investigating and understanding the experiential world of the patient, including especially so the specific felt sources and origins of that world. As we know, this necessitates the similar investigation and understanding of the *analyst's* experiential world as well, including the measured articulation of aspects of it in the context of the therapeutic dialogue. It also includes an ongoing appreciation for (and hopefully, articulation of) the implicit, nonsymbolized dimension of experiencing and relational learning that so powerfully and involuntarily contributes to the coadaptive, mutually organizing aspect of the relational world the two individuals coconstitute together. (By now it must be evident that to investigate the experiential world of the patient means also to explore and attempt to account for the greater context of which each of us is an integral constituent.) It also requires a continual sensitivity to and articulation of what is felt to be most affectively enlivening, self-expansive, self-integrative, and deepening of interpersonal contact. This is not news from the standpoint of a variety of psychoanalytic paradigms (see the work of Strachey, Stern, Winnicott, Kohut, Loewald, Gill, Stolorow, Atwood, & Orange, E. Shane, Mitchell, Aron, and Davies, just to name a few). But, more specifically, it is the *expansion* of the dyad's collaboratively arrived-at and felt awareness of these sources and origins—past, present, and imagined future—that plays an important role in the perturbation of the relational system such that the stage is set for the emergence of new, more useful patterns of experience. Importantly, these *more useful patterns of experience* should not be construed to mean *more reality-based, more objective*, or *more true*. Ultimately, these newer *experiential contours* are sustainable because they are reiterated, *over time*, and supported by and throughout by the interpenetrating relational systems in the patient's life.

What might this *expansion*, so central to therapeutic action, look like? And why is this expansion so pivotal to change? Let's return to Jack for a moment. For years, Jack's (and my) interest rested in not just *how* he experienced himself (heretofore forgettable and monstrous), his history (heretofore awful), and his environment (heretofore sometimes benign, sometimes dangerous) but also *why*. And for a long period, Jack was confirmed in the view that it was the emotional absence of his parents that could account for this. He pictured himself as unable to extricate himself from his historical milieu in which his sense of self remained shackled to *forgettable* and/or *monstrous* and in which his sense of the world remained obstinately *critical* and/or *abandoning*. As we explored these particular dimensions of his experience in the context of our relationship (in which these self-other configurations had intermittently come to life), what became increasingly evident to both of us was not just that our relationship was an evocation of and conduit for his relational history, effectively "drawing blood" and bringing to life the "ghosts of the past" (Mitchell, 2000), but also that we were both constituting his experiences, in *real time* and *over time*, such that we remained as integral a part of what was responsible for his experiential world as was his relational history *and* his sense of his relational future.[14]

The therapeutic relationship is not solely a means of "working something through" or "resolving conflict" but can more profitably be understood as being an essential source of an individual's experiential world, right along with one's history, and one's current state of mind. Therapeutically, we wish not to arrive and remain at conclusions about our emotional life together that are devoid of this sense of the ongoing complexity of its origins and sources, that have been stripped of its sense of context, past, present, and future, but rather to expand our awareness of the ongoing, continually shifting, multiple sources that contribute to such experience.

Alternatively stated, if *sustainable* change in perceptions, meanings, and ways of relating is more likely to occur within a complex adaptive system that is situated more or less in between order and chaos, or "poised at the edge of chaos," then it is desirable for both patient and analyst to be able to sense and acknowledge when their relationship is headed or is situated in that direction (i.e., away from too much order or too much randomness). This is accomplished through dialogue, yes, but also via the essential spirit that underlies the psychoanalytic relationship—the wish to be curious, to inquire, and to understand. Mitchell (1993) asks, "What is going on around here?" to which I would add, "And could things be different?"

It is not solely the therapist's willingness and capacity to tolerate the expectable painful affect—the inevitable doom and darkness that sometimes permeates our therapeutic work—but also the therapist's implicitly conveyed sense that there is more to the patient, and to us, than what we know thus far; there is more to us than our history, our enactments, and our current, arrived-at conclusions.

REFERENCES

Atlan, H. (1984). Disorder, complexity, and meaning. In Paisley Livingston (Ed.), *Disorder and Order*. Saratoga, CA: Anma Libri.

Atwood, G. E., Orange, D. M., & Stolorow, R. D. (2002). Shattered worlds/psychotic states: A post-Cartesian view of the experience of personal annihilation. *Psychoanalytic Psychology, 19*, 281–306.

Bacal, H., & Herzog, B. (2003). Specificity theory and optimal responsiveness: An outline. *Psychoanalytic Psychology, 20*, 635–648.

Bacal, H. (2006). Specificity theory: Conceptualizing a personal and professional quest for therapeutic possibility. *International Journal of Psychoanalytic Self Psychology, 1*(2).

Bak, P. (1996). *How nature works: The science of self-organized criticality.* New York: Copernicus.

Beebe, B., & Lachmann, F. M. (2001). *Infant research and adult treatment: A dyadic systems approach.* Hillsdale, NJ: Analytic Press.

Bohr, A., & Mottelson, B. R. (1957). *Collective and individual-particle aspects of nuclear structure.* København: I kommission hos Munksgaard.

Bonn, E. (2005). Turbulent contextualism: Bearing complexity toward change. Prepublished paper.

Chaitin, G. (1990). *Information, randomness, and incompleteness.* Singapore: World Scientific Co.

Cilliers, P. (1998). *Complexity and postmodernism: Understanding complex systems.* London, New York: Routledge.

Charles, M. (2002). *Patterns: Building blocks of experience.* Hillsdale, NJ: Analytic Press.

Coburn, W. J. (2002). A world of systems: The role of systemic patterns of experience in the therapeutic process. *Psychoanalytic Inquiry, 22*(5): 655–677.

DuBois, P. (2003). Perturbing a dynamic order: Dynamic systems theory and clinical application. Prepublished paper.

Galatzer-Levy, R. (1978). Qualitative change from quantitative change: Mathematical catastrophe theory in relation to psychoanalysis. *J Am Psychoanal Assoc, 26*, 921–935.

Gell-Mann, M. (1994). *The quark and the jaguar: Adventures in the simple and the complex.* New York: W. H. Freeman.

Ghent, E. (2002). Wish, need, drive. *Psychoanalytic Dialogues, 12*, 763–808.

Harris, A. (2005). *Gender as soft assembly.* Hillsdale, NJ: Analytic Press.

Kauffman, S. A. (1995). *At home in the universe: The search for laws of self-organization and complexity.* New York: Oxford University Press.

Kohut, H. A. (1959). Introspection, empathy, and psychoanalysis—An examination of the relationship between mode of observation and theory. *Journal of the American Psychoanalytic Association, 7*, 459–483.

Kohut, H., (1984). *How does analysis cure?* Ed. A. Goldberg. Chicago: University of Chicago Press.

Kuhn, T. S. (1962). *The structure of scientific revolutions.* Chicago: University of Chicago Press.

Lachmann, F. M. (2000). *Transforming aggression: Psychotherapy with the difficult-to-treat patient.* Northvale, NJ: Jason Aronson.

Lichtenberg, J. D., Lachmann, F. M., & Fosshage, J. L. (1992). *Self and motivational systems: Toward a theory of psychoanalytic technique.* Hillsdale, NJ: Analytic Press.

Loewald, H. W. (1972). The experience of time. *Psychoanalytic Study of the Child, 27,* 401–410.
Lorenz, E. N. (1993). *The essence of chaos.* Seattle: University of Washington Press.
Magid, B. (2002). *Ordinary mind: Exploring the common ground of Zen and psychotherapy.* Boston: Wisdom.
Merleau-Ponty, M. (1968). *The visible and the invisible.* Evanston, IL: Northwestern University Press.
Moran, M. G. (1991). Chaos theory and psychoanalysis: The fluidic nature of the mind. *Int Review of Psycho-Analysis, 18,* 211–221.
Miller, M. L. (1999). Chaos, complexity and psychoanalysis. *Psychoanalytic Psychology, 16,* 355–379.
Mitchell, S. (1993). *Hope and dread in psychoanalysis.* New York: Basic Books.
Mitchell, S. (2000). *Relationality: From attachment to intersubjectivity.* Hillsdale, NJ: Analytic Press.
Orange, D. M. (2001). From Cartesian minds to experiential worlds in psychoanalysis. *Psychoanalytic Psychology, 18,* 287–302.
Orange, D. (2003). Why language matters to psychoanalysis. *Psychoanalytic Dialogues, 13*(1), 77–103.
Orange, D. M. (2006). For whom the bell tolls: Context, complexity, and compassion in psychoanalysis. *International Journal of Psychoanalytic Self Psychology, 1*(1), 5–22.
Palombo, S. R. (1999). *The emergent ego: Complexity and coevolution in the psychoanalytic process.* Madison, CT: International Universities Press.
Percus, A., Istrate, G., et al. (2005). *Computational complexity and statistical physics.* New York: Oxford University Press.
Pickles, J. (2006). A systems sensibility: Commentary on Judith Teicholz's "Qualities of engagement and the analyst's theory." *International Journal of Psychoanalytic Self Psychology, 1*(3), 301–316.
Piers, C. (2005). The mind's multiplicity and continuity. *Psychoanalytic Dialogues, 15*(2), 229–254.
Poincaré, L., Guillaume, C. É., et al. (1900). *Rapports présentés au Congrès international de physique réuni à Paris en 1900 sous les auspices de la Société française de physique.* Paris: Gauthier-Villars.
Prigogine, I., & Holte, J. (1993). *Chaos: The new science: Nobel Conference XXVI.* St. Peter, MN: Gustavus Adolphus College.
Ricci, M., Trigault, N., et al. (1622). *Entrata nella China de' della Compagnia del Gesv.* Napoli: Lazzaro Scoriggio.
Sander, L. W. (2002). Thinking differently. *Psychoanalytic Dialogues, 12,* 11–42.
Sashin, J. I., & Callahan, J. (1990). A model of affect using dynamical systems. *Annual of Psychoanalysis, 18,* 213–231.
Scharff, D. E. (2000). Fairbairn and the self as an organized system. *Canadian Journal of Psychoanalysis, 8,* 181–195.
Seligman, S. (2005). Dynamic systems theories as a metaframework for psychoanalysis. *Psychoanalytic Dialogues, 15*(2), 285–319.
Shane, M., Shane, E., & Gales, M. (1997). *Intimate attachments: Toward a new self psychology.* New York: Guilford Press.
Shane, E., & Coburn, W. J. (2002). Prologue. *Psychoanalytic Inquiry, 22,* 653–654.

Spruiell, V. (1993). Deterministic chaos and the sciences of complexity: psychoanalysis in the midst of a general scientific revolution. *J Am Psychoanal Assoc, 41,* 3–44.
Steinberg, M. C. (2006). Language, the medium of change: the implicit in the talking cure. Prepublished paper.
Stern, D. N., Sander, L. W., Nahum, J. P., Harrison, A. M., Lyons-Ruth, K., Morgan, A. C., Bruschweilerstern, N., & Tronick, E. Z. (1998). Non-interpretive mechanisms in psychoanalytic therapy: The "something more" than interpretation. *Int J Psychoanal, 79,* 903–921.
Stern, D. N. (2004). *The present moment in psychotherapy and everyday life.* New York: W. W. Norton.
Stolorow, R. D. (1997). Dynamic, dyadic, intersubjective systems: An evolving paradigm for psychoanalysis. *Psychoanalytic Psychology, 14*(3), 337–364.
Stolorow, R. D., Atwood, G. E., & Orange, D. M. (2002). *Worlds of experience: Interweaving philosophical and clinical dimensions in psychoanalysis.* New York: Basic Books.
Sucharov, M. (2002). Representation and the intrapsychic: Cartesian barriers to empathic contact. *Psychoanalytic Inquiry, 22*(5), 686–707.
Taupin, B., & John, E. (1969). *Your song.* Dick James Music, Ltd., BMI.
Taylor, M. C. (2001). *The moment of complexity: Emerging network culture.* Chicago: University of Chicago Press.
Thelen, E., & Smith, L. B. (1994). *A dynamic systems approach to the development of cognition and action.* Cambridge, MA: MIT Press.
Thelen, E. (2005). Dynamic systems theory and the complexity of change. *Psychoanalytic Dialogues, 15*(2), 255–283.
Thom, R. (1974). *Modèles mathématiques de la morphogenèse: Recueil de textes sur la théorie des catastrophes et ses applications.* Paris: Union général d'éditions.
Trop, G. S., Burke, M. L., & Trop, J. L. (2002). Thinking dynamically in psychoanalytic theory and practice. In A. Goldberg (Ed.), *Progress in self psychology* (pp. 129–147). Hillsdale, NJ: Analytic Press.
Varela, F. J., Thomson, E., & Rosch, E. (1991). *The embodied mind: Cognitive science and human experience.* Cambridge, MA: MIT Press.
Waddington, C. H. (1966). *Principles of development and differentiation.* New York: Macmillan.
Weisel-Barth, J. (2006). Thinking and writing about complexity theory in the clinical setting. *International Journal of Psychoanalytic Self Psychology, 1*(4), 365–388.

NOTES

1. I am deeply indebted to Robert Stolorow, Donna Orange, Estelle Shane, Nancy Van Der Heide, Judy Pickles, Joye Weisel-Barth, and Richard Siegel for their passionate encouragement and close attention to detail that resulted in this chapter's many revisions.

2. William Coburn is editor-in-chief of *International Journal of Psychoanalytic Self Psychology* (Analytic Press) and is an editorial board member of *Psychoanalytic Inquiry* (Analytic Press). He is supervising and training analyst and faculty member at the

Institute of Contemporary Psychoanalysis, Los Angeles, and at the Northwestern Center for Psychoanalysis, Portland, Oregon.

3. Each of these designations technically refers to a different aspect of a broader contemporary systems perspective; see Taylor (2001) for a clear delineation.

4. For that deeper, multidisciplinary plunge, see Cilliers (1998), Kauffma (1995), Taylor (2001), and Prigogine and Holte (1993).

5. Some of these assumptions include the notions that intrapsychic life, and consequently the structuring of personality (or subjectivity), emanates from biological drives or from the internalization (and the resulting internal representations thereof) of self and object relations early in life; or that reality is objective, concrete, static, and verifiable, and that it is potentially distorted (hence, transference) via one's subjectivity; or that "the mind" is relatively isolated and/or protected from that which physically resides outside the cranium.

6. See Orange (2003).

7. Heisenberg's theory of indeterminacy (so named by Niels Bohr) or *uncertainty* pertains to the measurement of pairs of observables of a single particle such that increasing the accuracy of the measurement of one quantity necessarily increases the uncertainty of the simultaneous measurement of the quantity of the other.

8. I am deeply indebted to Paul Cilliers for his descriptive insight into the nature of open systems.

9. This is analogous to what Varela, Thomson, and Rosch refer to as *structural coupling* in the realm of biology (1991).

10. In chemistry, this phenomenon serves as a classical example of nonequilibrium thermodynamics to which complexity theorists refer as a visually dramatic illustration of nonlinear dynamics (see Thelen and Smith, 1994, p. 45).

11. The term *attractor state* can be understood as a preferred configuration of the constituents of a system or a patterning of emotional experiencing that is preferred (or reiterated) enough such that it is identifiable.

12. As a complexity-informed analyst, I am interested in the anomalies, the "noise," the occasional aberrations and departures from what we have relationally come to take for granted (i.e., the too much order or the too much randomness of a relational system). These departures may function as a systemic perturbation, a useful introduction of novelty into the system, consequently altering the emotional and relational landscape, or they may signal an important change in the landscape, one that has already emerged and that we are beginning to experience and experiment with. This is analogous to Winnicott's observation that an interpretation may often be the sign of a change having already occurred, as opposed to always understanding interpretative interventions as the cause for change. These autocatalytic events may or may not be usefully investigated with the patient.

13. Orange (2006, personal communication) points out that perhaps a more felicitous means of speaking about the notion of theory use is that we *live* theory, not apply it.

14. See Loewald (1972), Stolorow, Alwood and Orange (2002), and Stern (2004) for expanded discussions of the relationship between past, present, and future in the coalescing of human experience.

2

On Utilizing Attachment Theory and Research in Self Psychological/ Intersubjective Clinical Work

Shelley R. Doctors, PhD

This chapter focuses on the contributions attachment theory and research make to the self psychological/intersubjective approach to clinical work. Despite the impossibility of full theoretical integration, several overlapping, interpenetrating attachment concepts can be usefully adopted. For the sake of clarity, I group these ideas into three categories: 1) themes of safety, security, and the experience of felt security; 2) attachment research methodology, including the adult attachment interview; and 3) the various patterns that characterize how people organize maximal proximity to sources of safety and security. These patterns correspond to the attachment categories identified in research. Examples from adult, adolescent, and couples work will demonstrate my thesis[1]—one needn't aim for theoretical integration to borrow attachment theory and research understandings to enrich all varieties of clinical work.

As my focus is on clinical utility, I will only briefly address the theoretical obstacles to integrating attachment theory with self psychology or intersubjectivity. Though I will note conceptual *disjunctions*, there are also *conjunctions* among these theories. The disjunctions make total integration of attachment theory impossible, while the conjunctions highlight their overlap and define the areas in which attachment concepts can helpfully amplify self psychological and intersubjective clinical understanding.

INCORPORATION WITHOUT INTEGRATION

Attachment theory proceeds from the belief that the primary drive in human life is the need for safety and security and that this need is served in infancy and childhood by attachments to caregivers. Bowlby (1969) defined the need for attachment ties as a biological given. Attachment research explicates the styles of negotiating attachment needs that develop between children and their caretakers and sees the psychological patterns that form in this context as having long-lasting effects on psychological functioning. Children judged to have secure attachments are those who can freely express distress in anxiety-producing circumstances and who have confident expectations that their distress will elicit comforting responses. Insecure children are those who lack the confident expectation that they will be soothed and comforted and who have developed more convoluted modes to manage fear and distress.

Attachment theory privileges infancy and early childhood, while the very idea of privileging any developmental epoch is antithetical to the intersubjective approach. Rather than seeing development as dependent on infantile bonding, or the oedipal era, or any other key period, intersubjectivity is concerned more generally with the psychological field in which all of development, indeed all of life, unfolds. Similarly, though self psychology, like all psychoanalytic theories, is importantly interested in events occurring early in life, its main contributions, the selfobject concept and the distinctive role of empathy in human relations, are applicable throughout the life cycle. Additionally, intersubjectivity theory vigorously rejects the notion of biological givens (just as it rejects the notion of stages), for it rejects the idea that any psychological conflict or issue is inevitable or preeminent in human life in favor of a view of ongoing intersubjectively specific interactions through which distinctive meaning structures take form in all of us.

Phenomenologically, however, these theories all view development in the context of the interacting psychological worlds of children and caregivers. Attachment theory, just like self psychology and intersubjectivity, underscores the central role of relationships throughout life. Each focuses on *affective* exchanges and the patterns and expectancies formed therein. Granted, attachment theory (with its emphasis on affects of fear and anxiety) emphasizes a narrower slice of experience, while intersubjectivity offers a broader theory of affective experience and a more encompassing view of human interaction. Both, however, emphasize that *patterns* established through affective exchanges are responsible for creating forms of self- and interactive- regulation.[2] Typically, in the clinical population, patterns established early on have created ongoing relational difficulties. The *patterns established through affective interaction*, the common ground of attachment, self psychology, and intersubjectivity, is the main subject of this contribution.

Attachment-related behaviors were originally seen as strategies for maintaining proximity to caretakers, serving the biological function of protection from predators (Bowlby, 1969). Yet early on a more purely psychological view of attachment emerged, a view strikingly similar to our contemporary psychoanalytic theories. Sroufe and Waters (1977) placed affective interaction at the center of the attachment domain and advanced the idea that "felt security" was the goal and outcome of attachment-related interactions. They saw parental responsiveness and sensitivity to the child's affective communication as the context within which the child learns to organize emotional experience. Based on the caregiver's response, the child learns a set of "strategies for maintaining the self-organization and for maintaining proximity to . . . caretakers" (Main, 1995, p. 409). These strategies or "attentional/representational states" are eventually experienced as providing a kind of felt security (Main, 1995, p. 409). People then seek to maintain and perpetuate ways of being associated with a subjective sense of security.

In the language of nonlinear dynamic systems theory (Thelen & Smith 1994, see also Stolorow 1997), the states associated with felt security are called "preferred attractor states," ways of organizing cognitive and emotional experience and relating to others to which people return again and again. The phrase "felt security," coined to explain the psychological effects of attachment motivation, is experience near in the best self psychological/intersubjective tradition. Understanding that these ways of organizing experience are felt by the patient as necessary for safety and security and that they are coextensive with the only self-organization the patient has ever known helps the clinician appreciate the threat inherent in changing them. When the tenacity of entrenched maladaptive patterns are understood as *strategies for maintaining the self-organization, maintained by the threat of annihilation anxiety,* rather than as instances of the "repetition compulsion" (Freud, 1914, 1920), clinical work benefits.

Attachment theory, self psychology, and intersubjectivity are mining the same developmental interactions; all conclude that affect integrating interactions forge personality. In 1984, Daphne Socarides Stolorow and Robert Stolorow (Socarides & Stolorow 1984/85) linked self psychology to intersubjectivity theory, claiming that selfobject functions referred primarily to the integration of *affect* into the organization of self experience; the need for selfobject ties was conceptualized as the need for attuned responsiveness to affect states throughout the life cycle. From this vantage point, mirroring (Kohut, 1971, 1977, 1984) serves to integrate affects of pride, expansiveness, efficacy, and pleasurable excitement into the self organization while experiences of oneness with idealized sources of strength and calm (Kohut, 1971, 1977, 1984) refers to attuned, comforting responses that integrate affect states involving anxiety, vulnerability, and distress.

Indeed, self psychology and intersubjectivity are the psychological theories that best account for the relational phenomena that are the special purview of attachment theory and research. Mirroring and idealizing selfobject experiences seem the very modes by which secure attachment proceeds. In real life it is impossible to distinguish between the psychological conditions that eventuate in a "cohesive self" and those that lead to the development of a "secure" individual. For practical purposes, both theories speak to the same set of interactions and see problems in attunement and responsiveness to affect states as the key to understanding psychological troubles.

Not only does each theory account for psychological life similarly, but though intersubjectivity theory doesn't privilege any one issue, it virtually assumes the existence of attachment needs. Speaking of development in 1984, Atwood and Stolorow wrote, "When the psychological organization of the parent cannot sufficiently accommodate to the changing phase-specific needs of the developing child, then the more malleable and vulnerable psychological structure of the child will accommodate to what is available" (p. 69). While one need not account for *why* this is true in order to agree *that* it is true, this intersubjective developmental formulation dovetails with the first basic assumption of attachment theory and research, namely, that the baby is motivated to form, maintain, and preserve his primary relationships because his emotional and physical survival depends on his doing so (Slade, 1999). Attachment theory holds that the infant is motivated to do what is necessary (emotionally, cognitively, and behaviorally) to maintain his primary relationships. For that reason, disturbances in the actual lived experience of these relationships result in the formation of distorted interactive patterns. These *patterns* are slowly ingrained and routinized and then function to strongly bias an individual's functioning in later relationships. Except for the attribution of a *motivation* to maintain primary relationships, the developmental story of intersubjectivity theory (and its pathological consequences) is identical to that of attachment theory.[3]

ORGANIZING PRINCIPLES, INTERNAL WORKING MODELS, AND THEMES

The patterns that develop as distillates of lived experience are referred to in intersubjective theory as *organizing principles* while attachment theory uses the term *internal working models.* Though both have similar origins, function similarly, and are closely related to D. Stern's (1985) RIGS, they are conceptually distinct. Internal working models, the phrase that emerged from the analysis of research protocols, are general archetypes, while organizing principles are more personal, emerging as they do from specific intersubjective interaction. Two individuals who exhibit the same internal working model will nonetheless probably have different organizing principles. And, while some individuals manifest internal working models from more than one research category, all individuals have many different organizing principles. That said, organizing principles and internal working models must still be differentiated from the more common idea of psychological *themes.*

When someone jokingly says, "My organizing principle is, 'I shop until I drop,'" they are telling us about a *theme* in their life. A theme is like hearing the manifest content of a dream, while an organizing principle or an internal working model is like a dream's latent content. The organizing principle or internal working model contains the code for the specific developmental origins of the manifest theme. Many different organizing principles may possibly underlie the theme, "I shop until I drop." Is it, "When I feel sadly helpless, I try to feel my power to make things happen by giving to myself," or, "When I feel fortunate I must share my luck with others, lest I feel selfish and guilty." Is this a mode of self-care learned through deprivation that forestalls depression or might it be compulsive altruism necessary to regulate the undermining effects of envy and harsh criticism? Or is it something else entirely?

An organizing principle describes an individual's sequence of psychological reactions—a cascading chain of emotions and behaviors, typically condensing an interaction that once occurred, usually repeatedly, with another person. A feeling and the response to it become amalgamated and become the province of one individual. Recognizing that people have "feelings about their feelings" can be quite useful clinically. These tightly packed sequences may involve affective experience not directly related to attachment, though attachment issues often play a role in integrating interactive experience.

To illustrate: Helen, a middle-aged woman, spent a good deal of her childhood frightened and, when frightened, usually endured her parents' irritated deprecation of her fear. Though fear and self-deprecation are a *theme* in her life, long past childhood, her fear and her parents' response to it are amalgamated, entrained. In analysis she says, (attend to the affect), "I'm afraid to go back to school, but I'm so annoyed with myself. It's so stupid. No one else would feel that way." Her words reveal an organizing principle—an amalgamation of her own affect tightly coordinated with the emotional responses others have previously had to her affect. Her fear and her parents' responses to it are now entrained such that *when* she is frightened she reacts to her fear *as her parents once did,* with irritation and denigration. Attachment issues are implied in her accommodation to their view of her.

Internal working models, just like organizing principles, refer to representations of *all* experienced interaction patterns, though they have been most extensively elaborated in regard to models of self and other in attachment relationships. Like organizing principles, such models of prior transactions bias thoughts, feelings, and behavior.

The secure individual has confident expectations that one or more trusted persons can be counted on for emotional support and will come to their aid should difficulties arise. Such security allows one to function directly and creatively in the world of relationships and activities. As with Kohut's (1977, p. 253) analogy of selfobject experience being like oxygen, one isn't aware of its presence but becomes painfully aware of any shortages. While secure individuals can take emotional support for granted, those who have developed insecure working models create indirect strategies through which they can assure the maximal physical proximity and psychological availability of a needed attachment figure. Paradoxically, though insecure individuals are working harder at relationships, they are hobbled by expectations and strategies that limit their effectiveness in the here and now.

The internal working models that characterize insecure attachment are modes of organizing thoughts, feelings, and memories when the support of an attachment figure can't be taken for granted and are of particular interest to us in the understanding of the psychological fallout from dysfunctional families. Just like organizing principles, they are the result of one person's mind in interaction with another's. The degree and extent of affect attunement and the form of misattunement determines the shape of each individual's personal world of experience and their characteristic internal working models.

PATTERNS ASSOCIATED WITH ATTACHMENT INSECURITY

I will briefly review the types of insecure attachment identified by attachment researchers (Ainsworth, et al., 1978; Main, Kaplan & Cassidy, 1985) and demonstrate how I use some of the research methodology clinically before turning to case examples illustrating the internal working models that typify insecure attachment patterns.

Bowlby taught that children would organize themselves at great cost to their psychological functioning in order to maintain their attachments. He explained distortions in thinking and feeling as adaptations made in childhood to environmental failure. This was confirmed by researcher Mary Ainsworth and colleagues (1978) who demonstrated that variations in maternal responsiveness and sensitivity in the first year of life lead to differences in children's *patterns of seeking care and expressing affect.* Building on observational studies, she created a controlled separation and reunion research design for mothers and toddlers called the "strange situation" from which emerged the first attachment classifications—secure (B), avoidant (A), and resistant-ambivalent (C).

The column on the left side of table 2.1 describes children's behavior after separation from a parent and then upon reunion. The different patterns identified by Ainsworth exemplify ways children learn to organize emotional experience in response to variations in parental responsiveness; dif-

Table 2.1 (adapted from Hesse, 1999)

Ainsworth: Infant Strange Situation Response	**Main: Adult Attachment Interview**
Secure (B)	Secure/Autonomous (F)
Shows signs of missing parent on first separation, and cries during second separation. Greets parent actively, for example, creeping to parent at once, and usually seeks to be held. After briefly maintaining contact with the parent, settles and returns to play.	Coherent, collaborative discourse is maintained while speaker describes attachment-related experiences and their effects, whether favorable or unfavorable. Speaker seems to value attachment, while maintaining objectivity regarding any particular experience or relationship.
Avoidant (A)	Dismissing (Ds)
Does not cry on separation, attending to toys or environment throughout procedure. Actively avoids and ignores parent on reunion, moving away, turning away, or leaning away when picked up. Expressions of anger and distress are absent.	Normalizing, positive descriptions of parent ("excellent, very normal mother") are unsupported or contradicted by specific incidents. Negative experiences said to have had little or no effect. Transcripts short, often due to repeated insistence on lack of memory.
Resistant-Ambivalent (C)	Preoccupied (E)
Preoccupied with parent throughout procedure, may seem actively angry, alternately seeking and resisting parent, or may appear more subtly angry, while acting passive. Fails to settle or return to exploration on reunion, and typically continues to focus on parent and cry.	Preoccupied with experiences, seeming angry; confused and passive or fearful and overwhelmed. Some sentences grammatically entangled or filled with vague phrases ("dadadada") or psychological jargon. Transcripts long: some responses irrelevant.
Main & Solomon, 1986, 1990: Disorganized/Disoriented (D)	**Main & Hesse, 1990, 1992: Unresolved/Disorganized (U)**
The infant displays disorganized and/or disoriented behaviors in the parent's presence, suggesting a temporary collapse of behavioral strategy. For example, the infant may freeze with a trance-like expression, may rise at parent's entrance, then fall prone and huddle on floor, or may cling while crying hard and leaning away with gaze averted. Infant will otherwise fit A, B, or C.	During discussions of loss or abuse, individual shows striking lapse in the monitoring of reasoning or discourse. For example, individual may briefly indicate that a dead person is still alive in the physical sense, or that this person was killed by a childhood thought. Individual may lapse into prolonged silence or eulogistic speech. The speaker will ordinarily otherwise fit Ds, E, or F.

ferences in children's behavior correlate with differences in parental sensitivity to the child's affective communication.

Later research was even more interesting. Mary Main, et al. (1985) developed an interview protocol for use with adults called the adult attachment interview or the AAI (George, Kaplan, & Main, 1984, 1985, 1996). Analyzing the narratives obtained by asking adults about their relationships to caretakers in childhood demonstrated patterns analogous to the behaviors and states of mind characterizing the categories established for children. These appear in the right hand column in table 2.1. Over time, the researchers shifted their focus from the content of the memories elicited to the adult's capacity to integrate attachment-related experiences and to tell coherent stories in a collaborative manner, remaining aware of themselves, the interviewer, and their story, without becoming derailed by affect. The adults Mary Main characterized as secure/autonomous (F) seemed organized similarly to Ainsworth's secure (B) infants, while the affective patterns of dismissive (Ds) adults correspond to Ainsworth's avoidant (A) children. Similarly, Main's preoccupied (E) adults showed patterns analogous to those seen in resistant-ambivalent (C) children. This research was the first to show the far-reaching impact of attachment-related experience on the self-organization.

The AAI evaluates the *ways* in which attachment related events are remembered and organized, what Mary Main (1995, p. 409) has referred to as the attentional/representational states of mind associated with attachment experiences. The content of the memories reported, even extremely traumatic content, doesn't determine judgments about security and insecurity. As we shall see, secure adults have the capacity to express ideas and feelings around all sorts of early events in a *coherent, flexible,* and *related* manner. Such adults can relate coherent stories while remaining aware of the emotional implications of their stories on themselves and their listeners. Insecure adults attempt either to overregulate affects and feelings (like avoidant children) or are unable to contain and regulate thoughts and feelings, like resistant-ambivalent children. Insecure patterns of organizing thinking and managing emotion reflect specific child-caregiver systems for negotiating safety and security needs. Thus the patterns that characterize an individual's organization reflect earlier interactive, intersubjective systems.

Main and Solomon (1986, 1990) later identified a further insecure category—disorganized-disoriented, to describe fearful, odd behaviors in children that previously couldn't be categorized. The last box down in the left-hand column describes infant behaviors in the strange situation procedure identified by Main and Solomon as indicators of disorganized/disoriented (D) attachment. The bottom box on the right (next to it), describes parental behaviors identified by Main and Hesse (1990, 1992) characterizing unresolved/disorganized (U) attachment in the adult parents of the disorganized children. Disorganized behaviors in children were thought to arise in relation to parents who were vulnerable to dissociative states stemming from unresolved trauma and loss. Inexplicable, frightened states in such parents would be frightening to a child; an attachment figure who is "at once the source of and the solution to . . . alarm" (Main & Hesse, 1990, p. 163) presents an inherent conflict for a child.

Though parental physical or sexual abuse often structures this conflict, parents can be the source of alarm based on their psychological reactions alone; frightened and frightening behavior triggered in the parent by disorganizing thoughts or feelings associated with the parent's unresolved traumas creates interactive dilemmas for children. When children cannot find a solution to the paradox of fearing the person they might seek for comfort, organized strategies collapse and disorganized states of mind become part of the child's psychological repertoire. An example of a disorganized state of mind in an adult, obtained utilizing an adaptation of the methodology of the AAI, will follow.

ADRIANA Z. AND THE AAI

I sometimes incorporate aspects of the AAI methodology in my evaluation sessions and have found that the information I've gleaned has been useful in fine-tuning my clinical understanding.

Adriana Z., a fifteen-year-old Italian American, was generally anxious and showed signs of incipient panic disorder and phobic tendencies I thought might relate to her early history of painful medical procedures and hospitalization. She also had complaints about her mother. Adriana said, "She's crazy," but couldn't explain further, except to say, "She says things that don't make sense."

To investigate what Adriana was attempting to communicate, when I met with her parents, I utilized the structure of the AAI. I asked Mrs. Z. to tell me about her relationship to her mother and asked her to think of two adjectives that described her relationship to her mother in childhood. Her responses were "caring" and "sensitive." Then, again using the AAI format, I asked her to tell anecdotes, one at a time, that illustrated each quality.

To illustrate her mother's "caring," Mrs. Z. said, "I have a memory. I must have been five or six years old . . . and I suppose it was my first communion because I remember clearly that I was wearing a white dress. And I must have fallen in the mud or something because I remember the dress was all dirty. My mother. . . . I can remember her then . . . lighting matches and putting them out on my bare bottom."

Mrs. Z. seemed to notice neither her attentional shift nor her husband's shocked astonishment. She continued to smile, unfazed by the turn her narrative had taken. Remember, we are not focused on the content of the memory but on *how* the events are remembered and organized. Mrs. Z.'s response isn't *coherent*—the descriptor chosen and the story illustrating it don't match. The idealization of a troubled relationship is typical of an avoidant style but this example is more disturbed than that. It's not *collaborative*—there was no understanding of me or her husband as listeners. Was she able to *monitor* her functioning at that time? Could she *reflect* on her responses, her memories, her relation to herself and to those around her? Mrs. Z.'s response was so incoherent, so uncollaborative, she so lacked the capacity to monitor and reflect on her responses that I thought she was disorganized and even disoriented by her memory. Mrs. Z. went on to illustrate "sensitive" with a story of climbing into a window despite a broken arm rather than tell her mother she had had an accident, for she didn't want to worry her "too sensitive" mother! Adriana's mother's responses demonstrated disorganized, incoherent patterns of representation of thoughts and feelings—a disorganized, virtually dissociated state of mind with respect to attachment.

Mrs. Z. had not been able to integrate her traumatic experiences and was vulnerable to disorganization and disorientation when anxious. Extrapolating into Adriana's life story, Mrs. Z. had behaved chaotically when fear-provoking events in Adriana's medical treatment made her anxious. Her discombobulated responses frightened Adriana and complicated Adriana's capacity to function in the face of anxiety. When a parent's insecure mode of managing self-regulation is the interactive context for a child, intergenerational transmission of maladaptive functioning often results.

Using the AAI opened a window into Mrs. Z.'s reactions to fear and anxiety; her lapses allowed me to understand what Adriana meant when she said her mother didn't make sense. Clinically, I refined my hypothesis about the role of early hospitalization and medical procedures and focused on Adriana's memory of her mother's participation in those experiences. *That* led us to key traumatic memories, which became a cornerstone of the work that followed.

It's crucial to understand that someone with the same history of abuse could give a coherent account of it, *if* the associated thoughts and feelings were better integrated. Such a person might tell about the same experience differently. To illustrate, consider this invented example: "My mother . . . I'd say nervous, even impulsive, and I can tell you why. My mother had lived apart from her own mother and father for several years when she was little and never got over it. When something shocked her, she went into action, sometimes doing alarming things. She could be very scary and very hurtful. When I was little, I learned to stay away from her when I was upset or hurt so as to avoid her impulsive actions. I didn't even let her know when I broke my arm because she would make it worse. It was hard to get over that habit, but I've managed, for my sake, my husband's and my children's, thank goodness."

The AAI allows a direct window on the degree of *integrated access* the individual has to his own state of mind with respect to attachment. It allows us to see the degree to which that individual can simultaneously monitor the relation between his own state of mind and the current relational surround. Such competence is demonstrably independent of the effects of IQ, educational level, or social polish but is related to generally competent psychological functioning and, when absent, to the intergenerational transmission of incompetent patterns of affective functioning and self-management.

As will become more apparent, sometimes the organization that is heir to the negotiation of attachment needs is a "royal road" to intersubjective understanding. Two adult and two adolescent cases illustrating different forms of insecure attachment will demonstrate how knowledge of internal working models amplifies an understanding of organizing principles. Each case illustrates the long shadow cast by issues of safety and security and the patterns that characterize how maximal psychological proximity to sources of safety and security are organized. While all the cases center on patterns formed through affective interaction, the adolescent cases underscore the intergenerational transmission of insecure attachment from parent to child.

All these composite cases are constructed to illustrate patterns identified in research. In life, however, people frequently have different attachment styles with each attachment figure—for example, a secure attachment to one parent and an insecure attachment to another. Moreover, admixtures are more common than research might suggest, that is, an individual could have a largely secure relation to one parent with features of avoidant attachment, and a different combination characterizing the attachment to the other parent. It should be understood that real people can no more be reduced to examples of research categories than they can be to diagnoses. In this first case, attachment understandings helped me to understand the meaning of a rupture in treatment.

ADULT INDIVIDUAL PSYCHOANALYTICALLY INFORMED PSYCHOTHERAPY: JACQUELINE

Jacqueline had completed a successful two-year psychotherapy with me and had been free of her previously disabling panic disorder for several years when she returned following an excruciating breakup with the boyfriend she had expected to marry. Although her previous symptoms hadn't returned—she wasn't experiencing somatic symptoms and wasn't presenting at ERs expecting to die—she was profoundly depressed and terribly shaken.

Jackie is adventurous and tough-minded, hardworking, and well informed on an amazing variety of subjects. Self psychology and intersubjectivity had provided a solid basis for understanding her developmental predicaments—her fears of seeking comfort, her lack of idealizable figures and deficiencies in mirroring, and, in particular, how life with her extraordinarily timid, fearful mother had affected her.

Though initially Jackie had said she came from "the average American family, conventional and normal to the point of being boring," we came to see otherwise. Jackie's mother was easily shaken and her family tried to avoid circumstances in which she might "melt down." A restaurant waitress once brought her mother the wrong selection and, unable or unwilling to rectify the waitress's mistake, her mother collapsed into quiet tears. After gently but unsuccessfully encouraging her, Jackie and the rest of the family sat through her mother's tears in stoic silence, distracting themselves by eating or looking about, as they knew that further efforts to communicate with her mother would only make her more distressed.

In the first phase of treatment, we had discovered that Jackie had often worried that her emotional expression might distress her mother and precipitate the psychological collapse she always feared. To avoid helplessly experiencing her mother's distress, Jackie limited her expressions of affect to those she deemed not too threatening to her mother. In particular, when anxious Jackie feared it would show, just like when witnessing her mother's inexplicable breakdown. We had understood her panic disorder as constituting a "feeling about a feeling"—fear attendant on being afraid—fear her fear would trigger something more fearful. As Jackie became more aware of her reactions to anxiety and fear, her panic disorder subsided. Recognizing unarticulated aspects of her early affective experience had tamed her panic anxiety and opened the way to expanding her access to and expression of emotionality.

When she returned to treatment, to regain her social confidence she sought to understand her behavior with her former boyfriend, Michael. How could he have concluded she was sometimes emotionally uninvolved and uncommunicative when she was so glad to be with him and chattered happily with him at every opportunity?

Reviewing incidents in the relationship, we discovered she had experienced moments of insecurity with him when she had withdrawn, automatically assuming (as in the pattern established with her mother in childhood) that she couldn't deal with him in regard to the anxiety about the relationship he sometimes evoked but rather had to manage it herself. The problematic organizing principle we had previously recognized—reacting fearfully to her own anxiety—was further elaborated when we recognized the impact of her insecure internal working model. She was not only frightened when she was anxious but *withdrew* from the interaction in response to her own anxiety, unconsciously fearing her affective display would precipitate disorganization and then the loss of the attachment figure. Her attachment category is a variation on dismissive (D) or avoidant (A). Avoidant children do not express distress on separation or when it might be expected. Though they appear contained, physiologically they are highly aroused. When Jackie managed herself in accordance with an old danger situation, maintaining psychological and physiological proximity in an attachment relationship as she had learned to when frightened in childhood, she lost touch with the interactive consequences of hiding an important emotional reaction, allowing Michael the impression she was far less emotionally involved than she actually was.

The work progressed rapidly over nine months time and we were close to ending again. She was no longer depressed, and had begun a new relationship in which she was more successful at recognizing moments of insecurity and more effective in maintaining relational contact while speaking about her reactions within the relationship. Recognizing her bugaboo—the fear of stressing the relationship partner and the related fear of losing the attachment figure—she worked hard to change her pattern and was doing well. Further, she was concerned about finances, as the bill was mounting, her income was limited, and insurance had not yet paid a cent. I like this woman very much and had unhesitatingly taken her back into treatment when she was in trouble, assuring her that we would work something out.

After September 11, work pressures caused Jackie to cancel sessions, sometimes just hours before our appointment. After several such missed appointments, in a message to her I said I certainly wasn't charging for cancellations related to September 11 but wanted to talk with her to figure out how to see each other and how to avoid further cancellations, for eventually I would have trouble absorbing last-minute cancellations. She completely flipped out! In messages, in phone conversations, and then in the office, she expressed shock, disbelief, and outrage that any charge might *ever* be made for a missed session.

I was dumbfounded and unable to understand what had happened. I tried to shift from the concrete level of money and policies but found myself unable to understand how this sophisticated citizen-of-the-world did not know there could be a charge for a missed session. Could I have failed to mention it in either treatment? Hadn't she ever looked at a bill? I was ruffled and getting angry, too.

So there we were, in my office, me primed for "disruption and repair" (Beebe & Lachmann, 1994) work. Asking her what I had said or done or not said or done only kept us at the level of the concrete. But when I asked how the incident affected how she felt about me, she replied, sadly and soberly, "I thought I could count on you to look out for me, and . . . you didn't." Her disappointment and chagrin were palpable. At first I didn't follow what she was saying, but I stayed with it, for my lack of understanding alerted me to the possible presence of quite personal meaning. And then it fell into place and I said to her, "Oh, of course. Finally you could assume that someone was there, I was there, keeping an eye on things and managing what needed to be managed. At last you could operate freely, confidently knowing that if there were something worrisome I could be counted on to take care of things. You could go on with your activities, blessedly free from having to monitor other people—me. How wonderful it was to take that for granted and how awful it was to have that shaken. My message seemed to mean I needed you to attend to me, to take care that you didn't trouble me. No wonder it was so upsetting."

That broke the logjam, for both of us. To translate, the fee incident had disrupted a previously unrecognized developmental move forward. The selfobject dimension of the transference had been silently, blissfully in place and she was developing security in relation to me. She didn't have to worry about taking care of me and she could be confident in relying on someone to be able to look out for themselves and for her safety and security. There was a rupture in the idealizing selfobject transference and, in her distress, she was frantically trying to get me to "act right," to keep her safe so that she didn't have to second-guess her reactions for fear they would upset me.

The work with Jackie proceeded along self psychological/intersubjective lines but was helpfully enhanced by my understanding of specific attachment themes—safety and the internal working models of attachment she had developed in childhood and was in the process of remodeling in treatment. Through mirroring and idealizing selfobject experiences, Jackie was developing attachment security in relation to me. She was fighting with me to assure herself that she could count on me as a partner in the process and that she needn't return to the insecure stance in which she had to fearfully take care of everything herself and act as if things were okay when they weren't.

COUPLES' TREATMENT: GABRIEL AND SAM

In this next case, I focus on a different pattern of insecure attachment—the resistant-ambivalent (C) attachment category. While one might intuitively expect people who are avoidant and dismissive of attachment themes to be hardest to treat, research demonstrates that it is the resistant-ambivalent category that generally has the poorest outcome. As children, such people alternately seek and resist the parent. After separation and reunion they cannot be comforted, continue to cry, and fail to settle in.

Prior to couples therapy, Gabriel and George each had long-term individual treatment. They had been together for many years and while Gabriel felt their work lives had led them to drift apart, George thought the situation was quite grave.

An interactive dynamic was apparent from the first. George complained he didn't feel Gabriel was with him, yet knew his own pattern was to sulk for months before saying anything. Gabriel expressed interest in George's complaints and wanted George to tell him when he was unhappy. However

George couldn't ask for attention if he wasn't confident there was already interest directed toward him. Sam wanted to feel instantly settled in but Gabriel was more worried about being taken over. Gabriel needed more emotional space and wished to verbalize needs and wants, though George couldn't let himself ask directly for what he wanted.

Gabriel acknowledged his difficulties with trust and knew his fearfulness affected the relationship. As a boy whose interests were different from others, he evoked rage in his father, beatings from his peers, and was assaulted by men who were supposed to have cared for him. Gabriel needed time to develop intimacy but felt it was possible and progressing with George.

George's story was sad in a different way. His interest in neurochemistry was traceable to his sufferings with a schizophrenic mother who had been hospitalized innumerable times during his childhood, adolescence, and early adulthood. When she wasn't psychotic, their relationship was close and loving. In between episodes, she could be a doting, even protective mother. George's father's absorption in his own career and his implicit emotional abandonment of George and his mother was doubly hard, as it was a source of shame in his Midwestern Lutheran community. George had often been alone for long stretches while his mother was in the hospital. He seemed always to be imagining happy reunions and suffering shattering disappointments. Once, when he was excited to see her, she didn't even recognize him.

It was easy to understand George's need to feel that someone was really there, although he was unable to verbalize his desire for attention. It was equally clear that Gabriel's anxiety about being taken over had emerged from traumatic circumstances. He needed directness that George couldn't provide, for openness kept him abreast of the pace of a building intimacy and a steady, moderate pace reassured him that he wouldn't suddenly be overpowered by someone else's needs.

We began the work of helping them to understand the vulnerabilities each brought to the relationship and focused on how their needs and fears affected their current interactions with each other. One scene they repeatedly played out occurred while Gabriel was cooking. George would dance about nervously, in a manner both men recognized as a bid for attention. It was annoying to Gabriel and, though George was hurt by Gabriel's irritation, he regularly repeated the performance.

The work deepened as I spelled out George's fear of asking more directly for the attention he wanted. George was skittishly trying to make the contact he craved and to achieve a desperately desired proximity, but the possibility of not being met, not being recognized (which was signaled by Gabriel's distracted look) threatened him with utter psychological catastrophe. Tentatively maximizing proximity, while anxiously skirting disappointment, can be thought of as his organizing principle, even as resistant/ambivalent may describe his predominant internal working model of attachment.

George was faithful in opening up his inner experience and it is that process that I wish to highlight, for I believe it reflects the resistant-ambivalent pattern often seen in those who have experienced inconsistent parenting. We came to see that when the response George wanted wasn't forthcoming quickly enough, he began to feel frustrated and defeated and to tell himself, "Gabriel won't ever . . ." and then, "I don't want it anyway." The tiniest indication that Gabriel wasn't on George's wavelength was sufficient to initiate George's retreat. His avid interest in connection shifted quickly to angry withdrawal and to a state of mind in which he was quite resistant to engagement. If George did complain he felt alone, Gabriel's response (including loving interest and concern) was almost always experienced by him as "too little too late." George couldn't hear Gabriel, so involved would he already be in his lonely, resentful chewing over of injuries suffered. George's accurate recognition of any whiff of flagging interest would repeatedly lead him to grouse miserably to himself, "It doesn't matter what I say, nothing I say matters." George agreed with my interpretation that keeping himself company in that resentful way was actually enlivening to him.

The interaction between them was fascinating. George might recount a conversation in which he told Gabriel about a problem, would appear to have received thoughtful consideration, but nonetheless felt unheard, unrecognized, and angry. When George felt he wanted more of a response but was being overlooked by Gabriel he retreated. Gabriel was usually unaware that there was something left unfinished between them but wanted to know what it was so he could respond. As he began to make increasingly direct requests that George ask for what he wanted, George began to notice his vague sense that something would be spoiled, even ruined, were he to actively pursue Gabriel. I believe that what would have been violated would have been the attachment pattern acquired in traumatic circumstances, the loss of which would threaten a familiar sense of self. George's strategy for gaining as much attention as possible while risking rejection as little as possible, whether considered an organizing principle or an internal working model, provided a subjective experience of felt security.

To illuminate the components of George's mode of seeking emotional interaction, I spoke of George's exquisite sensitivity to distraction and preoccupation as his "early warning system." Acknowledging that he withdrew in response to a distracted partner to a self-encapsulated place in which he obsessively reviewed events himself, "licked his wounds," and built a simmering resentment, I spoke of his learned, vigilant attunement to the earliest signs of unresponsiveness in his mother. His unwillingness to pursue his needs directly had functioned to keep him from asking for something she *couldn't* give and protected him from a dreadful confrontation in which he would feel *all alone and bereft.*

At this point in the treatment I learned that his mother had also had a seizure disorder and that George's attunement was so incredibly acute he could tell a day before a seizure when one was approaching! Even though George is hypervigilant, he is accurate when he picks up low-level signs of distraction in Gabriel. However, he is not accurate in his automatic *interpretation* of the meaning of those signs in his current-day relationship. Helping him gain greater conscious awareness of this pattern and the flexibility to consider the choices open to him was the therapeutic challenge.

Here, again, is the overlap between what intersubjectivity theorists call organizing principles and attachment theorists call internal working models. George had learned that when he was desirous of contact, signs of unavailability in the other presage emotional disaster. At that moment, he shifted to a state of mind in which his emotional abandonment was a foregone conclusion. The absence of the other was experienced, regretted, bemoaned, and railed against. In this state of mind he was resistant to actual contact, though psychologically, as in childhood, he was maintaining the closest degree of proximity possible. What was once an interactive drama with his mother had become condensed into a personal pattern—a chain of automatic emotional responses. First he sought contact. Then, in reaction to a sense that wasn't forthcoming, he became hopeless about getting it and then didn't want it anymore.

What does attachment theory add to this picture? First, this story hinges on the seeking out of a secure connection. Second, it illustrates modes of achieving psychological proximity to an elusive object that had come to be associated with felt security, and third, understanding attachment ideas shapes interventions that focus on the regulation of distance—physical and emotional. Under terribly adverse conditions, George had negotiated a way of being as emotionally connected as his mother's psychological state allowed that simultaneously aimed to protect him from psychological devastation. His angry self-encapsulation functioned to maintain his private experience of contact when closer contact wasn't possible. In treatment, George had to come to recognize his fears of reaching out to Gabriel, his sense that self-containment was safer than trying to be with Gabriel. This has been crucial in complexifying their earlier formulation—that George craved contact and Gabriel feared it.

I used my sense of George's exquisite calibration of distance to illuminate the hair-trigger shift away from seeking Gabriel to resisting Gabriel. We developed a language of directionality in relationship, a fine-grained awareness of whether each was moving toward relationship or away from it. We considered the psychological conditions (around and within each partner) that produced withdrawal and spoke about what was required to encourage a movement into the relationship, transforming patterns that had been useful in incompetent systems but which guaranteed dysfunction in adulthood. Gabriel learned to modify his irritated responses to what he feared might be an impingement and, with the support of his partner and the treatment, George became better able to tolerate disappointment and developed some new faith in the expression of his needs. The old patterns lost their automaticity as they were illuminated and understood in the treatment and as the new intersubjective surround began to have an impact.

ADOLESCENT TREATMENT: AMANDA AND REBECCA[4]

Two fourteen-year-olds who presented with delicate self-cutting will illustrate the contribution of attachment-related understandings to work with adolescents. Behaviors that look alike may nonetheless have different meanings and respond to different interventions. The experiences that led to insecurity were different for each girl and the treatments that evolved were also different. Yet in each instance, aspects of attachment theory and research contributed to understanding each girl's subjective experience.

Amanda J. and Mrs. J.

Mrs. J. requested consultation after her daughter's friends reported Amanda had cut herself several times. Amanda was eating and sleeping erratically and not attending to schoolwork. Mother, described by the referring clinician as abrasive and controlling, said she knew that her relationship to Amanda had been disrupted by her live-in boyfriend's obnoxious behavior and her own inability either to effectively protect her daughter or to communicate openly with her about it.

In the initial meeting with Mrs. J., I was impressed by the contrast between her exceedingly high intelligence and the disturbed communication pattern she evidenced with me. Facial displays of affect were notably absent and those present did not match her words. Her narrative was not collaborative—she recounted bizarre behavior without a corresponding recognition that I might react to her report. Any attempt on my part to respond or participate was firmly brushed aside.

My thoughts about my observations drew on my knowledge of the AAI. Mrs. J.'s narrative carried the imprint of her interactive and self-regulatory disturbances (see Beebe & Lachmann, 2001). She seemed to squelch emotionality in herself and to disconnect from her surroundings when content was affect-laden. Such evidence of attachment insecurity made me wonder about the interaction between the mother and daughter and its effect on the daughter's self-regulation and to wonder whether Mrs. J. might have been a disorganized, disorienting parent to Amanda.

In our first session, Amanda described herself as often saying something "just out of the blue" that "made no sense." Indeed, her narrative was quite disjointed, but in contrast to her mother's, offered germinal insights that helped me understand her; she was more open than her mother and allowed me to connect with her, a good prognostic sign. Amanda spoke about circumstances in which her mother seemed to "freeze" dramatically and inexplicably, for example, when someone spilled something at the table. Though Amanda laughed, I commented that the intensity of her mother's reaction, the look on her face, and the sound of her voice were all frightening. She seemed pleased that I understood. As the session was ending, she blurted out, "Oh yes, one more thing. My mother is frightened of me, she really is . . . trust me" to which I was able to respond, "I think I understand. She's not only sometimes frightening to be around, she's also often frightened herself and you've been there when she appears frightened of you."

I believe this is an example of a mother's disorganized attachment pattern affecting the interactive and self-regulatory style of the daughter. Mother's narrative lapses reflect her lack of integration of her own attachment experiences (which are not described here). Simultaneously, this lack of integration disturbs her interactive process with Amanda. Amanda has had to cope with the subjective experience of a sudden loss of relatedness. Without warning, her mother would, psychologically speaking, disappear and she would be without a partner to manage her own affective reactions, including the fear inspired by her mother's inexplicable behavior. While secure children believe that when distressed, emotional support will be available, Amanda's insecurity reflected learning the opposite—when distressed, she didn't expect she could turn to anyone to help her manage her feelings.

The experience of feeling terribly alone while upset was the emotional center of the experiences of cutting we talked over together. My understanding of her state of mind at those times and my capacity to gently link those states to the many previous relational experiences they echoed helped Amanda. I was not merely providing insight, but introducing her to the novelty of the emotional comfort an understanding presence can provide. My emphasis on affect attunement and emotional integration in Amanda's treatment led to her reorganization in many realms.

Amanda showed the heartening capacity to use a new relationship that keeps us interested in working with adolescents. Disturbances in sleeping and working were ameliorated and cutting disappeared. Mood was no longer depressed. In less than six months, Amanda's communications became more fluent and more self-reflective. Family interactions remained disturbed but Amanda managed them more successfully (albeit through withdrawing). Her mother wanted mother-daughter sessions and I recommended them but Amanda refused. Though cutting was behind us, treatment continued. Whether we spoke about her girlfriends, her teachers, or her special "crush," the dyadic processes characterizing our interaction continued to contribute to the reorganization of her self- and interactive regulation.

Rebecca A. and Mr. and Mrs. A.

Rebecca's school suggested consultation after girls in her grade reported they were worried about her, for Rebecca, age fourteen, had cut herself, was using drugs and alcohol indiscriminately, and was involved in tremendous social turmoil. The initial consultation-evaluation sessions, first with Rebecca and then, with Rebecca's permission, with Mr. and Mrs. A., revealed an adolescent excited, confused, and overwhelmed by her relationships with both boys and girls and unable to believe either parent might help her to deal with her distress. While she expected her academically oriented father to dismiss social concerns as "silly," her frustrations with her mother were differently organized. Conflicts between Rebecca and her mother were prominent. When Rebecca shared a concern of her own, her mother tended to reframe it to fit a story or experience characteristic of her relation to her own mother.

Mrs. A. reported she had shared absolutely everything, even her first sexual experience, with her own mother. Speculations about her mother's probable reactions dominated Mrs. A.'s thoughts when interacting with Rebecca. Rather than respond to feelings her daughter was expressing and actual problems Rebecca had, Mrs. A. would begin to speak about what her own mother might have done in comparable circumstances, each time losing touch with Rebecca's actual problem and current situation. Together with other omitted details, I concluded Mrs. A. was preoccupied with her own maternal attachment. She behaved as if she expected Rebecca to relate to her as she did to her mother, with slavish devotion to her thoughts and mood; she was unable to recognize how different her daughter's circumstances actually were.

Though intelligent and high functioning professionally, Mrs. A. simply ignored inclinations and interests of Rebecca's that didn't coincide with her own. As Mrs. A. was intent on high academic achievement, she focused on grades. Not having been very "social" herself, and never having experimented with drugs, she was completely unconcerned about drug use, and asked only that Rebecca tell her whenever she drank or used drugs. Unconsciously she expected to control Rebecca as she was controlled by her mother's wishes.

Rebecca referred to her mother's insensitive substitution of her own interests and experience for Rebecca's as "intrusiveness" and dealt with these "intrusions" by precipitously dismissing them. Her attempts to escape her mother's frustrating failure to recognize her had left her unreflective and impulsive. Though also very intelligent and in some ways high functioning, she tended to be blithely dismissive of problems she encountered in interactions. In short, Rebecca paid little attention to how she managed herself—socially and academically.

Rebecca was insecurely attached to both parents, despite being able to converse more easily with her father. Insecure children come into adolescence with special needs to be valued and validated for who they are. As is often the case, Rebecca experienced the social milieu as a second opportunity to gain the recognition she craved. More comfortable with boys than the other girls were and very beautiful as well, by thirteen she was discovered by older boys and began to "fool around," to drink, and to use drugs. After a brief flirtation with an eating disorder, episodes of cutting began in the midst of social turmoil at school. Older girls resented her presence and Rebecca became the target of nasty, unflattering gossip. Yet her capacity to understand others emotionally and to anticipate their reactions to her behavior was poorly developed, so her own social blunderings complicated her misery.

Rebecca felt overwhelmed socially. Talking the problem over in individual treatment was eye-opening for both of us, for we came to see that Rebecca had often neglected to think through consequences and was unable to put herself in another's place, as other young adolescent girls could. Intergenerational transmission of modes of psychological organization can be seen when parents who fail to reflect on the minds and hearts of their children produce adolescents who lack the same capacities. Rebecca was neither self-reflective nor empathic toward others. She was miserable and confused and allowed me to know that.

Treatment took some interesting turns. I said I thought she needed all of her wits about her to cope effectively with her social predicaments and straightforwardly explained why refraining from drinking and smoking pot might help. Relieved to have something she could do to feel less lost, she adopted my suggestion.

Rebecca's interest in my comments about her family led to adjunctive family sessions. The task in family work was to encourage mother and father to allow room for Rebecca's point of view both in their thinking about her and in their communications with her. I attempted to facilitate an interaction within which Rebecca could begin to articulate her point of view, for herself as well as for them. My goal was to helpfully expand their repertoire and to draw attention to problematic interactions, so that Rebecca might better appreciate her emotional needs, frustrations, and choices.

In family sessions we could see the unbearable tension Rebecca experienced when she felt she couldn't get her mother to hear her, no matter how hard she tried. Previously Rebecca had "fled" from these experiences in a somewhat "hysterical" fashion and barely recognized their impact on her.

In concurrent individual treatment I told Rebecca I thought the terrible tension she had experienced in relation to frustration with her mother was somehow related to the states in which she had cut and she said excitedly, "Absolutely. I felt like I would burst. Think of it visually," she said, "I had to get it out. The blood would do that."

Her family began to "hear her" and as she articulated her point of view, she became more self-aware and more adept at self-management. Without telling anyone, Rebecca stopped taking the antidepressants that had been prescribed by her previous therapist. Despite this, her mood improved dramatically, as did her schoolwork. Rebecca took steps to calm her social life. She gradually withdrew from the social fast track, resumed friendships with girls she had dropped, and settled into relationships that helped her to further develop her social-emotional capacities.

DISCUSSION AND CONCLUSION

These cases illustrate my belief that the psychological organization emerging from the negotiation of attachment needs can be a "royal road" to self psychological/intersubjective understanding; self psychological/intersubjective understanding may be deepened by familiarity with affective patterns gleaned from the world of attachment theory and research.

Understanding the attachment-related structure of Jackie's affective inhibition guided the work that followed her breakup, while recognizing an attachment-related pattern made sense of a disruption that might have prematurely ended treatment. The organizing principle uncovered in the first phase of therapy—when afraid she feared that letting it show would make matters worse—was fruitfully elaborated and deepened by my understanding of avoidant-dismissive attachment style. When my phone message disrupted the selfobject transference, seeing the connection between idealizing and mirroring selfobject experiences and the development of attachment security was crucial in "repairing" our connection.

Attachment understandings were useful in identifying the origins and functions of ways of being developed by George to cope with inconsistent parenting caused by his mother's episodic bouts with mental illness. In addition to demonstrating an additional attachment-related pattern (George's is resistant-ambivalent, while Jackie's is avoidant-dismissive), the case provides a window into entrenched maladaptive psychological modes which resist change in treatment. As in this case example, a detailed dissection of these complex patterns allows patients to recognize and modify habitual, maladaptive routines. Understanding the felt security inherent in maximizing proximity to attachment figures deepens an appreciation of the fear of the loss of a familiar sense of self. Recognizing that these patterns are maintained by the anxiety attendant on losing an essential attachment bond contributes to the therapist's patience and reframes what might otherwise seem like a malignant resistance.

Reviewing both adolescent cases, one gains a sobering glimpse of the intergenerational transmission of insecure attachment patterns and the associated incompetent modes of self- and interactive regulation that is their legacy. Sometimes, as with Mrs. A. and Rebecca, the child's functional deficit flows directly from the parental interaction. Mrs. A. wasn't able to hold in mind and reflect upon the child Rebecca was and Rebecca grew into an adolescent who couldn't reflect upon her thoughts, feelings, and the consequences of her actions. At other times, "intergenerational transmission" operates more obliquely. Amanda's mother's disorganized attachment often effectively left Amanda without a relational partner, influencing her excessive reliance on managing herself by herself, thereby interfering with Amanda developing more competent modes of self-regulation.

An important proviso is in order. For the sake of illustrating the clinical utility of attachment-related understandings, I highlight *patterns,* making them the psychological foreground and relegating other details to the hazy background and I use categorical schemas to demonstrate my points. Yet the richness and complexity of an individual's psychological life can never be adequately captured by an attachment category.[5] Similarly, good clinical work never proceeds in preordained "cookbook" fashion, whether the book in question is an attachment handbook or a diagnostic manual.

My thinking about attachment categories is similar to my views on diagnosis. Though both can sensitize the clinician to styles of functioning, neither fully captures an individual personality and neither automatically prescribes a treatment. A map of North America provides an analogy. Knowing the location of a major city can orient you to temperature trends and general proximity. With greater sophistication about location, you may even anticipate regional accents, but maps can never provide the atmospheric details one discovers by being there. And it is new dyadic interaction around the distinctive details of the patient's experience that allows therapeutic reorganization.

To delineate my thesis from reductionistic "cookbook" approaches to clinical work, I selected examples of two young adolescents who each presented with symptoms of cutting and who each had features of insecure attachment to insecure parents. In each case, attachment theory and research amplified my psychological understanding of their subjective experience of interacting with their parents. Using my knowledge of the AAI to recognize that Mrs. J.'s behavior with me reflected significant problems in self- and interactive regulation was helpful in understanding Amanda's communication, just as recognizing Mrs. A.'s preoccupation with her own mother was helpful in eventually understanding the communication difficulties that so frustrated Rebecca. With each girl, attachment concepts helped me to understand the psychological problems their symptoms reflected and treated. While both psychotherapies were effective in opening adjunctive developmental opportunities, transforming ways of being that improved overall functioning and eliminated symptoms, there can be *no single* way to treat fourteen-year-old girls who cut themselves, even if one recognizes that insecurity is a factor. Though Amanda and Rebecca may at first glance seem similar, their insecure attachments arose from different subjective experiences, their cutting had different meanings and served different functions, and the treatments that suited them were geared to these differences.

In each case described, Amanda and Rebecca, but also Jackie, Gabriel, and George, and more briefly Helen and Adriana, *patterns* established through attachment-related, affective interaction were important in the clinical illumination and transformation of maladaptive modes of self- and interactive regulation. I have argued that attachment theory and research contributes to *pattern recognition* and can be helpfully incorporated into clinical work conducted from a self psychological/intersubjective perspective. Since the *patterns* created by affective interaction are central to the conception of psychological health and pathology in self psychology, intersubjectivity, and also attachment theory, if one eschews issues that pertain to full *integration, incorporation* of concepts gleaned from attachment theory and research should be welcome.

The purpose of this chapter is to suggest that understandings gleaned from attachment theory and research make important contributions to clinical work conducted from a self psychological/intersubjective perspective. Familiarity with the ways of being that emerge from the negotiation of attachment relationships can help the clinician recognize patterns and their significance more quickly and thereby support therapeutic efforts. The limitations of these schemas adds a cautionary note that need not curtail enthusiasm for theory and research that opens the clinician's mind and heart to new perspectives on old problems.

REFERENCES

Ainsworth, M., Behar, M., Waters, E., & Wall, S. (Eds.). (1978). *Patterns of attachment.* Hillsdale, NJ: Lawrence Erlbaum Press.

Atwood, G., & Stolorow, R. (1984). *Structures of subjectivity: Explorations in psychoanalytic phenomenology.* Hillsdale, NJ: Analytic Press.

Beebe, B., & Lachmann, F. (1988). The contribution of mother-infant mutual influence to the origins of self- and object representations. *Psychoanalytic Psychology, 5,* 305–337.

Beebe, B., & Lachmann, F. (1994). Representation and internalization in infancy: Three principles of salience. *Psychoanalytic Psychology, 11*(2), 127–165.

Beebe, B., & Lachmann, F. (2001). *Infant research and adult treatment, co-constructing interactions.* Hillsdale, NJ: Analytic Press.

Bowlby, J. (1969). *Attachment and loss, Vol. I.* New York: Basic Books.

Caligor, J., Fieldsteel, N., & Brok, A. (1984) *Individual and group psychotherapy: Combining psychoanalytic treatments.* New York: Basic Books.

Doctors, S. (2003). Advances in understanding and treating self-cutting in adolescence. In A. Streeck-Fischer (Ed.), *Adoleszenz-Bindung-Destrucktvat.* Germany: Klett-Cotta.

George, C., Kaplan, N., & Main, M. (1984). Adult attachment interview protocol. Unpublished manuscript, Univ. of California, Berkeley.

George, C., Kaplan, N., & Main, M. (1985). Adult attachment interview (2nd edition). Unpublished manuscript, Univ. of California, Berkeley.

George, C., Kaplan, N., & Main, M. (1996). Adult attachment interview (3rd editon). Unpublished manuscript, Univ. of California, Berkeley.

Freud, S. (1914). Recollecting, repeating and working through. S.E., Vol. XII, London: Hogarth Press, 1955.

Freud, S. (1920). Beyond the pleasure principle, part III. S.E., Vol. XVIII, London: Hogarth Press.

Hesse, E. (1999). The adult attachment interview: Historical and current perspectives. In J. Cassidy and P. Shaver (Eds.), *Handbook of Attachment.* New York: Guilford Press, 1955.

Kohut, H. (1971). *The analysis of the self.* Ed. A. Goldberg. Chicago: University of Chicago Press.

Kohut, H. (1977). *The restoration of the self.* New York: International Universities Press.

Kohut, H. (1984). *How does analysis cure?* Ed. Arnold Goldberg. Chicago: University of Chicago Press.

Main, M. (1995). Recent studies in attachment: Overview, with selected implications for clinical work. In S. Goldberg, R. Muir, & J. Kerr (Eds.), *Attachment theory: Social, developmental, and clinical perspectives.* Hillsdale, NJ: Analytic Press.

Main, M., & Hesse, E. (1990). Parents' unresolved traumatic experiences are related to infant disorganized attachment status: Is frightened and/or frightening parental behavior the linking mechanism? In M. Greenberg, D. Cicchetti, & E. M. Cummings (Eds.), *Attachment in the pre-school years: Theory, research, and intervention* (pp. 121–160). Chicago: University of Chicago Press.

Main, M., & Hesse, E. (1992). Disorganized/disoriented infant behavior in the strange situation: Lapses in the monitoring of reasoning and discourse during the parent's adult attachment interview and dissociative states. In M. Ammaniti & D. Stern (Eds.), *Attachment and psychoanalysis.* Rome: Gius, Laterza & Figli.

Main, M., & Solomon, J. (1986). Discovery of a new insecure-disorganized/disoriented attachment pattern. In T. B. Brazelton & M. Yogman (Eds.), *Affective development in infancy* (pp. 95–124). Norwood, NJ: Ablex.

Main, M., & Solomon, J. (1990). Procedures for identifying infants as disorganized/disoriented during the Ainsworth strange situation. In M. Greenberg, D. Cicchetti, & E. Cummings (Eds.), *Attachment in the preschool years: Theory, research, and intervention* (pp. 121–160). Chicago: University of Chicago Press.

Main, M., Kaplan, N., & Cassidy, J. (1985). Security in infancy, childhood, and adulthood: A move to the level of representation. In *Growing points of attachment theory and research. Monographs of the society for research in child development, 50* (1–2, Serial No. 209), 66–104.

Slade, A. (1999). Attachment theory and research: Implications for the theory and practice of individual psychotherapy with adults. In J. Cassidy and P. Shaver (Eds.), *Handbook of attachment: Theory, research and clinical applications.* New York: Guilford Press.

Socarides, D., & Stolorow, R. (1984/85). Affects and selfobjects. *Annual of psychoanalysis, XII/XIII,* 105–119.

Sroufe, L., & Waters, E. (1977). Attachment as an organizational construct. *Child Development, 48,* 1184–1199.

Stern, D. (1985). *The interpersonal world of the human infant.* New York: Basic Books.

Stolorow, R. (1997). Dynamic, dyadic, intersubjective systems: An evolving paradigm for psychoanalysis. *Psychoanalytic Psychology, 14*(3), 337–346.

Thelen, E., & Smith, L. (1994). *A dynamic systems approach to the development of cognition and action.* Cambridge, MA: MIT Press.

NOTES

1. Since privacy and confidentiality are the essential elements that make it possible for the patient to put his trust in another human being (Caligor, Fieldsteal, & Brok, 1984, p. xiv), the case examples are composites designed to illustrate attachment-related patterns.

2. Beebe and Lachmann's (1988, 2001) ideas about the reciprocal developmental co-construction of internal and relational processes mine this territory, too, and provide another congenial language with which to speak of patterns and expectancies that emerge from interaction.

3. Over the years, the work of intersubjectivity theorist Bernard Brandchaft describing pathological structures of accommodation has come to more clearly acknowledge the impact of attachment needs.

4. Some details of these case composites appear in Doctors (2003).

5. Indeed, one implication of this chapter is that attachment status may change as the result of psychological treatment, a view consistent with research showing that significant life events may change attachment status despite the general tendency for attachment categories to be continuous over time.

3

Moving Along: Reflections on Self Psychology and the Boston Change Process Study Group

Dorienne Sorter, PhD, and Jacqueline Gotthold, PsyD

> Out beyond ideas of wrongdoing and rightdoing there is a field. I will meet you there. When the soul lies down in that grass, the world is too full to talk about. Ideas, language, even the phrase each other doesn't make any sense.
>
> —Rumi

Flopping on the couch opposite an analyst, a seventeen-year-old girl—almost woman—announces her depression with a flourish. "I am sooooo depressed today," Becky wails. Becky's eyes are averted as she begins her bleating. Slowly, as she finishes her announcement, she raises her eyes, knowing she will meet her analyst's gaze. Her analyst almost welcomes, almost sighs, almost smiles as their eyes meet. "So . . . what's up?"

Years ago we might have asked what, if anything, could be said about these fifteen seconds of a forty-five minute session of a three-times-a-week, five-year treatment. We might have consulted the patient's history, the story of the transference and countertransference, and/or the complete transcript. Yet now, as we have refined our foci, these moments in the consultation room yield richness toward a sophisticated understanding of therapeutic action. In the above vignette the declarative content consists of only eight words. Yet volumes have been "spoken" in the exchange beginning with Becky's flopping on the couch, to the meeting of eyes between patient and analyst. How we understand the richness of such exchanges is the focus of this chapter.

We will examine in both the adult and child treatment process recent developments explicated by the work of the Boston Change Process Study Group. This group, hereafter referred to as BSG, has addressed the realm of treatment that lies outside the verbal, outside a consideration of conscious and unconscious, to the dimension of the implicit—implicit relational knowing. Or in the words of the BSG the "something more" in treatment. Clearly, as a field, psychoanalysis was ready to embrace such an explication and a language that enables an exploration of elements always in operation in the treatment process but heretofore elusive to capture. The multitude of articles, presentations, and classes dealing with this exploration confirms this conclusion.

In an earlier chapter we noted the applicability of the BSG's work to treatment informed by a broad range of psychoanalytic theories (Gotthold & Sorter, 2006). How can an analyst working from a self psychological framework integrate the findings of the BSG?

Contemporary self psychology and intersubjective theorists have been working to further refine the articulation of the unfolding mutative processes between patient and therapist. They have continued to explore and expand upon the cornerstones of self psychology theory: the function of empathy, the selfobject transferences and the cycle of rupture and repair in the patient/analyst relationship. Some of the contributors to the expanded self psychological brain trust include Stolorow (1997), Stolorow and Atwood (1992), Stolorow, Brandchaft, and Atwood (1987), and Orange, Atwood, and Stolorow (1997), who have directed our attention to the intersubjective and contextual realm of the treatment process. Bacal's specificity theory (1998) has pointed to the centrality of analyst's specific responsiveness to the patient's needs. Lichtenberg (1989) and Lichtenberg, Lachmann, and Fosshage (1992) have put forth a motivational systems theory. All of these new perspectives of self psychology have focused on the ongoing, dyadic, "relational" dimension of the psychoanalytic situation.

The infant research (Sander, Tronick, Stern) and systems theory (Thelen & Smith, 1994; Coburn, 2000; Fosshage, 1997, 2003, 2005) literature leads self psychology theory down another avenue for expansion. Lachmann and Beebe (1996a, 1996b, 2002) applied infant research findings and systems theory to adult treatment. The findings in these areas of research have led us to understand the treatment relationship in terms of it being a dyadic, bidirectional system of influencing and being influenced. The embodiment of these new areas of theoretical developments have contributed to our embracing ideas about the co-creation of expectancies in the treatment relationship, the role of self and other interactive regulation, and the inextricable role of the nonverbal in all interactions.

Resulting from the continued growth, expansion, and inclusiveness in self psychological theorizing, the findings of the BSG increase precision in articulating the dimensions of the treatment process that were not accounted for yet, always in operation. The BSG's work at the "local level" refocuses our attention to the "something more" than the global foci, that of attuned responsiveness, rupture and repair, and empathic immersion. Their highlighting of the interweaving of the explicit/declarative domain with the implicit procedural domain in all interactions gives new meaning and understanding to self psychology's bidirectional, interactively regulated, attuned-responsive treatment dyad.

In this chapter, we question whether in this exploration enough emphasis has been placed on 1) the "moving along" process, explicated in earlier papers (1998, 2002, 2005) by the BSG; 2) the interplay of declarative/explicit and nondeclarative/procedural dimensions in the treatment process; and 3) whether the recent expansion and application of the BSG's work toward the creation of a unified field theory is not premature.

The original participants of the BSG are well-known to members of the psychoanalytic community. Their varied backgrounds added fullness to their work. Lou Sander, Daniel N. Stern, Edward Tronick, Jeremy Nahum, Karlen Lyons-Ruth, Alexandra Harrison, N. Bruschweiler-Stern, and Alexander Morgan all have contributed to their evolving explication of therapeutic action. At the time of their early publications (Stern, et al., 1998; Lyons-Ruth, 1999; BSG, 2002), general agreement was growing in the field that "something more" than interpretation powers the treatment process.

The BSG initiated the close examination of clinical process toward the end of defining this elusive "something more." Drawing from developmental findings, systems theory, and psychoanalytic clinical process, they proposed new ways to understand therapeutic action. The BSG felt that verbal (declarative) interpretation was not sufficient to account for therapeutic action. The "something more," they felt, was not necessarily verbal. They found that, frequently, change was powered in the realm of the nonverbal, or what the BSG understood to be procedural. From the cognitive psychology literature, we know that the term "declarative memory" (Cohen & Squire, 1980) refers to "a memory system involved in the processing of information that an individual can consciously recall and declare to remember" (Davis, 2001, p. 451). Procedural memory, on the other hand, is one type of nondeclarative memory that influences experience and behavior, but typically cannot be explicitly or consciously recalled (Squire, 1994; Fosshage, 2005).

Procedural memory involves the acquisition of information in nonverbal form associated with highly practiced sequences of actions. Once learned, this kind of knowing becomes automatic and not necessarily ever symbolically encoded. This procedural encoding of information is how most sports are played. For example, once learned, riding a bicycle becomes procedural. One no longer thinks "I must push the pedals and I must steer the wheel." Once acquired, the procedures become part of a person's repertoire of actions requiring no conscious thought.

How we do things with others, the BSG suggests, may also be procedurally encoded. They called such procedurally encoded interactions "implicit relational knowing." We were struck by a vivid example from a recent highly touted film that demonstrated implicit relational knowing. In *The Devil Wears Prada*, an entire publishing house learned to turn aside quickly and avoid eye contact when "the devil," Miranda Priestly, the boss, made an appearance. Whoever is in the elevator when "the devil" steps in, simply steps out—without any thought. It is as if the "uh-oh here she comes" has been automated. Miranda appears, everyone scatters. These avoidance behaviors have become procedurally encoded.

In their endeavor to increase the precision in the understanding of therapeutic action, the BSG reviewed hours upon hours of psychoanalytic process. They were struck by those times when the consultation room seemed electrified, or when something very important seemed to be happening beyond the verbal interchange. What was discovered was that these "moments" often led to a transformation in the way patient and analyst had of being with one another. The BSG referred to these moments as "moments of meeting" or "now moments."

The following vignette serves as an example of such an electric moment. Joan (Gotthold & Sorter, 2006; Sorter, 1996) made a beeline for the corner of the sectional sofas in my office. Big-eyed, she sat with legs off the floor, as far into the corner as she could possibly move. My office chair is one with rollers. When I sat down, I initially rolled my chair forward slightly, to achieve what for me is an optimal and usually acceptable distance between my patient and me. Joan's eyes grew wider. She reared back, drawing herself as far from me as she possibly could, clearly indicating a need for distance physically and psychically. No words were spoken, nor were they necessary for me to understand that I had violated her space and she had done the best she could to escape me. Without premeditation, I immediately rolled my chair back. Joan visibly uncoiled and our session continued. This surprise action, unanticipated by either of us, was for both of us a now moment. A now moment, according to the BSG, is a special kind of "present moment" (Stern, 2004), one that is "lit up" affectively, resulting in the shared implicit relationship being called into the open. Within a few seconds, without uttering a word, Joan and I (DS) learned much about each other. This intersubjective sharing of experience was understood without having to be verbalized. The BSG has asserted that such crossings of the intersubjective field, of patient and analyst, lead to increasingly complex and coherent responses. This moment of meeting shaped our way of being together.

The spontaneity of the action in the moments of the session described above pulled both patient and therapist into what Stern (2004) would refer to as a "present moment, defined as a lived nonverbal moment." Moments of meeting, now moments, and present moments emerge in the context of the ongoing unfolding of the co-created, interactively regulated treatment process. These are steps in what the BSG and Stern (2004) refer to as the "moving along process," in other words, the stuff treatment is made of.

Stern (2004) devoted an entire chapter in *The Present Moment in Psychotherapy and Everyday Life* to the process of "moving along." He defines moving along as the everyday dialogue that moves the therapy session forward in time. It is the gathering of sentences, pauses, facial expressions that create what Stern termed the "local level." The local level was defined as "the second by second interchange between patient and therapist consisting of relational moves composed of verbal and nonverbal happenings, such as spoken phrases, silences, gestures and shifts in posture or topic." It is from this local level that "moments" emerge. The moments Stern refers to are "present moments" which consist of 1) relational moves, those present moments that one is aware of but that do not enter long-term memory; and 2) conscious present moments that are divided into the regular present moment, the now moment, and the moment of meeting. For a more detailed explanation of these particular moments we refer the reader to chapter 10 in Stern's 2004 book.

Subsequent work by the BSG highlighted the "fittedness" and "sloppiness" in the treatment process. Sander (1995a, 1995b, 1997, 2002) based on research examining parent/infant interactions, introduced the term "fittedness" into the BSG lexicon. . . . While Sander's initial work on fittedness was concerned with physiological regulation of states, especially sleep states, the BSG extended this term from physiological fittedness to include shifts in intersubjective states. Various other terms have been used to describe this phenomenon. The BSG (Stern, 2004) uses "fittedness of intentions," "recognition of fittedness," and "moments of meeting" almost interchangeably.

In the extension of the principles of nonlinear systems theory to the enactive theory of therapeutic change, the BSG embraced the notion of sloppiness (2005). This is their attempt to capture the improvisational, sloppy, messy, and spontaneous quality of the therapeutic relationship at the local level. Sloppiness, according to the BSG (2005), refers to the "indeterminate untidy or approximate qualities of the exchange of meaning between patient and analyst" (p. 694). In that 2005 article, they reiterated the belief that treatment takes place at the local level, where implicit relational knowing is enacted. A broad application of the local level envisions that traditional psychoanalytic concepts such as conflict and defense emerge from and are transformed at the local level. This implies a shift from a depth psychology to psychoanalysis at the local level. The topography of psychoanalysis is thus inverted by the BSG.

Our earlier work (Gotthold & Sorter, 2006) examining the BSG's constructs was in a questioning spirit. We wondered whether constructs such as implicit relational knowing, moments of meeting, now moments, terms conceived by the BSG, added specificity and clarity in describing the process of change. Then, as now, we feel their additions to the psychoanalytic lexicon capturing that "something more" are invaluable.

Once again we want to refocus attention on the importance of "moving along" which we feel to be central in the understanding of therapeutic action. We understand implicit relational knowing—not to be confused with unconscious process—to be the result of a co-created, interactively regulated process originating between infant and caregiver. This rule-based set of expectancies form the child's emergent implicit relational knowing and is procedurally encoded before symbolic language develops. It is this rule-based set of expectancies that each member of the treatment dyad brings to the consultation room. As Lyons-Ruth (1998) stated, "If all goes well, the child develops 'implicit relational knowing'" that becomes gradually "more articulated, integrated and complex" (p. 285). We believe the same holds true in the treatment situation. The vitality and therapeutic action of the treatment emerges from the uniquely, intersubjectively, co-configured dyadic procedural, as well as explicitly encoded ways of being together. If all goes well in the treatment process, implicit relational knowing for both patient and therapist becomes increasingly articulated, integrated, and complex.

We continue to question the underplaying of the moving along process. The moving along process, articulated by Nahum (1998), Tronick (1998), and Stern (2004), accounts for the gradual treatment process whereby a sense of self and agency can become increasingly coherent through a series of inevitable mutually regulated sequences. We believe that not only is this process essential to the understanding of those moments, but also that the unfolding of the co-created, interactively regulated, dyadic relational experience provides a priming of the therapeutic canvas where patient and analyst develop a context—a way of coming to know each other—such that these implicit relational moments can be transformative. We suggest that each moment is embedded within the procedural and declarative, ongoing context, co-created by the particular dyad. The following vignette is an example of this process.

Years into a treatment, more fully developed below, Paul, a rose expert, told me about a gift he thought of buying for his partner. "Dori, this exquisite little vase, with the perfect rose would fit right there on your mantle." Resulting from the multitude of our past interactions, I understood the shift and softening in the tenor of his voice to be indicative of his caring for me, caring developed with much struggle over many years. He, based on his sense of our past interactions, knew how meaningful this thought was to me. I knew, while he could never actually bring me a gift, this verbalized thought was an intimate and deeply felt communication. It spoke volumes about how far our relationship had evolved. There was no need to explore the actual giving of the gift. I suspect that such exploration may well have been destructive. It was known, by both of us, that no gift would be given.

There was no need to declaratively indicate my understanding of the meaning of the communication. The deeper meaning, the felt experience (the strength of the selfobject bond), was known between us. It reflected an implicit relational knowing—our way of being together. This moment was made possible by our respective procedurally encoded set of expectancies, transformed by the moving along—canvas priming process—and resulted in a transformation and expansion of our implicit relational knowing. We want to emphasize that the "ongoingness" (moving along) of the interactively regulated treatment process that occurs through the interweaving of nonverbal communication, such as facial expressions, shifts in tones of voice, the adoption of each other's way of being together, and declarative communication, is transformative. While change results from both the moving along of treatment, as well as the emergence of special moments, we believe the crafting of the co-created way of being together to be central to both.

In the above vignette this interweaving of explicit and implicit communications shaped the ongoing clinical process. Earlier we had advocated, as did the BSG, a collaborative handling of moments such as the one in the vignette above. Such handling may or may not involve a declarative interpretation of the treatment relationship. It was a collaborative process that took place over time and not simply a collaborative handling of a specific moment that resulted in the expansion of our implicit relational knowing.

The following question emerges: Must the implicit relational/declarative interactive sequences of treatment (what has been felt or discovered) be verbally articulated in order to be transformative? Stern, in his recent book (2004), argues both sides of this declarative/nondeclarative debate. Stern states that "change is implicit. It need not be made explicit and talked about. It becomes part of the patient's implicit relational knowing" (p. 152). He goes on to say that as a result of this transformation there is a preparation for "new explorations of explicit material and the way for interpretations" (p. 165).

We do not argue both sides of this debate. We believe that the moving along process results in transformation in *both* patient and analyst's implicit relational knowing, affecting the context and the way they are together. We further assert that co-created, interactively regulated interchanges occurring procedurally are transformative in and/of themselves and are, thus, interpretive. These formulations lead us not down the linear path, the procedural paving of the road to the declarative world of verbal interpretation. It is not a one-way street. There is a bidirectional influencing of procedurally encoded interchanges along with declarative interchanges. We believe, at times, remaining in the realm of the procedural process is imperative. As we demonstrated with our vignette, to say what does not need to be said can diminish both the shared experience of each participant.

From a slightly different perspective, that of Beebe and Lachmann (2002), the above vignette could be thought about as part and parcel of the ongoing regulations in the dyadic system. They would agree, as we suggest above, that therapeutic action can occur in an implicit form of processing without the necessity of translation into an explicit verbal mode (p. 209).

It is through our appreciation of the often separated worlds of child and adult psychotherapy that we have come to value both realms, procedural and declarative, as they contribute to the interpretive and transformative processes. We note that the field created by the intersubjective crossing of both the child and adult analysts' implicit relational knowing is essential to the inclusion and understanding of the procedural realm in play or nonverbal treatment process. Clearly evident in the treatment of children, development resumes, behavior and psychic change occurs, and a sense of agency returns without the primacy of the declarative realm.

What follows is a presentation of two cases: work with an adult and work with a child. It is our intention to demonstrate the universality of the underlying process of the interweaving of both declarative and procedural dimensions of the clinical process regardless of the specific developmental capacities brought to the consultation room. Our emphasis in these cases is on the moving along process.

PAUL

Orange (2006) suggested that the whole is more than the sum of its parts. In so doing she reminds us that all our moments take place in an overall context. Paul is now close to sixty years old. He has been in treatment with me for more than twenty years. Now when we sit together, I am amazed at what he has accomplished and at the relationships he has developed. Paul and I can note with pride and sometimes amusement how much his context has changed.

This treatment began with a referral from the school Paul's child attended, suggesting that Paul and his wife would benefit from couples therapy. During the couple's treatment, Paul developed a sense of trust that I was consistently present and reliable. He had never before experienced this sense of trust. That experience allowed Paul to consider beginning treatment with me. The potential for the formation of a selfobject experience with me felt present and I agreed to see him.

When the couple's treatment ended, Paul entered analysis with me. His early life had been filled with traumatic disruptions. I did not understand the enormity of its impact on him until we began to unravel and make some order of his history. As we tried to put a narrative together, both of us were confused. Paul's difficulty creating order out of the chaos was matched by my difficulty remembering the details of his narrative. Still, we moved along. I came upon a solution to my problem of retaining the details. I began to make notes, in a somewhat sloppy but yet orderly fashion. When I decided to write up this case, I found all these little slips of paper with events and dates listed.

What follows is part of a lengthy co-creation of his life's story as he told and retold it with me as a participant and witness. When Paul was four years old, his brother Johnnie (age six) died. There was massive confusion about the cause of Johnnie's death, including Paul's conviction that his father had killed his brother. Following this tragic event, Paul's family fell apart. The content of some of my notes follow: "After my brother died, my mother left home, leaving my younger brother and me. Every now and then she would show up but each time it was with a different man. . . . I had a nanny I loved. I think my younger brother and I even went to her house to live—or maybe it was for a few weeks. Suddenly our nanny left too. She was gone."

Paul's confusion showed in his eyes as he tried to understand how this possibly had happened. I wondered as well. Paul felt the chronology was important in order to make order out of his chaos. Thus, we searched for the actual dates of these events. "My father must have gone somewhere too. Maybe he moved into the hospital where he had an office. I guess that's when my nanny was there. . . . He would show up and take us to a beach. I was terrified. He would swim out and I was certain he would drown leaving me alone to take care of my brother."

Paul and I struggled along (moved along) with many repetitions of these occurrences. It was painful for Paul to recall them and painful for me to listen, but we kept at it for months. Another note read, "I didn't know where my father was but then he married Ava and he sent for us. We were put on a plane and got off in Guam. Ava was beautiful and let us do whatever we wanted. We had no hours, no regular meals, we could smoke, do whatever we wanted. I was going to grow up and marry her."

He wept as he finally was able to tell me that his beloved Ava committed suicide, leaving a trail of pills from the front door to the bedroom. My note read, "Our father retreated into a darkened study and alcohol. When I had to go into that room and ask for money to buy a hamburger for us, I was terrified. My brother and I were so confused; we would wander through the jungles and beaches and collected boulders (large rocks). I kept them in my dresser drawer."

Ultimately, Paul's father was hospitalized for alcoholism. Strangers appeared in Guam, swooped up the boys, and put them on a plane. When they got off the plane they discovered they were now to live with relatives in the "States." These exchanges took place over years.

Paul and I began to understand that those heavy rocks, collected during the black period following Ava's death, represented the only solid matter in their lives. Together we understood those rocks were concrete evidence that he existed. He could open the drawer and feel them. He could see them, and if he lifted them, he could feel their weight. As our relationship solidified over time, Paul experienced me as a rock, solid matter in his life. An idealizing selfobject tie allowed Paul to trust that together we could create some coherent narrative of his life. That is the moving along process and it is transformative.

Later, as Paul told and retold his story, the narrative began to have some coherence. We realized that the slips of paper provided concrete evidence, as did the rocks, of the reality of his experiences. Each time we pulled out one of the sheets of paper to order it chronologically, we would refer to them, see what was missing, modify what needed modification, and extend the narrative.

In the confusion of this tragedy, no one in the family had told Paul the correct story, nor was anyone available to verify or correct Paul's understanding of it, that his father had killed his brother. Everyone in the family had his or her own version of why Johnnie died. One relative, in the spirit of talking to young children, said Johnnie fell out of a tree on his head. That was not true. Over time Paul, as he realized that his father had not killed Johnnie, began to trust his own perceptions. Johnnie apparently had a seizure, hitting his head on the corner of a table as he fell. His father, present at the time, picked up his son, and distraught, tried to wake him. At this point in the treatment, Paul was able to follow the sequence of events and have some understanding of the wild confusion the family was thrown into with Johnnie's death. He was able to understand that his original view of the events was through the eyes of a four-year-old.

Of all the moments in the ongoingness of this co-created narrative, one sticks out for me. Describing a quiet moment Paul said, "You know, I was lying in my bed this morning just relaxed and thinking, when I 'knew' with a visceral certain sensation that my father did the best he could under the circumstances." I didn't feel the need to question this reflection. Our eyes met and I nodded. We sat quietly for a number of moments soaking in this profound observation. This was an amazing moment of meeting. It was almost as if we said, "Ah, yes, we have it. Now we know and we can move on with life." Declarations from me would surely have undone the profundity of his statement of knowing.

How can we understand a process such as the one above? In our work together we stumbled along. It was certainly messy, and very choppy. The work described above represents a major ongoing theme among many others in this treatment. Our work together included traditional psychoanalytic themes such as those surrounding the guilt he felt at moments of secret happiness that his older brother had died. He revealed this with shame as he recalled being told by his father, "Now you are my oldest son." The thrill of being the oldest son also terrified him. These feelings overwhelmed him leaving him fearful of being alone with his father. His fear that his father could now kill him as he had killed Johnnie with all its various permutations served as a backdrop to the psychoanalytic process. At moments when Paul was filled with shame over his confession, his dread that I would shame him, as he had felt shamed as a child would permeate our sessions. We would, in fits and starts, also come back to the trying to make sense of the chaos of his early life.

In any lengthy treatment there are disruptions and repairs of those disruptions. There were heightened moments (Beebe & Lachmann, 2002) such as the one described earlier about the "perfect rose vase." There were other moments when both of us were joyous over recovered abilities long dormant. There was, for instance, his description of writing a paragraph about a bird he had seen in the garden. The ability to make a statement, even a simple one about a bird in the garden, had been lost in the confusion of his mind and his fear about saying something that would bring on some dreaded event.

From a retrospective look we both feel pleased by what we have accomplished together. During the moving along dyadic process of this treatment, Paul and I have come to know each other very well. Paul now has a more cohesive narrative of his history. He is no longer afraid to "make a statement" and in fact now holds the title of executive director of his organization. Paul can now "read people," understand them, and talk to them without fear of retribution. His "implicit relational knowing" has expanded exponentially. I believe if I were to discuss this case with Karlen Lyons-Ruth she would say that Paul and I were participants in an ongoing process leading to "increasingly integrated and complex content." That's how I see it.

I had completed this report when we had one more opportunity to see where we were together. Paul was rereading a three-volume biography on Lyndon Johnson, a man he admires greatly. As he was regaling me with Johnson's virtues, I asked Paul if he thought he and I had together come to know nearly as much about him (Paul) as the author of the book knew about the workings of President Johnson's mind. He said the following:

> I've learned to be strategic. I used to think I had to do things indirectly. [He made the shape of an arc in the air.] I couldn't get from one thing to another because I was so fearful [paranoid, he added] about the consequences. Now I know I can trust myself and I can trust people. I can get from A to B in a direct manner. I understand people and I am not afraid to act. I can make a statement and know that someone will listen.

From a self psychological point of view, my emphasis is, in part, on my patient's subjectivity along with my contributions to the dyad. Paul's subjective experience, as communicated both declaratively and procedurally, was always in the forefront of our work together. As highlighted in this vignette, the moving along process facilitated the emergence of the selfobject transferences.

LITTLE HENRY

The following child case is offered as an example of both ongoingness or moving along process and a situation where the action sequences, in context, speak for themselves. Armed and ready, Henry, Little Henry as he was known in his family, entered our tiny consultation room, three times a week, in a determined manner. Armed, by his mother, with an "after school snack special" from a shop across the road from the clinic. Ready for me to appear in the waiting room, Henry clutched the bag containing the frank, the drink, and the chocolate chip cookie. Once in my office, Henry set up shop. He placed the frank, the drink, and the cookie in a neat row on the edge of my desk. Little Henry stood, wordlessly, in front of his materials and systematically ate each item in succession. Initially, there were never any deviations from his plan. As our time together grew, the rate of consumption deviated depending on what was on Henry's mind. Had the school day been upsetting? Did he need time to regroup before an interaction with another human? Or, did he recognize, want to be recognized, and count on the recognition by this now-familiar human? Following this voiceless, wordless, meaningful opening action sequence, Henry would greet me and give the "signal" that connection, verbal connection, was possible.

Our co-created opening ritual emerged early on in the treatment process (after the first three months or so) and continued until our summer break some seven months later. How did I come to participate in this mime-like drama? Initially, I felt constrained by the role of silent observer. However, the part I felt to be thrust into became my own. I knew we were always together, always engaged, and I was ready. I came to know the importance of waiting—of sitting silently, meaningfully—waiting for the final cookie crumb to be consumed, waiting for my cue, waiting for Henry to be ready.

In our wordless state, I understood Henry's need to feel in full control of his advances and responses to me. As much as possible, Henry tried to protect himself from my responses, initiations, or, as he could feel, intrusions. I experienced him as "titrating our connection" in order to make it possible for him to remain within a sphere of relatedness with me. Henry clearly knew how to psychically detach himself from potentially painful, overwhelming experiences with others. Yet, his desperate wish to know and be known powered his attempts at self-regulation in our budding relationship.

This work with Henry dates back to a time when communicating the power and meaning of such communications, therapeutic action sequences, or moments to the field was harder. Henry's sequences, pauses, glances, transformations, and resulting increased self- and interactive regulation were difficult to make understandable to other analysts and at times, even myself. Yet, as his therapist, even in silence, I experienced him as an "other" in our dyadic interactively regulated treatment relationship. I was acutely aware that only in his silence, in the actions sequences and in those moments, could selfobject transferences unfold, such that both mutative experiences and declarative interpretations would be transformative. Both the field and the treatment were at a loss for words.

Little Henry was a bright, verbal, and very troubled child when he began treatment at age eight. He was referred to treatment by his school, because he was distracted and distracting in the classroom. When he was able to be in the classroom, Henry would lurch around in his seat, often pretending to machine gun down his classmates. While his parents felt that "boys will be boys," the school expressed great concern. Henry was small for his age, thus the family's nickname. His self-contained stance rendered him so small he seemed almost nonexistent. His father, Big Henry, was very tall, large and booming. He demanded that Little Henry was and had to be "just like me." This demand extended to the point of Little Henry being dressed for school in a blazer and tie, when he attended a school without uniforms. Big Henry could not be denied or disappointed. Little Henry practiced meeting his father's emotional needs while protecting himself by retreating to violent, fantastical expansive scenarios. Little Henry and I later understood this dynamic as contributing to his feelings of nonexistence, fears of intrusion, and impulsive, seemingly random moments of anger.

Little Henry's mother, Doris, attempted to "run interference" for him in the home, in spite of her overwhelming fear, fragility, and disorganized thinking. Doris would plead with her husband to allow their son to "be a child." Big Henry's booming response often sent her to bed for a week, leaving Little Henry to fend for himself. Henry seemed to experience his mother's presence as, at best, minimally protective and at worst an intrusive betrayal. At times, Little Henry focused his rage at her, rendering her even more tentative and ineffective in her forays into what she felt was "mothering."

For Doris, as with many mothers, bringing her child to treatment was experienced as a referendum on her capacity as a mother. Doris spoke of feelings of inadequacy, fear, and guilt, while simultaneously searching my responses for signs of my valuing and appreciating her maternal instincts. I understood her provision of nurturance—the snack—was a concretization of her maternal role. Her snack set the wordless stage for our sessions. In some way, Henry brought Doris into session with him, as he regulated his hunger, his connection with me, his sense of purpose and separateness.

In a session nearing the end of the school year, Little Henry was in the midst of the snack when he looked in my direction, picked up the cookie, and said, "Want a piece?" While startled, I tried to respond in a matter of fact manner: "Sure . . . thanks." Henry broke off a piece of the cookie and watched expectantly as I ate it. "This sure is a good cookie," I said, with the satisfaction of having finished a huge meal. Little Henry broke out into one of his rare smiles. I noted how engaging and present he seemed when he managed a smile. He seemed to recognize me—a moment of bidirectional recognition, a moment of engagement, a now moment, a present moment? Is this an indication that Little Henry was now capable of an increasingly flexible, coherent, and complex response with a known other?

At the time the treatment was in progress most child therapists would have "gotten the drift" of my work with Henry. However, the means of rendering these sequences meaningful and accessible for discussion among all psychoanalysts was not readily available. The mutative effects of the treatment were in evidence, while the treatment process remained elusive.

One might wonder why being a therapist standing armed and ready, silent, attentive, careful, and respectful, watching a child eating an afternoon snack is considered treatment. "It just is" is not a sufficient response. Dramatic though Henry's smile was heralding in a seemingly new relational capacity between us, months of my standing armed and ready was the essence of the work—moving along.

The current conceptual formulations and lexicon of the BSG provides the means for discerning the formation and meaning of those interactively regulated therapeutic action sequences. The rich, transformative, moment-by-moment action sequences are important to understand not only in terms of the nonverbal or the unconscious dimensions but also in terms of the procedurally encoded ways of being with other—the implicit relational knowing dimension. This is clearly the "something more" that begged for explication.

This vignette illustrates a nondeclarative interpretative process. I never interpreted Henry's "resistance" or verbalized my observation that he seemed to need to protect himself from perceived intrusions or demands from me. I communicated my respect for his need to control the timing, distance, and pace of our interactions in silence and in stillness. If I had commented on our process, I would have re-created a familiar and familial situation where my explicit demands overrode his implicit relational capacities in an unattuned, nonempathic manner. Henry and I co-created a place where he could "just be" and experience his sense of being with another.

This clinical vignette demonstrates that empathic attunement and the unfolding of the selfobject transferences occurs within the inextricable weaving of procedural and declarative domains. In an earlier paper Gotthold (1996) addressed the need for the analyst (child analyst) to communicate his or her understanding of the child's subjective experience to the child, such that it is felt and understood by the child. It was noted that the analyst's understanding and resulting interpretations could be offered by way of nonverbal "play" or verbal communications. Fast forwarding to a more contemporary self psychological understanding of the child treatment process, we now account for the bidirectional, dyadic, dynamic ongoing process of self and interactive regulation that occurs, again, in the interwoven realm of play, procedural, and declarative communications. Henry's silences, beckoning me to play and speak, my careful attuned affective responsiveness to being offered a piece of cookie and our co-creation of a unique dyadic system of safety and freedom all occurred in a procedurally and declaratively intertwined realm of a system of influence and influencing.

CONCLUSION

Our highlighting of the moving along process and the nondeclarative dimension of interpretation that emerges from implicit relational knowing results from our conviction of the depth and richness of those processes. We feel that much is yet to be understood about the inextricable weaving of implicit relational knowing and the declarative dimension in any relationship.

In our earlier work, we noted the broad pan-theoretical value in the BSG's work. It seemed to us applicable regardless of one's psychoanalytic flavor. However, as demonstrated in the clinical vignettes presented, we find that their contributions fit well with a self psychological theoretical framework. As we continue to applaud, apply, and extend their constructs, we simultaneously fear the rush toward broad-stroke application of this model to an ever-widening range of clinical phenomenon. We wonder about the advisability of moving toward a "unified field" approach stemming from this work. The exquisiteness of their constructs lies in the precision and detail, locating the ever-smaller components of the something more. For example, implicit relational knowing more and more gets referred to as "the implicit," thus creating a danger of losing the exact meaning of the term and replacing the unconscious with the implicit. The BSG's creation of a viable lexicon for use in the field enabling the examination of therapeutic action to occur at close range is in fact its contribution. Flexibility, concealed dimensions of interaction, and richness emerges when any treatment conducted from any theoretical stance is explored from within this framework. We wonder what is to be gained if the BSG's research findings about the co-created moment-to-moment processes are stretched and pulled prematurely to neatly cover a wide range of older, dearly held constructs such as defense and conflict?

REFERENCES

Bacal, H. (1998). Optimal responsiveness and the specificity of selfobject experiences. In H. Bacal (Ed.), *Optimal responsiveness: How therapists heal their patients* (pp. 141–170). Northvale, NJ: Jason Aronson.

Beebe, B., Knoblaluch, S., Rustin, J., & Sorter, D. (2005). *Forms of intersubjectivity in infant research and adult treatment.* New York: Other Press.

Beebe, B., & Lachmann, F. (2002). *Infant research and adult treatment: Co-constructing interactions.* Hillsdale, NJ: Analytic Press.

Boston Change Process Study Group: Bruschweiler-Stern, N., Harrison, A., Nahum, J., Sander, L., Stern, D., & Tronick, E. (2002). Explicating the implicit: The local level and the microprocess of change in the analytic situation. *Int. J. Psychoanal., 83*, 1051–1062.

Boston Change Process Study Group. (2005). The "something more" than interpretation revisited: Sloppiness and co-creativity in the psychoanalytic encounter. *JAPA, 53*(3), 691–729.

Coburn, W. J. (2000). The organizing forces of contemporary psychoanalysis: Reflections on nonlinear dynamic systems theory. *Psychoanalytic Psychology, 17*, 750–770.

Cohen, N. J., & Squire, L. (1980). Preserved learning and retention of pattern-analyzing skill in amnesia: Dissociation of knowing how and knowing what. *Science, 210*, 207–209.

Davis, J. T. (2001). Revising psychoanalytic interpretations of the past: An examination of declarative and non-declarative memory processes. *Int. J. Psychana,, 82*, 449–462.

Fosshage, J. L. (1997). Listening/experiencing perspectives and the quest for a facilitating responsiveness. In A. Goldberg (Ed.), *Progress in self psychology, vol. 13* (pp. 33–55). Hillsdale, NJ: Analytic Press.

Fosshage, J. L. (2003). Contextualizing self psychology and relational psychoanalysis: Bi-directional influence and proposed synthesis. *Contemporary Psychoanalysis, 39*, 411–448.

Fosshage, J. L. (2005). The explicit and implicit domains in psychoanalytic change. *Psychoanalytic Inquiry, 25*, 511–539.

Gotthold, J. (1996). It's as easy as child's play: Play, a self psychological approach. *Psychoanalysis and Psychotherapy, 13*(1).

Gotthold, J., & Sorter, D. (2006). Moments of meeting: An exploration of the implicit dimensions of empathic immersion in adult and child treatment. *International Journal of Psychoanalytic Self Psychology, 1*, 103–119.

Lachmann, F. M., & Beebe, B. (1996a). Three principles of salience in the organization of the patient-analyst interaction. *Psychoanalytic Psychology, 13*, 1–22.

Lachmann, F. M., & Beebe, B. (1996b). Self and mutual regulation in the patient analyst interaction: A case illustration. In A. Goldberg, (Ed.), *Basic ideas reconsidered: Progress in self psychology, vol. 12* (pp. 123–140). Hillsdale, NJ: Analytic Press.

Lichtenberg, J. (1989). *Psychoanalysis and motivation.* Hillsdale, NJ: Analytic Press.

Lichtenberg, J. D., Lachmann, F. M., & Fosshage, J. L. (1992). *Self and motivational systems: Toward a theory of psychoanalytic technique.* Hillsdale, NJ: Analytic Press.

Lyons-Ruth, K. (1999). The two-person unconscious: Intersubjective dialogue, enactive relational representation and the emergence of new forms of relational organization. *Psychoanal. Inq., 19*, 576–617.

Orange, D., Atwood, G., & Stolorow, R. (1997). *Working intersubjectively: Contextualism in psychoanalytic practice.* Hillsdale, NJ: Analytic Press.

Orange, D. (2006). The whole is more: The "local level" and Heinz Kohut's psychoanalysis. International Self Psychology Conference, Chicago.

Sander, L. (1995). Identity and the experience of specificity in a process of recognition. *Psychoanalytic Dialogues, 5*, 5579–5593.

Sander, L. (1997). Paradox and resolution. In J. Osofsky (Ed.), *Handbook of child and adolescent psychiatry* (pp. 153–160). New York: John Wiley.

Sander, L. W. (2002). Thinking differently: Principles of process in living systems and the specificity of being known. *Psychoanalytic Dialogues, 12*(1), 11–42.

Sorter, D. (1996). Chase and dodge: An organization of experience. *Psychoanalysis and Psychotherapy, 13*(1), 68–75.

Squire, L. R. (1994). Declarative and nondeclarative memory: Multiple brain systems supporting learning and memory. In D. L. Schacter & E. Tulving (Eds.), *Memory Systems* (pp. 203–232). Cambridge, MA: MIT Press.

Stern, D. N., Sander, L., Nahum, J., Harrison, A., Lyons-Ruth, K., Morgan, A., Bruschweiler-Stern, N., & Tronick, E. (1998). Non-interpretive mechanisms in psychoanalytic therapy: The "something more" than interpretation. *Int. J. Psycho-Anal., 79*, 903–921.

Stern, D. (2004). *The present moment in psychotherapy and everyday life.* New York: W. W. Norton.

Stolorow, R. (1997). Dynamic, dyadic, intersubjective systems: An evolving paradigm for psychoanalysis. *Psychoanalytic Psychology, 13*, 337–346.

Stolorow, R., & Atwood, G. (1992). *Contexts of being.* Hillsdale, NJ: Analytic Press.

Stolorow, R., Brandchaft, B., & Atwood, G. (1987). *Psychoanalytic treatment: An intersubjective approach.* Hillsdale, NJ: Analytic Press.

Thelen, E., & Smith L. (1994). *A dynamic systems approach to the development of cognition and action.* Cambridge, MA: MIT Press.

II

APPLICATIONS TO CHILD TREATMENT

4

A Peek into the Playroom: A Contemporary Self Psychological Approach to Work with Children

Rosalind Chaplin Kindler

For the self psychologically oriented child and adolescent therapist, these are exciting times. The world of adult analysis has become attentive to the significance of spontaneity, creativity, improvisation, the use of metaphor, playfulness, music, and art in the treatment of adults (Kindler, 2005; Knoblauch, 2000; Lachmann, 2001; Lichtenberg, 1999; Ringstrom, 2001). The importance of nonverbal, noninterpretive modes of communication, as well as what can be implicitly known and co-constructed in the analytic encounter, is now well recognized (Stern, 1998, 2004; Gotthold & Sorter, 2006). Since these elements have long been the bread and butter of work with children and adolescents, this bodes well for a new collaborative and inclusive relationship between adult and child therapists, bridging the gap between the psychoanalytic worlds of adult and child treatment.

Many eminent writers have paved the way by describing work with children and adolescents from a self psychological point of view (Marohn, 1997; Palombo, 2001; Ornstein, 1974; Tolpin, 2003; Miller, 1996; Shane, Shane, & Gales, 1997; Schave & Schave, 1989). However, with some notable exceptions (Doctors, 1995, 1999, 2000; Gotthold, 2006; Hilke, 2004; Lewinberg, 1995; Smaller, 2003), relatively little has been written about work with children from the standpoint of contemporary self psychology.[1]

For the purposes of this chapter, I will borrow from Coburn's (2005) description of contemporary self psychology as "[being] increasingly distributed across a variety of creative, innovative points of view (in addition to the broader categories of the traditional, the intersubjective and the relational)." Coburn further states that "at this point, [self psychology] cannot be found exactly anywhere."

Such conceptual uncertainty does not faze child therapists. Contemporary self psychological child therapists, already comfortable with the creative and the innovative, also find themselves working within a happy confluence of relationally based theories. This confluence is comprised of developmental theories, such as attachment and infant research, which have important areas of overlap with clinically based theories, such as intersubjectivity and traditional self psychology (Doctors, this volume). How do these concepts help us in the clinical situation with children? Doctors suggests that this "clinical overlap," which occurs among the relational theories, informs and contributes to our understanding of the clinical picture. For example, in discussing how attachment theory and research contributes to the self psychological/intersubjective approach, Doctors argues that "phenomenologically, [these] theories all view development in the context of the interacting psychological worlds of children and caregivers. Attachment theory, like self psychology and intersubjectivity, underscores the central role of relationships throughout life." Further, the increase in our understanding of development based on direct observation of the "clinical child" as well as the "observed infant" has allowed a far more sophisticated identification of normative versus pathological behaviors in children. This chapter will offer some clinical examples to demonstrate the application of this theoretical confluence, in short, a peek into the contemporary self psychological treatment room.

The difficulty, expressed by Coburn (2005) in precisely locating contemporary self psychology, has ironically resulted in a remarkable transformation in psychoanalytic thinking and practice with adults. However, for those of us who work with children, the advent of many of these overlapping contributions has been welcome and perhaps even felt to be somewhat overdue. Moreover, for many child therapists, the introduction of certain of these concepts has been received as an acknowledgment and affirmation of what we have intuitively known and practiced in our work with children, but had not found a way to conceptualize.

We now have the benefit of a language and a literature to describe the complexity of our interactions with our child patients. One of the most comprehensive and innovative providers of many of these conceptualizations was the Boston Process of Change Study Group (1998). This group was comprised of representatives from the fields of psychotherapy, psychoanalysis, developmental psychology, and pediatrics. Their goal was to study the elements that brought about change in the psychotherapeutic encounter. From Stern came such notions as the improvisational nature of the therapeutic process and such concepts as "moments of meeting," "now moments" (Stern, 1998, 2004), and "the something more than interpretation" (Stern, 1998). The group assimilated from cognitive psychology (Epstein, 1994) the concepts of implicit (procedural) knowledge, that which is "known" or remembered, but is out of awareness, into the spectrum of contemporary psychoanalytic thought. These concepts resonated powerfully with child therapists. Now we had a language for those "moments" when we just "knew" that something unnameable had happened between child and therapist; those moments when we felt "in our bones" that something important and reciprocal had been communicated. We did know that in those moments words were not necessary. Lyons-Ruth (1998) described these meaningful moments, so familiar to child therapists, as experiences of "implicit relational knowing," moments that occurred and were experienced at a presymbolic or nonverbal level.

Researchers following mother-infant moment-to-moment interactions brought us the concept of self and mutual regulation (Beebe & Lachmann, 1988). Stern (1985) introduced the notion of affect attunement (p. 138) and RIGS (Representations of Interactions that have become generalized) (p. 97). These concepts provided us with a language to explain our experience when we kept so tightly in touch with the child's emotional tone and subtle shifts in state. We could recognize the positive outcome as emerging from our being reliably available to a child through experiences of misery, unhappiness, and disappointment. We could now understand our therapeutic work as contributing to the child's "lived moments," changing the child's implicit rules of relationship. We could recognize these building blocks of experience in therapy as crucial to the child's recovery with or without the addition of verbal explanations.

Further, the "baby watchers" (infant researchers) gave us a language for so much that we "just did" with children. For example, whether engaged in play with toys, art, music, dramatic role-play, or simply talking, we can now be aware that the quality of "being with" the child depends not only on our capacity to attend to the child's needs for our attuned empathic immersion into his or her subjective experience, but also on our capacity to find meaning in all of the child's communications and responses in the interactive process across the verbal and the physiological realms. That is, body position and movements, tone of voice, and tempo and quality of speech and movement. So, for example, when we lower our vocal tone and/or slow the tempo of our speech to match the child's, when we move our bodies to find just the right proximity for the child's comfort, we now understand how and why this is an effective tool for affect regulation (Stern, 1985).

At around the time the Boston Change Process Study Group, as it came to be known, was publishing its ideas, the work of developmental psychologist Peter Fonagy and his collaborators emerged, providing an innovative and influential contribution to the field of child psychoanalysis and the question of how and why therapeutic change happens. Fonagy's research examined the links between the quality of attachment between child and parent and the development of the capacity for mentalization or reflective function in the child, thus combining a psychoanalytic perspective with a cognitive affective developmental view. "Mentalization enables children to 'read' other people's minds" (Fonagy & Target, 1998, p. 92). In other words, the capacity for reflective function allows the child to "hold the experience of the other in mind" (Coates, p. 120). Importantly, this "thinking about thinking" (Fonagy, 1991) also allows the child the sense that he or she can be kept in mind by the other. This question of keeping the other in mind has been addressed and defined by many theoreticians throughout the literature, for example, Bowlby's (1973) concept of internal working models, the representational world of ego psychology, Stern's (1985) RIGS, and the organizing principles of intersubjectivity theory (Brandchaft & Stolorow, 1990). However, the capacity to mentalize has emerged as a crucial instrument in the assessment and treatment of children and adults.

Significantly for child therapists, self psychology's emphasis on relational development provides a natural area of overlap with attachment theory. Child and adult therapists alike have been powerfully influenced by the revolutionary contribution of Bowlby and his followers. For the contemporary self psychologically oriented child therapist this has been a crucial aid in understanding the child's experience of his/her relational world. A key addition was the adult attachment interview (Main & Goldwyn, 1991), a research instrument designed to measure the attachment patterns of adults in their families of origin, which found co-relations and predictable attachment patterns that prevailed cross-generationally. This important area of study was incorporated and elaborated by Fonagy, et al. (1995). This body of knowledge has further shaped the thinking of child therapists, allowing them to gain insights into the attachment patterns of the parents of their child patients, and thus be alert to the possible cross-generational implications for attachment pathology.

The cases presented here will illustrate how these overlapping theoretical and clinical ideas have influenced my understanding and ways of responding in the clinical situation.[2]

Simon is a nine-year-old boy with rosy cheeks, quite small for his age, but with a solid frame. He has straight blond hair, cut quite short, and light blue eyes which meet my gaze, then dart away when I approach him in the waiting room. His mother, who has brought him, flashes me a brilliant smile. She and I have already met several times. I have also met with Simon's father. Simon, I know from his parents, has been having a terrible time these days, particularly in school. He resists going, gets into a lot of trouble when he's there, and is frequently sent to the principal's office or is sent home, suspended. He is teased by other kids and is aggressive and destructive in class, ripping up his own and others' work. He often gets out of control and puts himself in danger, running outside or up and down the hallways.

Simon's presenting picture triggered certain thoughts and questions for me. I thought of his behavioral symptoms in terms of affect regulation and impulse control. I wondered about his vulnerability to specific kinds of injuries that would trigger rage and shame reactions and which he tried to counteract with aggressive and oppositional behavior. I also wondered about the various contexts in which these behaviors took place and with whom (signs of selfobject failures). Further, as a nine-year old, Simon's successful passage along the developmental path seemed under threat. Optimally, this developmental stage should be a time of significant relational, psychological, and cognitive growth, a time when the child can develop a new sense of independence, competence, and efficacy through activities outside the home with peers and alternative adult role models.

Simon seems to quickly get comfortable and settles on play with the Play-Doh. I sit beside him. We settle into a rhythm of light conversation while, with great purpose and concentration, he makes one-dimensional Play-Doh faces and attaches them to Popsicle sticks. He is quiet. I tell Simon how his parents had both been to see me and how they agreed that he should come and meet me. He makes a smiling face with the Play-Doh and then says he's going to make a sad face. My heart sings. "Great!" I think, "This boy is going to be a gift to work with."

I felt excited and encouraged because Simon seemed to be capable of both appropriately identifying affect states and of expressing them in play, an indication that he has a sense of his affective life.

I wait. Then, feeling hopeful, I ask him if anything ever makes *him* feel sad. "No." "No?" I wait some more. "Scared?" "No." He works away stolidly. There's something about this exchange, which, in spite of his flat denial, somehow leaves me feeling invited in. In fact there is a nice rhythmic, playful feel to this. I decide to play on. "Worried?" I venture, keeping it light. By now I get that they're rhetorical questions, and I think he knows this. "No." "Hmm," I say. And I wait in what now feels like a playful silence.

Simon then volunteers that they used to have Play-Doh like this at his school, but he doesn't get to do that stuff any more. I ask him about what it's like for him at school these days. He tells me he likes school a lot, likes doing work at school. It seems that there's nothing about school he doesn't like. He continues to work with great concentration, but soon asks me to tell him again about the fact that both his parents had come to see me. He asks me to repeat what I'd told him earlier about how they had both agreed that they wanted him to come and see me to get help with his worries. This is new in his experience. His parents are divorced and Simon knows they do not agree about anything much. I wonder if he's trying to find out if I know this too.

I ask him if he would like to see the other part of my office where I met with his parents. I show him which chairs they had sat on. Although he understands that they had not come together, Simon asks me several times to show him exactly which chairs they had used. He is like a child who needs to hear his favorite story over and over. The fact that both parents had sat down in my office was terribly important to him.

> I believe that asking direct questions of children about their presenting symptoms is generally a counterproductive pursuit. The child who has been brought to see you with encopresis is unlikely to respond happily to direct questions about this shame-filled symptom. Most agree that what generally works best is to wait for issues to emerge from the child. We have all had the experience of parents informing us of the latest misdeed committed by their child, with instructions to the therapist and the child to "talk about it in therapy." My experience is that the feelings of shame stirred up by such confrontations, can often be more harmful than useful. However, in the session just described, I found myself pulled into this playful, rhythmic, "question and answer" back and forth with Simon. And the experience of mutual recognition that occurred in this sequence carried us forward to something: a spontaneously arrived at "moment" resulting in my decision to show Simon where his parents had sat. This "moment of meeting" (Stern, 1998, 2004), although spontaneously arrived at, was also fueled by my conviction that, for children of divorced parents, particularly in cases of high conflict, it is extremely important that they be given any information which may provide them with a sense that their parents have agreed on something, that their mother and father can unite with a common purpose: their child. This experience can do a lot to alleviate feelings of self-blame, resentment, and hopelessness, and may provide the child with a much-needed opportunity to feel affirmed and acknowledged and to experience both parents as equally idealizable. Simon is the only child of this divorced couple. Many separated or divorced parents feel fearful, angry, and deeply wounded by each other, but are nonetheless loving parents. However, it is often the case that their engagement in protracted and painful legal battles can leave the child extremely anxious, disturbed, and sometimes traumatized.

Satisfied about his parents' meetings with me, Simon moves over to the toy shelf and chooses to play with the rescue helicopter and ambulance. The play has a mechanical feel to it. People are injured and must be rescued, but there is no narrative to flesh out the play. He is unable to provide any affective content and has no interest in adding the how or why they got hurt, never mind how they may feel about it. People need to be rescued. He can't say why. They need to be taken to hospital. But the ambulance driver is "crazy." He doesn't even have a license, and repeatedly crashes the ambulance and its patients, often running over their bodies. After watching this as it is repeated again and again, I comment, "Everyone is having a horrible time here, including that driver." He nods in agreement. When the play is complete, Simon (the driver) mutters an apology as he tosses the toys back onto the shelf. I ask Simon about the apology. He says that the driver had been causing a lot of trouble, acting crazy, and everyone was mad at him. I respond that the driver seemed to be very upset and was having to drive without even a license. He didn't even have a co-driver. I am to see a great deal of this crazy ambulance driver as Simon moved through his therapy. He appeared, as if on cue, whenever events (i.e., parental disputes), in Simon's life erupted anew.

The sequence just described grew out of what went before: the sequence of the Play-Doh faces, the "question and answer game," his telling me something about school, his disavowal of his experience there and my spontaneous decision to show him the place where his parents had sat to talk about his problems. Having established for himself that this was a place where he could play as he wished, Simon then set about telling me what his life was really like through his play, describing the turbulence of his subjective world. This was his way of symbolically representing his self-experience, communicating to me his sense of himself as being responsible for the damage and trauma of his parents. Ambulances are supposed to help people, but he was unable to do this and in fact, was sure that he caused them more pain. Although Simon had allowed me to witness his play, he did not actually invite me to actively participate with him. Unlike the previous sequences, he seemed to need me solely as an observer. This left me feeling somewhat at odds and out of touch, since my personal style tends to be more active. Further, it was difficult to be with him in this painful world, while relegated to the role of bystander. The intervention I did make, following his discarding of the apologetic ambulance driver, was designed to help Simon know that, although he might need to discard that painful part of his experience, as he had disavowed his miseries in the early part of the session, I could recognize the pain and shame in his experience, and I would not discard him.

As well as the school behavioral difficulties Simon was an isolated child, who did badly socially. His mother reported that, at home with her, Simon was a "perfect child," who presented no problems, was caring and solicitous and who took care of her when she was ill. He slept in mother's bed most nights when staying with her. His father reported that when staying with him, Simon slept alone and well. This need to preserve the connection, to protect and stay close to his mother, and his expectation that all would not be well for her (or him) in his absence, was also expressed in his school refusal.

For the first six months of therapy Simon's play centered around expressions of rage and helplessness. Puppet shows consisted entirely of one violent enactment after another, all of the puppets inflicting pain on each other, receiving terrible injuries and having to go to the hospital. During these shows Simon kept his eyes on me as if checking my reaction. Could I tolerate this? Would I disapprove and throw him out of my office? However, as the audience, my contributions to these enactments were to applaud, ask questions, and add the affective content where possible, as in, "Wow! That must really hurt!" or "He looks like he's really mad now." Or simply, "What happened?" Subsequently, there gradually began to emerge, the sprouts of narrative and the seeds of some affective content in Simon's play.

Simon had, from quite early on, taken to fixing things in the playroom. This began when one day a piece of dollhouse furniture broke. Together we glued the damaged piece and Simon was eager to check it when he next came. One day, about six months into treatment, Simon said it was a pity we couldn't play at having a store. I responded that indeed we could, and together we constructed a drama in which Simon had a fix-it shop, and I was the customer. Simon now adopted the persona which evolved and developed over the following months, that of the horribly overworked tradesman who works alone, has no sleep and no rest, but who speaks of these hardships in a matter-of-fact way. He is incredibly skilled at his job and in such demand that he has no alternative but to serve the public demand for his services at all hours, paying no heed to his own need for rest. He is overworked and exhausted but not angry, simply quietly resigned.

Only one call was required from me at any time of the day or night and Mr. Fix-It was at my door in seconds with his tools attached to his waist. I would tell him what needed fixing and he'd slide under the couch, as a mechanic under a car, and tinker and bang with his tools, until he would pronounce it fixed. Then he would say, "Well, what else do you have that needs fixing, ma'am?" Pretty soon, he has fixed everything in sight. His conversation is always very unemotional and calm. No, he has no help. Yes, he does get lonely. Yes, he does work very hard. Indeed, he only sleeps for maybe ten minutes every day. Yes, he is tired. He soon also reveals that everything I have in my "house" is exactly the same as he has in his. On another fix-it call he invites me under the couch with him to learn and see how to fix things, and soon he has offered me a job. I can take the night shift. These dramas were co-constructed by us both, but always initiated by Simon, and they continued in one form or another up to the end of Simon's therapy, which lasted about a year.

Simon's expectancies (Beebe & Lachmann, 1988) or organizing principles (Brandchaft & Stolorow, 1990) were reflected in the way the transference was played out with me. He would often ask me what I was going to do after our session was over. Would I go home or stay in the office? Would I be alone? As if, as with his mother, he might worry if this were so, because he was not certain that I would be all right without him. Another dimension of the transference could be understood by his careful monitoring of my reaction to the violent enactments in his puppet play. Could I tolerate his expressions of aggression? Would I see him as a bad kid, a troublemaker, and then reject him? Both the selfobject and the repetitive dimensions of the transference are evident in these communications. Simon's selfobject needs for mirroring, as well as idealizing and twinship experiences were played out in the co-constructed dramas he created. Indeed, his role as the ever-ready fixer of everything could also be understood to reflect what Tolpin (2003) describes as a "forward edge" experience of self-expansion in the transference. Simon had adopted an insecure attachment pattern that relied on accommodation as a way of keeping connected with mother; one which compromised and thwarted his age-appropriate developmental strivings (Brandchaft, 1993).

Simon and I did not talk very much about his troubles at school. But we did talk about his success when things were going well. And we did talk about his parents. The crazy driver, always arriving along with news of a new parental conflict, later became part of our language which, after a while, needed little further elaboration. We both "implicitly knew" all that was contained in this symbolic character. The shift from my role as non-participating witness to actively invited participant provided a myriad of selfobject experiences for Simon. His play reflected a shift in self-experience from crazy to competent, from destructive to constructive, and although his external world continued to seethe and churn, reports from parents and teachers were that he was doing better. My work with Simon led me to reflect again on the question of what it is that is curative in therapy. Although I was unable to effect any change between the parents, perhaps the fact that each parent maintained a positive alliance with me allowed Simon to be successful in fixing, or righting himself (Lichtenberg, 1989, p. 327).

One of the defining elements of work with children is the work with parents. Winnicott famously said "There is no such thing as a baby" (Winnicott, 1985). But until relatively recently, it did not naturally follow that parents were welcomed as participants in the analytic work with their children. In the child analyses of Klein, Anna Freud, and even Winnicott, parents were seen only as necessary supports to allow therapy to proceed, but peripheral in terms of their inclusion in the process. Altman, Briggs, Frankel, Ginsler, & Partone (2002) describe this important shift: "'To the extent that the traditional models are one-person models, the analytic situation could appropriately be thought of as consisting solely of the child and the analyst. [Accordingly] work with parents was seen by Freudian and Kleinians alike, as necessary only to secure their financial and moral support for the analytic process. . . . In our view, by contrast, parents and other caretakers are intrinsically parts of the analytic relational field" (p. 11).

The importance of this aspect of child work cannot be overestimated. Moreover, the means of bringing the parents into the treatment process will vary with each child and family. Possibilities range from weekly or monthly meetings with parents to conjoint sessions with parent and child together, to parenting sessions, which do not include the child. Whichever modality is used, work with parents is informed by the same range of theoretical and clinical concepts as those which guide all our clinical experience. In the following vignette, I present a fragment of a child-mother treatment, which illustrates how the convergence of some of the theoretical ideas presented here can be brought to bear to bring about change in the clinical picture.

Tessa is a startlingly beautiful child of six. She has deep brown eyes and dark curls which reveal her South American ethnicity. Her parents describe her as a "hellion." Her mother Paula reports that she feels "held hostage" by her daughter, either engaged in constant and often grim battles over control or in a state of apprehension, "walking on eggs," lest she set off another screaming tantrum. Paula, Brazilian by birth, is a bright intense woman who worked for many years in the fashion industry. She perceives her daughter as in need of discipline. Paula says that she wants some help in getting Tessa to concede that she, Tessa, is not the authority in the household, that this should be the mother's domain. But she feels uncertain when to be more (or less) firm, always second-guessing herself. Tessa's father, Frank, is a teacher of linguistics at a major university. He seems to be less worried by his daughter's behavior, feeling that his wife just needs to be firmer with her. They both describe Tessa's difficulties with transitions, with settling at bedtime, and her increasingly rough use of her mother's hair, which she has always used for self-soothing purposes along with thumb-sucking. Paula feels that, currently, there is an assaultive quality to this experience, with Tessa now increasingly holding her mother's hair so vigorously that she often hurts her. Paula feels guilty and angry and helpless. Tessa's behavior often leaves Paula feeling puzzled. First, because it never occurs in school where she is experienced as cooperative and unusually well-behaved, but also because Tessa is, in turn, either fiercely fighting with her mother over "silly little things" or desperately clinging to her, to such an extent that Paula often feels trapped and helpless.

Tessa has a sister, Sonia, six years her senior, who has a severe disability which requires constant and ongoing care and attention. Tessa walked at nine months and began to speak in sentences at around sixteen months. Conversely, Sonia's lagging development became more and more marked in contrast to Tessa's fast-track development in both the verbal and physical realms. Her parents describe Tessa's dawning awareness of her older sister's "different-ness" as she overtook her developmental milestones. However, Tessa's battles with her parents never involve her sister. They report that, quite the opposite, she is very helpful and even solicitous in contributing to Sonia's care and learning, but recently her controlling and oppositional behavior has become worse.

Tessa's parents did not initially come seeking treatment for their daughter. Paula's goal was to make some changes through strategies learned from parenting sessions. Several meetings took place with parents, both together and separately, during which the problems as they described them, were deconstructed to help them better understand the meanings and contexts in which the difficult interactions occurred. My sense was that Paula felt overwhelmed, powerless, and ashamed at her perceived incompetence in the face of her daughter's behavior. One day, after several sessions with Paula, she spoke urgently of her wish to do something to improve her relationship with Tessa, and suggested she should bring her in so that I could meet her. As we talked about this, Paula suggested that she might "set up" some circumstance that would be sure to create a "meltdown" just before bringing her, so that I could see it firsthand. While appreciating her need to have me as a witness, I firmly vetoed this idea. But we agreed that it might be useful to have Paula join Tessa in the playroom so that I could see how things went between them.

However, on the day of our session, Paula called me, saying that, although Tessa had previously responded well to the idea of their coming to see me, when reminded of our appointment earlier that morning, Tessa had refused to come, warning her mother that she would kick and scream and yell when she came to pick her up after school to bring her to my office. From our phone discussion Paula had seemed to handle the situation well, but was worried and wanted to warn me. I found myself preparing mentally for their arrival, limbering up, so to speak, in my mind, anticipating Tessa's resistance and its possible manifestations and meanings, thinking of all the different ways I might handle it and of the different ways this might play out. This situation is one that child therapists encounter on a regular basis, but it always requires a lot of mental preparation and self-monitoring. It seemed that, after all, Paula's call was to prepare me to meet the "hellion" in full force.

I was however, surprised to be met in my waiting room by Paula, accompanied by a calm, if somewhat wary, little girl with dark curls tied up in a rather funky ponytail. Tessa stood uncertainly at a little distance from her mother when I came to meet them. She returned my gaze and responded to my greeting by proffering for my inspection some small toys she had brought with her. I was struck by how immediately and comfortably she engaged with me. Once in the playroom Tessa seemed to quickly settle in, checking out the toys and commenting on this or that, to both her mother and me. Paula, although understandably somewhat diffident in this new situation, seemed able to participate and responded appropriately to her daughter's remarks.

However, after a few moments of comfortable exchange, mother and daughter entered into a low-key but gradually intensifying argument about Tessa's view of the purpose of a toy, which was similar to one she had at home. In this exchange I noted a sense of barely restrained antagonism between them, with Tessa adamant that she had it right, and Paula refusing to concede. However, although it was clear they were both on their best behavior, I assumed this to be prototypical, albeit in a low-key, of the kind of interaction which so often escalated into what Paula had described as "meltdowns." I also noted that, of the two, Paula seemed the more unsteady and unsure. In contrast there was, in Tessa's eyes, the glint of determination and a kind of excited anticipation. After a few moments of watching this exchange, and thinking that any further escalation was not going to be constructive, I decided to intervene with a mediating comment ("Sometimes we remember things differently"), which seemed to leave them both satisfied and able to move on.

Tessa then settled on play with the puppets. With her mother and I sitting on the floor, she quickly devised a "tricking" game which took the form of first building herself a multilayered tent-like thing in which she could "hide," then diving inside the tent, taking two puppets with her, which she first showed us and asked us to note.

As Paula and I sat together, there was a sense that we were engaged in a positive collaboration, which required little in the way of elucidation between us. We exchanged glances, which allowed us to implicitly agree that we would stay within the rules of Tessa's game. Neither of us knew exactly where it would lead, but we both knew we were willing to follow her lead. Tessa reemerged after a few moments, holding the two puppets behind her back. "This is the game I made up," she confidently announced. "You have to guess which of these puppets I'm thinking about." She will award a first prize to whoever guesses right and a second prize to the other. This game was repeated many times over. The score was an easy win for mother, with an occasional first-prize nod to me. Tessa also created another variation which consisted of her choosing particular pieces of play jewelry, earrings and so on, up to twelve, laying them out in order of preference, then mixing them up and asking us, in turn, to remember her preferences in the correct order. Again, Paula scored very well.

Only when the play was ended did we move beyond the play metaphor to articulate her experience more directly. As we cleaned up, I commented on the things we had said and done together, and Paula spontaneously asked Tessa about how she may feel about her sister's needs for so much attention. Tessa responded that it did sometimes "make her a bit mad." Tessa left my office calmly.

I was struck by the dramatic impact and the possible meanings of Tessa's play. My response was one of excitement and wonder at the magic of how beautifully things can sometimes work for some children in a therapeutic setting. Tessa was one of those children who seem to recognize immediately that something good might happen here, that here is an opportunity for self-expression in a safe environment. In thinking about the work with Paula and Tessa, three moments emerge as pivotal points in the process.

Each of these pivotal moments illustrates how the theoretical confluence plays out in the clinical situation.

The first pivotal moment was the shift in Paula from a stance in which she did not want me to see her daughter, to one in which she did. Second was the innocuous, but clearly important comment I offered to deflect the mounting tension between mother and child: "Sometimes we remember things differently." Third was the emergence of Tessa's game, which she played out almost as if she had devised a script, using both of us as participants.

What happened in our work that gave rise to this change of heart in Paula? This first shift reflected some change in Paula's capacity to reflect on the quality of her relationship with Tessa, to think about how each reacted and responded to the experience of the other, in other words, how their affective states were mutually regulated (Beebe & Lachmann, 1988). But one could also speculate that Paula's suggestion that she bring Tessa was an expression of her growing trust that, if I were to witness her humiliation and see her and Tessa at their "worst" during one of Tessa's "meltdowns," I would not judge her negatively or blame her as a "bad mother." There might also have been a gleam of hope flickering in Paula that such a meeting could ultimately be useful. In technical terms, the emergence of a selfobject transference allowed Paula to feel free to include her child in the work with herself. Also, given the prevailing quality of Tessa's attachment (insecure-ambivalent in Ainsworth's language), my thoughts further led me to the notion of the transgenerational transmission of attachment patterns (Main & Goldwyn, 1991; Fonagy, et al.,1995) and their implications for this mother-daughter dyad. Paula had described her own history of disturbed attachment. As a young and only child she had repeatedly been left alone and isolated for hours while her parents went out. She described herself pacing back and forth in fear and anxiety, certain they were dead and would never return, and her parents' chronic obliviousness to her experience.

The second pivotal moment, my remark, "Sometimes we remember things differently," had the twofold effect of first, modeling for Paula an alternate way of responding and deflecting conflict. But it also seems that this minor intervention, which expressed empathic understanding of both points of view and modeled acceptance of differences, allowed Tessa the freedom to move forward and engage mother and myself in her play, which became for her, a crucial vehicle for expression.

The third critical moment came with Tessa's game. This game had, in fact, all the hallmarks of a game show, featuring Tessa in the role of host, as she set the tough questions and announced the winners and losers, but managing never to lose her benign good humor. The game also captured something essential about their relationship. Tessa seized this opportunity to convey to her mother something about her experience of herself in relationship to her mother. But particularly relevant for the therapeutic process, Tessa's play provided her with the opportunity to articulate, within her chosen metaphor, something of her self-experience. This is play in the service of mastery. The implied meanings go further, into the realm we have already discussed of attachment and mentalization (Fonagy & Target, 1998).

In children's dramatic play, role reversal is a familiar phenomenon. Configurations of self and other can be reversed. The game seemed to capture a powerful theme in their relationship: Could her mother hold her in her mind, "think about her thinking" (Fonagy, 1991), and therefore, know her experience? The play was enacted by Tessa, and facilitated by Paula and myself. In this way, Tessa's message could be kept within the metaphor of her play. Paula later reported that, although they still had difficulties, she'd felt relieved to be able to be with Tessa in this way and, remembering the intervention I'd made ("Sometimes we remember things differently"), had recently made successful use of it to avoid another conflict. One could hope that this idealizing selfobject experience had contributed to Paula's growing capacity to respond empathically to Tessa.

Contemporary self psychology currently resides within the confluence of a range of innovative theoretical concepts from the canons of the relational and developmental theories. Each informs and enhances the other, enlightens our clinical judgment, and provides us with a background sensibility from which our interventions emerge. These concepts have provided self psychological child therapists, along with their adult-treating counterparts, with a new conceptual framework which affirms and enriches their clinical work. These are indeed exciting times.

REFERENCES

Altman, N., Briggs, R., Frankel, J., Gensler, D., & Pantone, P. (2002). *Relational child psychotherapy*. New York: Other Press.

Beebe, B., & Lachmann, F. (1988). Mother-infant mutual influence and precursors of psychic structure. In A. Goldberg (Ed.), *Frontiers in self psychology: Progress in self psychology, vol. 3* (pp. 3–25). Hillsdale, NJ: Analytic Press.

Boston Process of Change Study Group. (1998). Non-interpretive mechanisms in psychoanalytic therapy: The "something more" than interpretation. *International Journal of Psychoanalysis, 79*(5), 903–921.

Bowlby, J. (1973). *Attachment and loss. Vol. 2: Separation*. London: Hogarth Press.

Brandchaft, B. (1993). To free the spirit from its cell. In A. Goldberg (Ed.), *The widening scope of self psychology: Progress in self psychology, vol. 9* (pp. 209–230). Hillsdale, NJ: Analytic Press.

Brandchaft, B., & Stolorow, R. (1990). Varieties of therapeutic alliance. *The Annual of Psychoanalysis, 18*, 99–114.

Coburn, W. (2006). *Int. Journal of Psychoanalytic Self Psychology*, 1 (1), 3.

Doctors, S. (1995). Rachel's struggle: A self psychological perspective on late adolescent pathology. *Psychoanalytic Review, 82*(4), 499–513.

Doctors, S. (2000). Attachment-individuation: Clinical notes toward a reconsideration of "adolescent turmoil." *Adolescent Psychiatry, 25*, 3–16.

Doctors, S. (2007). On utilizing attachment theory and research in self psychological/intersubjective clinical work. In P. Buirski & A. Kottler (Eds.), *New Developments in Self Psychology Practice* (pp.). Lanham, MD: Jason Aronson.

Fonagy, P. (1991). Thinking about thinking. *Int. J. Psychoanalysis, 72*, 639–656.

Fonagy, P., Steele, M., Steele, H., Leigh, T., Kennedy, R., Mattoon, G., & Target, M. (1995). Attachment, the reflective self and borderline states: The predictive specificity of the adult attachment interview and pathological emotional development. In S. Goldberg, R. Muir, & J. Kerr (Eds.), *Attachment theory: Social, developmental and clinical perspectives* (pp. 233–278). New York: Analytic Press.

Fonagy, P., & Target, M. (1998). Mentalization and the changing aims of child psychoanalysis. In S. Mitchell (Ed.), *Psychoanalytic Dialogues*. Hillsdale, NJ: Analytic Press.

Gotthold, J., & Sorter, D. (2006). Moments of meeting: An exploration of the implicit dimensions of empathic immersion in adult and child treatment. *International Journal of Psychoanalytic Self Psychology, 1*(1), 103–119.

Gotthold, J. (1996). It's as easy as child's play: Play, a self psychological understanding. *Psychoanalysis & Psychotherapy, 13*, 19–26.

Hilke, I., Chaplin Kindler, R., Gottlieb, J., Smaller, M. (2007). How Does Analytic Child Therapy Inform Adult Treatment? Miss Nicht. In *Int. Journal of Psychoanalytic Self-Psychology 2*, 2, ed. W. Coburn.

Kindler, A. (2005). Improvisation and spontaneity in psychoanalysis. Presented at the twenty-eighth International Conference on the Psychology of the Self.

Knoblauch, S. (2000). *The musical edge of therapeutic dialogue*. Hillsdale, NJ: Analytic Press.

Lachmann, F., & Beebe, B. (1992). Representational and selfobject transferences: A developmental perspective. In A. Goldberg, (Ed.), *Progress in self psychology, vol. 8* (pp. 3–15). Hillsdale, NJ: Analytic Press.

Lachmann, F. (2001). Words and music. *Progress in self psychology, 17*, 167–178.

Lewinberg, E. (1995). Jacquie: The working through of selfobject transferences with a latency-aged girl. In A. Goldberg (Ed.), *Progress in self psychology, vol. 11* (pp. 125–140). Hillsdale, NJ: Analytic Press.

Lichtenberg, J. (1989). *Psychoanalysis and motivation*. Hillsdale, NJ: Analytic Press.

Lichtenberg, J. (1999). Listening, understanding and interpreting: Reflections on complexity. *Int. Journal of Psychoanalysis, 80*, 719–737.

Lyons-Ruth, K. (1998). Implicit relational knowing: Its role in development and psychoanalytic treatment. *Infant Mental Health Journal, 19*(3), 282–289.

Main, M., & Goldwyn, R. (1991). Adult attachment classification system, version 5. Berkeley: University of California Press.

Marohn, R. (1997). Failures in everyday psychotherapy. *Adolescent Psychiatry, 21*, 289–303.

Miller, J. (1996). *Using self psychology in child psychotherapy*. Lanham, MD: Jason Aronson.

Ornstein, A. (1974). The dread to repeat and a new beginning. *Annual of Psychoanalysis, 2*, 231–248.
Palombo, J. (2001). *Learning disorders and disorders of the self in children and adolescents*. New York: W. W. Norton.
Ringstrom. P. (2001). Cultivating the improvisational in psychoanalytic treatment. *Psychoanal. Dial., 11*, 727–754.
Schave, D., & Schave, B. (1989). *Early adolescence and the search for the self: A developmental perspective*. New York: Praeger.
Smaller, M. (2003). Working with adolescents. In M. Gehrie (Ed.), *Progress in self psychology, vol. 19* (pp. 155–169). Hillsdale, NJ: Analytic Press.
Stern, D. (1985). *The interpersonal world of the infant*. New York: Basic Books.
Stern, D. (2004). *The present moment in psychotherapy and everyday life*. New York: W. W. Norton.
Stolorow, R., & Atwood, G. (1987). *Psychoanalytic treatment: An intersubjective approach*. Hillsdale, NJ: Analytic Press.
Tolpin, M. (2003). Doing psychoanalysis of normal development: Forward edge transferences. In A. Goldberg (Ed.), *Progress in self psychology, vol. 18* (pp. 167–190). Hillsdale, NJ: Analytic Press.
Winnicott, D. (1985). *The maturational processes and the facilitating environment*. London, Hogarth Press.

NOTES

1. With their book, *Relational Child Psychotherapy*, Altman, et al., (2002,) have provided a valuable contribution from the relational point of view.

2. A version of this case material was presented at the 28th International Conference on the Psychology of the Self. Baltimore, 2005.

5

A Girl, Her Mother, and Her Analyst: A Study of Self- and Interactive Regulation in Child Treatment

Amy Joelson, LCSW

Self- and interactive regulation is crucial to the therapeutic process. In working together, patient and analyst strive continually to regulate themselves as well as their interactions. In their dance of self- and interactive regulation, which is often nonconscious and nonverbal, they co-create a sense of relatedness. Regulatory patterns emerge that are unique to each dyad or, as in the case to be discussed, triad.

The concept of self- and interactive regulation emerged out of infant research and has been applied to adult treatment (Beebe & Lachmann, 2002; Fivaz-Depeursinge & Corboz-Warnery, 1999). In the child literature, however, further study is necessary. In the enthusiastic leap from infant research to adult studies, the fun and dramatic years of childhood often receive short shrift (Gotthold, 2005). In this paper I apply the concept of self- and interactive regulation to child treatment. In a case illustration, I elaborate on the complexity of the regulatory processes when the patient's mother is in the room.

Having the patient's mother present in session can occur unexpectedly in child treatment but is rarely discussed. Whether or not she actively engages in her child's therapy session, her presence impacts on the process and outcome. The mother's presence increases the complexity of the analytic exchange, transforming a dyadic system (therapist and patient) into a triadic one (therapist, patient, and patient's mother, and all the sub-relationships among them). Furthermore, her presence amplifies the emotional experience for each participant.

In working with children, the implicit dimension of communication reigns. This implicit dimension is salient in play and other interactions, both verbal and nonverbal. It is most readily observed when the emphasis is on process rather than content, that is, on how a child plays rather than what she plays. However, process and content are inextricably linked and equally significant.

In the process of playing, child and analyst communicate implicitly as they coordinate patterns of self- and interactive regulation—moment to moment, session to session. Inevitably, they experience disruptions in these ongoing patterns. As they negotiate each disruption, the child alters expectations of how other situations will be managed. These ongoing implicit relational processes create therapeutic action, as they generate new ways of playing, new ways of relating.

To discuss this treatment, I put the implicit dimension of self- and interactive regulation in the foreground and dynamic content in the background. I describe the way one child uses play to regulate her experiences of herself as well as her interactions with others. Two pivotal moments in the treatment of this passionate little girl are examined. The mother was present for both. In the first moment her mother cried, and in the second moment her mother laughed. During these two heightened affective moments (Beebe & Lachmann, 2002), the mother's facial expressions provided a focal point of reference. Her expressions highlighted the processes of self- and interactive regulation among the three of us. This paper elaborates on the experience within the triad. It explicates a more nuanced understanding of the therapeutic action of play and of nonverbal implicit interactions in general.

THE TREATMENT OF ISABEL

Isabel came for therapy at three-and-a-half when her parents were beginning a tumultuous divorce. Her parents described her as having frequent tantrums and being easily agitated. The way each member of this family communicated distress would often inadvertently escalate the familial conflicts. Trouble erupted in their glances, their voices, their movements, and their rhythms. Each found it difficult to regulate the emerging distress, not having anyone to whom they could reliably turn for help.

Isabel's state of affairs was complex. On the one hand, she was challenged by the torn loyalties, abandonment fears, and reunion fantasies, which are typical for children of divorce. These are the themes that constituted much of the content of her play. On the other hand, however, Isabel needed to find ways to better manage the passionate emotions that overwhelmed her. This was especially difficult in the context of her overwhelmed and combustible family. There seemed to be no way for her to feel comfortable given how agitated her parents were. For this reason, treatment has focused on her ongoing processes of self- and interactive regulation.

Isabel's parents tried to resolve their conflicts through divorce. However, this model for resolving conflict left Isabel anxious about abandonment and urgent to figure out how her own emotional turbulence would be handled. Her tantrums increased. As she strained to negotiate the increasingly tense interactions with her parents, she faced increased difficulties in managing her own agitation. As Isabel battled for a different resolution, her fits of temper perturbed the family system.

THE FIRST SESSION

In playing together, Isabel and I tried different ways of interacting, ways that eventually led to new patterns of procedural knowing (Lyons-Ruth, 1998). The first session set the stage for our further play:

> Isabel: This is Captain Hook. He's on his pirate ship, sailing around. Here is the wicked witch. [She gets on his ship.] Here are the lost children [in the house]. The mother is trying to put them to bed, but the kids are scared. Captain Hook and the witch are coming. They are coming to get the lost children. Captain Hook and the witch get into a fight. Hook throws the witch overboard. [Hook is back on his ship now.] He's sailing to the house to get the mother. The children are scared: "Wah!" The mother can't protect them. They try to protect her. "Oh, mommy, mommy!" [They cry.] Let's cover up the house. Put this fabric over it. Let's put the other dolls in the house. And the horses [and other toys]. We have to protect all of them. More fabric. All these velvet pieces too. [And the felt.] Captain Hook is coming. Oh no! Help! He wants to get her. He's going to make her walk the plank. He's going to force her to marry him. Captain Hook wants to marry their mother! Oh, no! The mother hates him. She doesn't want to be married to him! The kids are upset: "Wah, wah!" Call the police! Put him in jail! [Then Isabel puts Hook into the house. He goes upstairs and captures the mother.] Captain Hook and the mother kiss! They kiss! And the kids—they cheer happily! Yeah! The kids are happy because they're getting married. That's the end. [All smiles.]

In this session, Isabel clearly established the themes, fears, and longings that would dominate the treatment. In my participation, I tried only to facilitate her narrative.

In my initial meetings with Isabel's parents, I learned that her mother anxiously wanted to divorce, but her father, who got into violent rages, wanted to stay married. They never explained this to Isabel. However, Isabel's Captain Hook story demonstrates how well she understood her parents' emotional states, even without explicit communication. The final kiss performed in the play was her effort to repair the violent ruptures experienced at home, kiss and make up. However, Isabel's choice of a happy ending contrasted sharply with how supportive I felt of her mother's decision to divorce.

Over the months, Isabel and I replayed this Captain Hook drama with many emotionally charged variations. She enjoyed helping me safeguard the growing number of "lost babies." We would layer many fabrics over the house—a creative undertaking that could take up most of a session.

Captain Hook was a major focus of our play, and he terrified Isabel. During some sessions Isabel dived into the playhouse, curling up under the fabrics we had laid out. She directed me to cover her up, and, then, to face the threat of Captain Hook. Her trembling voice from under the covers grew bolder with each command. As ordered, I would punish Captain Hook, reprimand him, tell him to get out, and put him in jail. In this process, Isabel expressed feelings of desire, terror, and rage. Through my participation, taking Isabel's orders, we could observe her emotional states and implicitly begin to regulate them.

Ending sessions became increasingly difficult. Telling Isabel we had to stop could send her into a rage. To prepare for this, we established a routine of drawing during the last ten minutes. We discussed how this helped her to calm down. Sometimes, Isabel initiated the shift to drawing, shifting what had been primarily an interactive regulation (my helping her to calm down) into self-regulation. Clearly, her self-regulation functioned interactively as well, as it would calm down our interactions.

Drawing also provided Isabel with a connection to her parents. She often took a picture home with her to give to one of them, confirming how important they are to her. Drawing thus became an important transitional activity, providing multiple levels of self- and interactive regulation, and bridging her two worlds of home and therapy.

THE MOTHER CRIES

Several months into treatment, a dramatic change took place. Isabel was four-and-a-half. Over the course of these months, her father had moved out and her visits with him became increasingly sporadic. She missed him badly, but both his visits and his absences seemed to agitate her. One day he arrived unexpectedly at her home. Her mother refused to let him enter.

The next day, Isabel demanded that I let her mother come into our session. This was unusual. I welcomed her. As we sat down to play, Isabel kicked off her pink plastic party shoes. Her mother observed from a chair. Isabel announced that she's not taking out Captain Hook today because he's too scary. I understood this announcement, as her effort to regulate her level of anxiety and as a communication to me about how precarious she felt. It was clear that we would not be playing in our usual way. She became angry with me when I let a small doll slip, accusing me of bonking her mommy on the head. "This mommy?" I asked, holding up the toy figure. "No!" She told me I bonked her real mommy and pointed to her mother sitting in the chair. Enraged, she blamed me again: "You let my daddy go. You let him slip away." I recalled how he had brought her to one session but did not come in or even wait in the waiting room. In an effort to calm down, Isabel shifted the play away from the dollhouse. She moved to my desk to paint a picture. It was for her father. We sat side by side. Isabel concentrated on painting hearts. I concentrated on her. Gradually I became aware that her mother, watching from a chair behind us, was silently crying. I felt torn between the needs of mother and daughter. When the mother excused herself to the bathroom, Isabel continued to paint, seemingly unaffected by her departure. It was not until later that I realized the impact of this moment. It was a turning point. I explore it in detail in the discussion section that follows.

With her mother out of the room Isabel played more freely, repairing the disruption that had taken place in our earlier dollhouse play. We returned to the dollhouse. This time she introduced Frankenstein. Frankenstein was coming after the mother and baby. Police and doctors intervened. When I told Isabel that our time was up, she had a flash of inspiration. She grabbed the monster and placed him in the bedroom to get the mother. And then, they kissed! I said, "What a surprise ending!" She was gleaming. I acted incredulous that the mommy and the monster kissed, and she let me know that "He's not a monster anymore": cured by a kiss. In this play, Isabel conveyed her belief in the healing power of her mother's kiss. She anxiously needed her mother to forgive monster-like behavior, whether it was her father's or her own. As in our first session, Isabel used play to regulate her despair about her parents' divorce. She restored her sense of comfort in the context of the play's final loving scene. However, when her mother returned to help her with her coat and shoes, Isabel didn't want to leave. She refused the practical shoes that her mother offered, insisting instead on walking out with her high-heel, slip-on, pink, plastic, party shoes.

Working with Isabel became more challenging after this. She insisted her mother come to each subsequent session, and her mother no longer sat as an observer. Instead, I became the observer outside Isabel's play with her mother. I came to understand Isabel's worry about leaving her mother out. Isabel turned on me if I did not understand her precisely, or if she felt I intruded on her relationship with her mother. She often told me to shut up and would sentence me to jail for my misdemeanors. She raged against me and, at the same time, delighted in her mother. Soon I was the one to "cry." She delighted in the play when I cried about how lonely I felt, how left out, and how misunderstood.

THE MOTHER LAUGHS

A profound shift in Isabel's therapy took place four weeks after her mother cried. It happened the day that Isabel turned me into a rabbit. In this session, her mother laughed. Her laughter was in response to how Isabel and I were playing. In turn, Isabel responded to her mother's new emotional state. As for my part, I broke out of my restricted state, opening the therapeutic space with a spirit of playfulness and curiosity.

When I had greeted Isabel in the waiting room, she seemed angry and defiant. She refused to come to my office, but, when I looked away, she became calmer. By averting my gaze, I gave her an opportunity to regulate her tension without the added intensity of having to interact directly with me. She raced ahead of me into my office. Then she continued her tirade from our previous session, telling me how rude I was. She worked at my desk with her back to me. Her mother sat on a chair. I sat on the couch.

I thought about how angry she had been with me for letting her father go, how she thought that if I cared, I would get her father back and her parents back together. I told her that I had written to her father and invited him to come to our sessions. She turned around and screamed, "You liar!"

I was dumbfounded for a moment and then asked, "How am I supposed to feel?"

"Bad! Sad!" According to her commands, I expressed how bad, sad, and lonely I felt. I threw myself into this drama: I pretended to cry and she loved it. I sobbed about how all alone I was, with no one to play with. She clearly resonated with my grief. This interaction was vitalizing to Isabel, enabling her to engage with me more fully.

My pretend crying functioned as an implicit interpretation. It captured a complex transference emerging among the three of us, as it echoed the difficult and complex dynamics between her mother, her father, and herself. Isabel's angry reactions to me represented both sides of her dilemma with her father. On one hand, she raged at me as if I were an abandoning father. Accordingly, she could understand my outcry as expressing the pain her father would have felt for being exiled. On the other hand, Isabel treated me in the way that she had felt mistreated by her father. From this perspective, my pretend crying and my explaining in the play just why I was so upset gave voice to Isabel's distress. She yearned to feel accepted and included by her father while worrying that he might angrily reject her.

In play, I acknowledged Isabel's anger and her fear of retaliation. In words, I shared how hard it is to feel left out when wanting to be included. My crying elicited her compassion both for herself and for her father. Apparently Isabel understood the predicament that I was conveying, and felt understood by me. She calmed down, momentarily.

When I spoke to Isabel directly (outside our playful dialogue), she punished me: "I'm turning you into a frog!"

I put on a frog voice and asked, "What am I supposed to do? I've never been a frog before. How am I supposed to feel now?"

She was curious but wary: "Hungry!"

"Hungry for what?"

"Hungry for bugs!"

Isabel's mother laughed loudly at my frog imitation, and pointed out the bug design on Isabel's shirt. Isabel glanced at her mother's face. Then, in a sudden uninhibited move, she ran up to me, chest forward, so I could eat the dragonfly on her shirt. I started to bite with my mouth open and she said, "No, catch it with your tongue!" So I stuck out my tongue to catch her dragonfly. She was brazenly playful for a moment and then retreated. Soon, she issued me another punishment and turned me into a rabbit. While I worked on my new rabbit voice, I asked, "What do I do? I keep changing! First I was a frog and now I'm a rabbit! I've never been a rabbit before. What's going on? Work with me. I don't know what to do." Her mother laughed heartily.

"Jump!" So I jumped and hopped around the office trying to get it right, "Like this?" Isabel gave me jumping lessons. Her mother laughed harder.

Isabel held up a princess puppet and ordered me, "Play with your friend!" I put the puppet on my hand so that the princess could be my friend, or, more accurately, be Bunny's friend. I was now Bunny. I asked about the princess's name and she told me to name her. This play marked the birth of Princess Lily, and the fabulous friendship between the princess and Bunny. I spoke for both of them.

This sequence—beginning when Isabel turned me into a frog and ending with the birth of Princess Lily—was transformative. It marked the emergence of our new way of playing. This is the "moment #2" described in detail in the discussion section.

Just as the previous shift in Isabel's therapy seemed to be triggered by her mother's tears, this shift was highlighted by her mother's wholehearted and uncontrollable laughter. Clearly, Isabel was expert at tuning into her mother's emotional state. She worried about her mother and, in these moments, they tracked each other closely. Her mother's laughter relaxed Isabel so she could more freely engage with me. Consequently, she became increasingly spontaneous and creative.

With the princess puppet on my hand, as I hopped about the office as Bunny, Isabel told her story: "The princess is mad. She goes back to the palace and there are bad people there. She's angry with her mother and father, the king and queen." As Bunny, I commiserated with the princess. I said, "It's so hard to be so mad at people you love." Isabel agreed, resonating with my words. Finally I was allowed to talk again! Through Bunny and Princess Lily, I now had a wonderful medium for communicating with Isabel.

Isabel loved Bunny and Princess Lily, but continued to be irritated with me, as Amy, if I slipped out of my two new roles. During the following months, she often reminded me to be Bunny and to keep the puppet princess on hand. Sometimes she hugged the Princess on my hand and told her how she loved her. Once, while squeezing her arms affectionately, Isabel said, "I can feel your bones!" We both knew of course that the bones she hugged were mine.

During the next few months, Isabel brought her mother into session, except for two times when her father did join us. After that, Isabel resumed meeting with me individually.

DISCUSSION

I now examine in detail the two moments described above. Each of these moments, co-created by Isabel, her mother, and me, were defined by the mother's emotional outbursts. In the first moment the mother cried, and in the second she laughed. In each case she was responding to interactions she observed between Isabel and me—functioning like a Greek chorus that comments on the action of the play. The mother's presence became an integral part of this phase of therapy. Her expressive responses intensified Isabel's experience and mine, and they contributed to dynamic change in the way we all worked together. As Tompkins (1980) has stated, "Affects amplify experience. They either make good things better or bad things worse" (p. 140).

Moment #1: The Observer Is the Observed

In this first moment, Isabel sat quietly by my side, painting at my desk. The moment was preceded by her unprecedented attacks against me. It was brought to a close by her mother's tearful response and departure from the room.

As we sat together, I reflected on Isabel's decision to shift our play from the dollhouse to my desk. Isabel's move served both self-regulatory and interactive functions. It helped her to lessen the intense stimulation and disorganization she had experienced at the dollhouse (self-regulation). Quietly painting hearts at my desk, she could realign herself with me after her angry attacks (interactive regulation with me), and be better situated to tune into her mother's increasingly distressed state (interactive regulation with her mother).

However, in the midst of this effort to calm down, Isabel again erupted with fury. I had started to get the paper for her painting, but she wanted to get it herself. She began to punch me wildly, threatening to box my ears. She begged me to remove my hands from my ears, which I had instinctively covered. When she promised not to hurt me, I took a chance and withdrew my hands. We were both wide-eyed, not knowing what would happen next. She gently touched my ears with her fists and withdrew them. "See? I told you it wouldn't hurt!" We were staring into each other's eyes. We both smiled, happy to have survived her violent impulse, and to thus renew our confidence in each other. Such disruption and repair of our ongoing regulatory processes (Beebe & Lachmann, 1994) occurred continuously. The process of reorganizing after each disruption contributed to my optimism about our work.

In the moment at my desk, Isabel commented on her painted hearts, "How cute!" Her voice sounded like an imitation of a grown-up. She was clueing me into her fantasy of an adult admiring her painting. However, the artificial tone in her voice communicated to me how her heart was elsewhere. Mine, too, had been elsewhere earlier in the session, during the dollhouse play. It was then that I had let one of the dolls slip, suggesting that I had not been fully immersed in that play. My distractedness had contributed to Isabel's fury. At the time, I had been trying to sort out what was different about how she and I were interacting. In retrospect, I realize that Isabel and I had both been preoccupied trying to track her mother's state.

Tears rolled down her mother's face. She cried silently, trying to hide her emotion. Isabel absorbed herself in her painting, trying to hide her concern. I tried to hide my uncertainty.

I was struck by the discrepancy between the mother's appearance and my experience. How could she feel such despair while I felt so optimistic? Her tears surprised me. My optimism waned. I subdued myself to tune into her need. I tend to do this in critical moments, such as at times when Isabel yells, or her mother cries. In lowering my arousal rate (self-regulation), I hoped to lower Isabel's distress and her mother's distress (interactive regulation). With this action, I could think more clearly.

I recalled how earlier in the session, Isabel's mother had been blankly staring into space. I had noted but ignored her depressed reverie. I now realized how much effort she had exerted to regulate her level of tension.

Isabel's mother and I made eye contact. We didn't want to disturb Isabel, who finally seemed calm, no longer erupting. The mother had needed her daughter to calm down with me before she could fully experience and express her own distress.

Isabel's mother was tearful in response to the aggressive way that she saw Isabel interact with me. She later told me her fear that the father's behavior was traumatizing to her daughter. She also conveyed how vulnerable she felt, after suffering similar attacks from Isabel on the previous day.

Isabel's mother excused herself to go to the bathroom. She needed to be alone to further experience and manage her emotion, without worrying about interactive consequences, especially regarding Isabel. The mother was accustomed to keeping her feelings to herself. However, in crying, she did communicate her despair. By leaving us to go cry alone, she conveyed her expectation that her suffering would burden us, and that we would not help her. Her crying thus contributed to Isabel and me feeling helpless and constricted.

Respecting the mother's need for privacy, and trying to preserve the connection that Isabel and I were forging, I joined the mother in pretending that nothing was unusual in her wanting to leave the room. As I tried to remain balanced in the context of competing demands for my attention, I overlooked a major piece: Isabel quietly drawing at my desk, seemingly unconcerned, was having a powerful reaction. She too was pretending that nothing was wrong. In the service of interactive regulation, all three of us constricted ourselves. I wanted to say something "psychoanalytic" to regulate my self-esteem and to impress her mother. But nothing came to mind. We were all in a state of alert, high-tracking one another.

Isabel's anxiety was part of an interactive systemic process. She needed her mother not only for maternal comfort, but to make sure that her mother was okay. Mother and daughter each looked to the other to know how to feel. They each struggled with how to feel all right when the other was not.

By bringing the mother into this session, Isabel began to establish her as an integral part of treatment. This shifted the treatment from a dyadic system, with Isabel and me working together in an atmosphere of general harmony, to a triadic system set in a conflictual atmosphere in which I became the object of Isabel's fury. Beginning with this session, a complex transference emerged. Isabel treated me as she felt her father had treated her, and responded to me as she would have liked to respond to her father but was afraid to. By bringing her mother into the treatment, Isabel created an ideal opportunity for us to elaborate and negotiate these triangular transferential issues. We explored the challenging and disruptive dynamics in her family by re-creating them in session. In time, we fashioned new ways of three people being together, ways that were new to all three of us.

Moment #2: Transformations

The second moment to be discussed took place four weeks after the first. The moment began with her turning me into a frog. My new frog voice (which took us all by surprise) breathed life into her command. Her mother laughed. Isabel became more courageous. She turned me into a rabbit. The moment came to a crescendo as Isabel gave me jumping lessons, to the chorus of her mother's sidesplitting laughter. The outcome of this moment was the creation of Princess Lily.

When Isabel turned me into a frog, her explicit intention was to punish me for talking. Her effort to silence me was not new. It functioned as both self- and interactive regulation. Opposing me seemed to solidify her sense of agency. Quieting me, which was part of her effort to lessen interactive stimuli, also served to stabilize her precarious equilibrium. Treating me as an enemy helped her to ally with her mother, who was also forbidden to speak with me.

In this moment #2, however, I would not allow myself to be constricted. Implicitly, I understood Isabel's turning me into a frog as a demand for change. I welcomed this opportunity. Although her tone of voice was harsh, I detected room for play. Isabel's body language, with her outstretched arm and hand gesture (the one people use when turning a person into a frog), contributed to my reframing her punishment as an invitation to engage. As I became transformed in this play, so did our relationship.

Elements of surprise and spontaneity contributed to the therapeutic impact of this moment (Reik, 1937; Taerk, 2002). Isabel's mother was surprised and delighted by my ridiculous play. Similarly, I was surprised and delighted to see her laugh so heartily. Isabel was also surprised by the sudden changes—to find me talking like a frog and her mother laughing so vehemently—changes that she herself had initiated.

Her mother's long chorus of laughter had profound interactive consequences. Isabel scanned her mother's face for the meaning of it: was the mother laughing at her, at me, or laughing with us? I looked at Isabel's searching face, then to her mother's, and back to Isabel. This three-way social referencing (Emde & Sorce, 1983; Klinnert, Campos, Sorce, Emde, & Svejada, 1983) took place procedurally. It cued each of us on how to move forward with one another. The mother's smile assured Isabel that it was safe to jump into the play. Isabel then moved closer to me, and tracked her mother a little less closely.

The mother's laughter, which was in response to my frog and rabbit imitations, also encouraged me to become more theatrical. My new animal voices, gleefully joined by the mother's increasingly elated mood, prompted Isabel to play with increasing gusto. Each of us felt emboldened by the interactions of this moment.

Isabel did not laugh. She played seriously. Again, as in moment #1, I had to find a balance between competing demands for my attentiveness. I made gleaming eye contact on the side with the mother, but I did not laugh. I respected Isabel's sense of gravity and performed my new animal roles in earnest.

I did make a mistake as a frog when I used my teeth instead of tongue to eat the bug on Isabel's shirt. Although she quickly corrected me—"No, use your tongue!"—she was able to tolerate my error. Her ability to good-humoredly accept my error stands in sharp contrast to her previous enraged responses. In this interactive "sloppiness" (Stern, 2004), we were each striving to get things right between us.

Accepting the roles Isabel assigned me, such as thief, liar, frog, or rabbit, served to open up communication and to expand the interactive possibilities between us. This is the concept of "wearing the attribution" (Lichtenberg, Lachmann, & Fosshage, 1996) applied to child therapy. As I jumped into each role ascribed by Isabel, I not only explored the meanings for Isabel, but I also added my own embellishments. Pretending to be a frog enlivened me—I had been waiting for an opportunity to jump in and engage more freely with Isabel. In turn, my increasing liveliness enlivened them. Through the frog play, I fostered an atmosphere in which Isabel and her mother both could increasingly experience and express their own vitality.

Moment #2 was a "moment of meeting" (Sander, 1998). Stern defined this as "a moment that implicitly reorganizes the intersubjective field so that it becomes more coherent, and the two people sense an opening up of the relationship, which permits them to explore new areas together implicitly or explicitly" (2004, p. 220). Our moment of meeting, however, involved three people, with an opening up of triadic ways of relating and new ways of playing.

CONCLUSION

The two moments examined in this paper are "heightened affective moments" (Beebe & Lachmann, 2002). Together, they describe a cycle of disruption and repair (Beebe & Lachmann, 1994), and of a "sloppy process" (Stern, 2004) leading up to a "moment of meeting" (Sander, 1998).

I have used the mother's face as a focal point of reference in discussion. Her face functioned as a visual metaphor expressing the affective atmosphere, and it functioned as a guide for Isabel to know how to feel and how to act. The sounds and rhythms of her tears and laughter also contributed to this ongoing dance of self- and interactive regulation. This is the nonverbal implicit stuff that makes up implicit relational knowing (Lyons-Ruth, 1998), providing the cues for how to be in a relationship.

In retrospect, I realized that to influence the atmosphere I had regulated myself differently in each moment. Reflecting on moment #1, I realized later the extent to which I had subdued myself. My efforts to lower the general level of stimulation were, in part, procedural. I entered into Isabel's dramatic affective state and slowly tried to bring it down (Beebe, personal communication, 2002). In moment #2, I enlivened myself to stimulate contact. I matched Isabel's constrained affect and playfully tried to bring it up. Similar to the way Isabel scanned her mother's face for guidance, I, too, kept watch on both Isabel's face and her mother's face to guide my interventions.

According to what I perceived, I adjusted the volume of my voice, the tempo of my speech, the intensity of my affect, or the pace of my movements. Such social referencing (Emde & Sorce, 1983; Klinnert, et al., 1983) and subsequent relational adjustments (cf. Tronick, 2003) often took place outside of my awareness.

Moment #1 led to increased constriction and tension. My increasing understanding of Isabel's agitation informed my interventions. As I playfully communicated my understanding of her difficult situation, I enabled her to experience herself as understandable. The mother seemed moved by my ability to stay attuned to Isabel's needs, even while Isabel rejected my advances. Moment #1 was part of a complex relational dance in which we each tried to negotiate the movement from a single dyad (Isabel and me) to three sets of dyads (Isabel and her mother, Isabel and me, her mother and me).

Moment #2 marked the transition from an atmosphere of constriction, apprehension, and conflict to a state of expansiveness and congruence. Each of us became able to interact more freely, spontaneously, and collaboratively. This moment repaired the disruption experienced by Isabel in moment #1. She was able to renew her tie with me, no longer needing to distance me in order to maintain her attachment to her mother. Her mother's laughter assured her of this. The playfulness of this moment marked a shift in the way we related to one another both individually and as a triad.

In the play that emerged, Isabel was able to experience her subjective world as sharable (Stern, 1985). In fact, in that moment we each experienced our worlds as increasingly sharable. Her mother experienced me as a coparent who intimately understood her relationship with her daughter. And I experienced her mother as a coanalyst, who witnessed, cherished, and shared my analytic world of play. In this moment #2, we transformed from a disjointed group of three competing dyads into a more comfortable and cohesive triangle group.

Viewing shifts in the play in terms of self- and interactive regulation organized my treatment of Isabel. I attended to the procedural ways in which Isabel managed her shifting affective states and I focused on her regulatory strivings. Rather than emphasize pathological implications, I helped her to experience her behaviors and moods as understandable and effective ways of managing her affects and experience. For example, rather than viewing Isabel's insistence on bringing her mother into session as an interference with our therapeutic alliance, I focused on how Isabel employed her mother's presence to regulate her experience. Isabel's regulatory efforts were thereby enhanced. The mother's inclusion in the treatment contributed to therapeutic change, as the interactions among the three of us led to Isabel and her mother experiencing their relationship in a new light.

As Isabel felt increasingly effective and understood, she developed an increasingly intimate connection with both her mother and with me. This was evidenced by her warmer tone of voice, increased eye contact, more relaxed and playful facial expressions, and increasingly inclusive play. Her greater sense of connectedness led to new expectations of a reliable and responsive environment.

In highlighting the implicit process of play, my approach differs from those who prioritize the symbolic content of play. Process does not substitute for content. Rather, there is a shift in emphasis. It was Isabel's subjective experience of herself with her family that defined the content of her treatment with me. This content was always present, even when the implicit dimension took the foreground. However, rather than emphasize the role of play in symbolically working through unconscious conflict, I highlight the role of play in facilitating new ways of relating, new ways of managing affects within relationships, and new patterns of self- and interactive regulation. New lived experience emerges in the therapeutic relationship, as patterns of interaction get established, disrupted, and reorganized. This sets up new expectations that are, hopefully, less grim. It is in this process, with the analyst functioning as a new play partner, that implicit relational knowing can be transformed. This process, crucial to adult and child treatment alike, is most clearly observable in child treatment where the implicit level of communication reigns.

In attending to the interplay of one's own self-regulation, the patient's self-regulation, and the co-created interactive regulation between patient and analyst, the analyst sets the stage upon which the patient can feel safe, understood, and not alone. In this setting, a greater sense of vitality and relatedness can emerge.

REFERENCES

Beebe, B., & Lachmann, F. (2002). *Infant research and adult treatment.* Hillsdale, NJ: Analytic Press.

Beebe, B., & Lachmann, F. (1994). Representation and internalization in infancy: Three principles of salience. *Psychoanalytic Psychology, 11*, 127–165.

Emde, R. N., & Sorce, J. E. (1983). The rewards of infancy: Emotional availability and maternal referencing. In J. D. Call, E. Galenson, & R. Tyson (Eds.), *Frontiers of infant psychiatry, Vol. 2* (pp. 17–30). New York: Basic Books.

Fivaz-Depeursinge, E., & Corboz-Warnery, A. (1999). *The primary triangle.* New York: Basic Books.

Gotthold, J. (2005). *Progress in self psychology, vol. 21.*

Klinnert, M. D., Campos, J. J., Sorce, J. F., Emde, R. N., & Svejda, M. (1983). Emotions as behavior regulators: Social referencing in infancy. In R. Plutchik & H.

Kellerman (Eds.), *Emotion, theory, research, and experience* (pp. 57–86). New York: Academic Press.

Lichtenberg, J., Lachmann, F., & Fosshage, J. (1996). *The clinical exchange.* Hillsdale, NJ: Analytic Press.

Lyons-Ruth, K. (1998). Implicit relational knowing: Its role in development and psychoanalytic treatment. *Infant Mental Health Journal, 19,* 282–291.

Reik, T. (1937). *Surprise and the psychoanalyst: On the conjecture and comprehension of unconscious processes.* New York: Dutton.

Sander, L. (1983). Polarity paradox, and the organizing process in development. In J. D. Call, E. Galenson, & R. Tyson (Eds.), *Frontiers of infant psychiatry* (pp. 315–327). New York: Basic Books.

Stern, D. (1985). *The interpersonal world of the infant.* New York: Basic Books.

Stern, D. (2004). *The present moment in psychotherapy and everyday life.* New York: Norton.

Stolorow, R., & Atwood, G. (1979). *Faces in a cloud: Subjectivity in personality theory.* New York: Jason Aronson.

Taerk, G. (2002). Moments of spontaneity and surprise: The nonlinear road to "something more." *Psychoanalytic Inquiry, 22*(5), 728–739.

Tomkins, S. (1980). Affect as amplification: Some modifications in theory. In R. Plutchik & H. Kellerman (Eds.), *Emotion, theory, research, and experience* (pp. 141–164). New York: Academic Press.

Tronick, E. Z. (2003). "Of course all relationships are unique": How co-creative processes generate unique mother-infant and patient-therapist relationships and change other relationships. *Psychoanalytic Inquiry, 23,* 473–491.

III

APPLICATIONS TO THERAPEUTIC MODALITIES

6

Toward a More Optimal Selfobject Milieu: An Intersubjective, Self Psychological Approach to Family Treatment

Carla Leone, PhD

Acknowledgments: I would like to thank James Sands, PhD, Diana Beliard, PhD, and especially Jill Gardner, PhD, for their support and helpful comments on previous drafts of this paper.

Portions of this chapter were previously published in the *Journal of Clinical Social Work*, vol. 29, pp. 269–289, and are reprinted here with permission of the publisher, Springer Science and Business Media.

INTRODUCTION

The emphasis in contemporary psychoanalytic theory on the contexts in which experience emerges and is co created leads naturally to a greater focus on the quality of patients' primary relationships. In the treatment of children and adolescents, this means increased recognition of the importance of family work as a crucial component of the treatment.

Yet conjoint work can be a daunting task, especially for clinicians used to the relative safety and predictability of individual treatment—and those whose psychoanalytic training did not include training in conjoint modalities. Working with two adults in couples therapy can be difficult enough, but family work involves people of very different ages, roles, and developmental levels. "Can I really hold all those people well enough?" the therapist/analyst may worry. "What if they mistreat each other and I can't stop it?" These and other concerns can understandably lead psychoanalytically trained clinicians to avoid or underutilize parent-child or larger family conjoint modalities.

Contemporary self psychology and intersubjective systems theory (Stolorow & Atwood, 1992) provide a theoretical framework that can "hold" the therapist as she struggles with the multiple demands and challenges of family treatment. The concepts of selfobject experience, affect attunement, and optimal responsiveness (Bacal, 1998) add to our understanding of what family members of all ages need from each other emotionally—and what they may need from their family therapist as well. Self psychological views of narcissistic injury, aggression, and defensiveness (Kohut, 1972, 1984) also make the theory particularly applicable to the treatment of troubled relationships, which frequently involve one or more of these.

The concept of experience as co-created and emergent from an intersubjective field (Stolorow & Atwood, 1992) draws the therapist's attention to the complex verbal and nonverbal, conscious and unconscious influences on family interactions. Increased awareness of the unique unconscious organizing processes that affect subjective experience and behavior and of the processes of reciprocal mutual influence that comprise interactions help us better understand why family members experience each other and interact with each other as they do. This framework can also shed light on our own responses to patients and their families.

From this theoretical framework comes a treatment approach designed to help family members function as a more optimal source of selfobject experience for each other, individually and together. Through the addition of the family therapist as an additional source of such experience and the establishment of a therapeutic dialogue with and between family members, family members' experience and needs can be clarified and their unconscious organizing frameworks and implicit relational patterns can be identified, explored, and understood. New relational experiences between the therapist and family members and eventually between family members can gradually lead to the development of new, more adaptive organizing frameworks and patterns of relating.

LITERATURE REVIEW

Interestingly, there is considerably more literature on the application of self psychology and/or intersubjective systems theory to couples or marital therapy (Howard, 2004; Leone, in press; Livingston, 1995, 1998, 2001; Mitchell & Wilson, 1998; Ringstrom, 1994, 1998; Rubalcava and Waldman, 2004; Schwartzman, 1984; Shaddock, 1998, 2000, 2002; Solomon, 1985, 1988a, 1988b; Solomon & Weiss, 1992; Trop, 1994, 1997) and to group therapy (Bacal, 1985, 1992; Harwood, 1983; Harwood & Pines, 1998; Livingston, 1999, 2004; Livingston & Livingston, 2006; Schwartzman, 1984; Shapiro, 1991; Stone, 1992, 2001; Weinstein, 1987, 1991) than to family therapy, especially recently. This may be due at least in part to the historical division between psychoanalysis and family systems theory,[1] but it is unfortunate since this approach is certainly at least as useful with families as it is with couples and groups.

Ornstein (1981, 1985) was the first to address the application of Kohut's ideas to work with children and families, with her "child centered family treatment" model. Eldridge and her colleagues later addressed the application of self psychology to understanding child abuse (Eldridge & Finnican, 1985) and to work with high-risk parents of young children (Eldridge & Schmidt, 1990). More recently, Beebe and her colleagues have incorporated findings from infant research into a psychoanalytic approach to work with mothers of infants that is grounded in self psychology (e.g., Beebe, 2003). Other relevant works include a paper on the application of self psychology and intersubjectivity theory to work with parents of children with learning disabilities (Amerongen & Mishna, 2004), and Joelson's (2005) recent description of the treatment of a young girl and her mother.

Only a handful of papers have specifically discussed family therapy from a self psychological or intersubjective perspective (Jacobs, 1991; Shaddock, 1997; Unger & Levene, 1994), including the previous version of this paper (Leone, 2001) and my previous discussion of the treatment of conflictual siblings (Leone, 2004). The present paper seeks to highlight and integrate this previous work and build on it in several areas.

FAMILIES AS A SOURCE OF SELFOBJECT EXPERIENCE AND SELFOBJECT FAILURE

People need and seek selfobject experience—experience that is strengthening, restorative, or vitalizing—in all intimate relationships, including family relationships. Children clearly need empathically attuned selfobject responses from their parents and caretakers, but the self psychological view of lifelong, ongoing selfobject needs means that all family relationships can have a selfobject dimension.

Parents seek affirming, affect-regulating, twinship and other selfobject experiences from their children and from the experience of parenting (Eldridge & Finnican, 1985; Eldridge & Schmidt, 1990). They may idealize their children and feel soothed and comforted by them at times, and may feel a profound sense of essential likeness and belonging with their children that is like no other. Siblings and extended family members also need such experiences from each other (Leone, 2004). Finally, the family as a whole can provide family members with the experience of being affirmed by and belonging to an entire group of others. Families can also be idealized for their ancestry, heritage, or other admired characteristics.

Although he did not discuss families or family therapy specifically, Kohut referred to individuals being "born in to a matrix of responsive selfobjects" (Kohut, 1985, p. 257). The healthy family can be seen as such a matrix: a web of relationships that individually and together serve as a source of selfobject experience for family members (Unger & Levene, 1994). The family ideally functions as a team of individual selfobject relationships, such that family members can access different selfobject experiences from different members. Also, when any one family member is less available as a source of selfobject responsiveness, another family relationship may provide it instead.

Unfortunately, many families do not function this way. Rather than a crucial source of selfobject experience for family members, families can instead become a source of selfobject failures and narcissistic injuries. These are especially painful because they occur in the very place—the family—that selfobject experience is typically most needed and expected. Many of the affective, behavioral, and interpersonal difficulties commonly seen in children and families presenting for treatment can be understood as stemming from chronic misattunements or selfobject failures between family members. For example, in the case of the teenage girl described below, her presenting problems of moodiness, irritability, depression, and frequent conflicts with others were understood as related to chronic, co-created selfobject failures in her family and, to a lesser extent, her peer group. The case will be introduced here and discussed further throughout the paper.

CLINICAL EXAMPLE—INTRODUCTION

"I'm not the problem, she is," fifteen-year-old Kate tells me in our first session, referring to her mother. "She's crazy!" Kate presented as an attractive, angry, depressed-looking teenage girl who was reticent at first but fairly quickly warmed to her subject of complaining about her mother. She described her mother as constantly critical of her dress, friends, academic performance, and so forth, and reported that the two frequently engaged in screaming matches which at times involved mother threatening to leave the family. "I do give her attitude," Kate admitted readily, "and I feel bad about it, but she deserves it!"

Kate had been brought for treatment at her mother's insistence, due to what her mother described as Kate's rude and unpleasant "attitude" and their increasingly frequent and intense conflicts. Mother reported that she and Kate had been very close until the last year or two, a description with which Kate generally agreed. The presenting problems reportedly developed approximately one year prior to the family seeking treatment, about the time Kate entered her freshman year of high school.

Kate was the daughter of middle-class, well-educated parents, both of whom were employed in professional careers. She had one older stepbrother, the product of her father's first marriage, who was married and living out of state. She had had a number of medical problems as a child, requiring several short hospitalizations, but had recovered fully (medically) and was in good health at the time of the treatment.

Kate's mother, Mrs. S., was a slim, attractive, intense, immaculately groomed woman who seemed to dominate my office and our interaction. She asked a number of questions about my credentials and approach and repeatedly emphasized that Kate needed a therapist who would take her firmly in hand and "teach her coping skills" rather than "one of those therapists who just listens, smiles, and nods."

Mrs. S. reported a history of depression and anxiety related to a very conflictual relationship with her own mother—a relationship she was determined not to replicate with Kate. She described her mother as very critical, hostile, and "crazy." She had adored her father, who she felt had taken good care of her in all areas except for protecting her from her mother.

Mr. S. was a relatively quiet, contained man who seemed caring and concerned but very stressed by work-related difficulties. The couple had been married for seventeen years and appeared to have a loving and committed relationship that was marked by periodic conflict and fighting. Rather than engaging in the conflict as Kate did, however, Mr. S. seemed to take a more soothing, deferential stance toward his volatile wife, taking pains to avoid upsetting her. He said he was worried about Kate, who seemed unhappy, and about the frequent conflict between Kate and her mother because "I know it's not good for either of them."

As noted above, Kate's difficulties were understood in this model as related to previous and current selfobject failures within and outside of the family. Both parents clearly loved her and wanted the best for her, but were having great difficulty empathically appreciating her experience and needs and responding to her accordingly. The reasons for such selfobject failures and the basic tenets of a self psychological, intersubjective treatment approach will be detailed, before returning to a description of the work with Kate and her parents.

CAUSES OF SELFOBJECT FAILURES IN THE FAMILY

Selfobject failures and misattunements in the family have multiple origins—detailed below—which must be identified and targeted in family treatment. These failures and injuries are seen as co-created (not necessarily in a symmetrical manner) and emergent from an intersubjective field.

State of the self of family members: First, relationships are highly influenced by the extent to which each participant has developed a positive, cohesive sense of self and an adequate ability to regulate and integrate affect. People who have not done so (like Kate and her parents, especially Mrs. S.) are more intensely dependent on others for affirmation, validation, and help with self-regulation. They are more reactive to injuries or selfobject failures, have more difficulty responding to feedback nondefensively, and are either too overwhelmed by their own affective experience (like Mrs. S.) or too affectively deadened (like Mr. S.) to grasp and respond to the experience of others. More simply, people have difficulty providing for others what was not available to them.

Family members' organization of experience: People whose experience of others is negatively colored because of previous painful or negative relational experience (negative transference) also have difficulty responding to others in an optimal manner. Transference, in this model, is understood as family members' unconscious organizing principles about themselves, others, and relationships, which color their current experiences of each other. Thus, early disappointments or selfobject failures can leave individuals especially prone to expect and selectively attend to similar disappointments in future relationships. This was certainly the case with the S. family, as Mrs. S.'s early experiences with a highly critical mother left her prone to perceiving criticism even when it had not been intended. Her reactions to criticism were also painfully heightened.

Learned relational patterns: Unconscious organizing processes—or transference—not only influence how we perceive and experience others, they also affect our behavior in interactions. Early patterns of interactions with parents and others that the developing child witnesses and is part of become part of the child's typical patterns of relating—implicit or unconscious "procedures for being with" others (Lyons-Ruth, 1999).[2] These influence, for example, how we respond to others when upset or hurt, how anger is expressed, how we signal or cue others to our needs and respond to such cues from others, and so on. In the case of Kate and her mother, despite Mrs. S.'s conscious desire to avoid replicating the troubled interactions she'd experienced with her own mother, once upset or injured she often found herself engaged in a painfully similar interactional "dance" with Kate.

Physiological characteristics: Physiological characteristics, such as temperament (Chess & Thomas, 1986), psychosis (Cozzarelli & Silin, 1984), or neurocognitive deficits (Palombo, 1985) can also affect the degree of successful empathic attunement between individuals in a number of ways. These disorders or deficits can interfere with an individual's ability to self-regulate and to perceive cues from others accurately. They can also cause people's subjective experience to be so idiosyncratic or unusual that it is more difficult for others to grasp and respond to. The match or degree of similarity of various temperament characteristics between any two particular individuals can also influence the ease with which they can easily understand and respond optimally to each other. For example, the fact that Mrs. S. was faster-paced, more intense, and more reactive than Kate contributed to their difficulties understanding and responding to each other.

Overall selfobject milieu: People have difficulty responding optimally to others when their own selfobject needs are not adequately met. The ongoing lack of an adequately responsive, reliable selfobject milieu is eventually likely to result in depletion, anger, or self-focus for anyone, even people without significant self-deficits, maladaptive ways of organizing experience or problematic implicit relational patterns.

By overall selfobject milieu I am including the quality of relationships outside the family, such as relationships with peers, teachers, and co-workers, as well as the impact of larger societal and cultural influences on the family—which Altman (1995) has termed the social-cultural "third" in psychoanalytic treatment. These include the impact of poverty, discrimination, immigration, and so on. A fuller discussion of the impact of these factors on family relationships is beyond the scope of this paper, but certainly they influence family members' abilities to respond optimally to each other.

Selfobject failures also frequently lead to other selfobject failures in families (and other systems), often in an escalating, vicious cycle. Lack of adequate selfobject experience for one family member leaves that person injured, angry, or depleted and thus less ability to provide needed responsiveness for other members. The others then become injured, angry, or depleted and have less to offer the first person, and the cycle continues or spirals in a domino-like effect. This often occurred with Kate and her family.

Lack of knowledge: In some cases people fail to provide adequate selfobject experiences for each other in part because they simply do not know what is needed or how to provide it. This lack of knowledge is usually secondary to other difficulties, such as an inadequate selfobject milieu (e.g., no one to ask or learn from) or entrenched organizing principles that interfere with the ability to take in new information. However, in some cases, new information can help people respond more optimally to each other. This may include information about what particular others feel or need, or general information about developmental or cultural norms, alternative discipline methods, physiological factors, and so on (Suskind, 1998). For example, as will be seen in the example to follow, Mr. S. benefited from information about what his wife and daughter needed from him when they were fighting. Later in the treatment, Mrs. S. also benefited from having Kate's behavior framed in terms of normal adolescent development.

In sum, selfobject failures in the family occur for a number of reasons. In many multiproblem families, several causal factors are involved for many or all of the family members. In other cases, only one factor may be relevant for one member. Either way, the treatment must identify and target these underlying causes of selfobject failures before family members are able to learn new and better ways of responding to each other.

FAMILY THERAPY: INCREASING SELFOBJECT EXPERIENCE IN THE FAMILY

How Does Family Therapy Cure?

From the perspective of self psychology, family therapy helps by improving the ability of family members, individually and together, to function as a source of selfobject experience for each other, as appropriate to the ages, capacities, and roles of each. How this goal is achieved depends on the causes of the selfobject failures, outlined above.

Specifically, when failures in empathy and responsiveness appear to be due to deficits in self-esteem and/or affect regulation, the treatment must facilitate the development or remobilization of these capacities. These occur through new relational experiences between the therapist and family members, and hopefully eventually between family members, that gradually lead to the internalization of functions initially provided by others. This process can also be thought of as the reorganization of the experience of the self and the development of new implicit procedures for processing affect.

Difficulties resulting from family members' particular ways of organizing experience and/or problematic implicit relational procedures are addressed through the gradual illumination, understanding, and transformation (Stolorow, Brandshaft, & Atwood, 1987) of those phenomena. New relational experiences destabilize existing implicit relational patterns (Lyons-Ruth, 1999) and organizing frameworks and lead to the gradual development of new organizing principles and new relational patterns.

When problems are due to a lack of sources of selfobject experience for one or more family members, the treatment naturally focuses on broadening and strengthening the current selfobject milieu, beginning with the addition of the therapist as a reliable source of selfobject responsiveness. Finally, educating, coaching, or advice-giving interventions are most indicated when misattuned responses are primarily due to a lack of knowledge or skill, and not primarily to one of the other factors just listed. Several of these types of interventions may be needed in any given case.

It is notable that the curative processes or goals just described differ from those of most other models of family therapy, as well as from those of most individual psychoanalytic treatment. Family systems theories focus primarily on changing the dynamics or behavior of the family through structural, strategic, or behavioral interventions (approaches which may also be understood as improving the selfobject functioning of the family), while placing less emphasis on the intrapsychic characteristics of the individual family members that may underlie their relationship difficulties. Conversely, psychoanalytic treatment of individuals generally focuses on addressing intrapsychic issues—and perhaps problems in relating as they are replicated in the treatment relationship—without addressing the ability to be more empathically responsive to particular others. Incorporating aspects of both approaches, self psychology–based conjoint treatment involves improving participants' abilities to provide needed selfobject responses for each other by addressing both the intrapsychic and interpersonal causes of selfobject failures between them.

When to Do Family Therapy and with Whom?

In contrast to the one-patient/one-modality world of individual treatment, in the treatment of children and families there are both more potential patients and more possible treatment options. These include individual treatment for one, some, or all family members, parenting-oriented sessions or couples therapy for the parents, conjoint treatment for some or all family members, and so on. In many cases, it is hard to decide who should be seen, how often, in which modalities, and by whom. While these decisions are rarely easy, careful consideration of the underlying causes of the difficulties and assessment of family members' abilities to address these issues effectively in each possible modality can help guide the clinician through the maze of treatment options to those likely to be most effective.

Overall, family intervention in one form or another is indicated whenever the presenting problems appear to be caused or maintained to a significant degree by a lack of adequate selfobject responsiveness between family members. The greater the impact of the failures on the identified patient's optimal functioning, the more family work is indicated. However, in this model, family intervention does not necessarily mean sessions with all family members present. Traditional systems-based family therapy understandably required the presence of all members of the family system so the therapist could observe and intervene in the theorized problematic system's dynamics. However, the present goal of helping family members become more attuned and responsive to each other's selfobject needs may be accomplished by meeting with family members individually, in subsystems, or all together, depending on the following considerations.

First, the treatment should focus most intensively on the primary selfobject breakdowns in the family—the relationships that appear to be the most troubled or those most impacting the present problems. This is usually, but not always, the parent-child relationship(s). While certainly helpful and informative at times, the presence of siblings or other family members, with their own needs and subjectivities, can dilute or distract from the focus on the most significant selfobject breakdowns or failures. In other cases, when the primary misattunements occur between siblings or between a number of family members, sibling or larger family sessions would be indicated.

Second, the format of the family work naturally depends on the particular treatment goals of a given period of the treatment. Establishing a selfobject relationship and therapeutic dialogue between the therapist and each family member, understanding and making sense of each member's subjective experience, illuminating unconscious organizing principles or transference-countertransference phenomena, identifying needs, and so on, can be done in either separate or joint sessions, depending on family members' willingness and abilities. However, directly modeling or facilitating more attuned interactions—or establishing new implicit patterns of relating between family members—is only possible in joint sessions. Family members' implicit or procedural patterns of relating also only become evident when seen in action, live and in color.

Third, successful work in joint sessions generally requires that participants share the goal of improving their relationship and be able to work toward this goal without constant traumatic selfobject failures during sessions. Family members are sometimes too angry, depleted, injured, or needy to be able or willing to respond empathically to each other, or even to tolerate witnessing the therapist's empathic responses to another. In such cases, conjoint sessions can do more harm than good. When traumatic injuries or failures occur in the therapist's presence, the tie to the therapist is jeopardized as well.

Rather, the goal of improving the degree of attuned responsiveness between family members can often best be achieved by initially seeing individuals or subsystems separately, then bringing them together once they become more able to work constructively on improving their relationship. The separate work may take anywhere from several years, in the case of individuals with very severe deficits or entrenched problematic relational patterns, to a few minutes in the case of those who can fairly quickly reaccess their well-developed capacities to regulate self-esteem and self-right. As will be discussed further below, Kate was seen individually and her parents were seen separately for six months before the first conjoint session was held.

Fourth and finally, a related issue involves family members' expectations or preferences about treatment modalities. Family members often enter treatment with particular images of how the treatment will or should be conducted—which may differ from those of the therapist. Examples include parents who expect their child to be seen individually and do not wish or expect to be part of the treatment themselves, parents who want to be part of all sessions and feel offended or excluded when the child is seen alone, and children or teens, like Kate, who want individual treatment with no conjoint work with parents or others. In such cases, insisting on treatment modalities or participants that differ strongly from family members' expectations or wishes is likely to be experienced as a narcissistic injury or selfobject failure by the therapist and is thus contraindicated. As it was in Kate's case, it is often necessary to work over time toward the modality the therapist believes will be most effective, once family members' concerns and preferences have been carefully understood and responded to.

TREATMENT METHODS IN FAMILY THERAPY

Equal empathic immersion: One of the hallmarks of self psychology is its emphasis on the therapist's empathic immersion into the patient's experience from within the patient's subjective perspective. Not surprisingly, then, self psychological family work involves empathic immersion and inquiry into the unique subjective experience of each family member being treated. This is admittedly a tall order, especially when family members have opposite or conflicting experiences of the same event or of each other. However, just as parents of several children find a way to empathically appreciate the experience of each one, sometimes simultaneously, sometimes in turn, so can the family therapist endeavor to do so as well.

It is particularly important that the therapist's empathic understanding be fairly equal across family members, so that a greater understanding of or identification with one member does not interfere with appropriate attuned responsiveness to the selfobject needs of the others. While naturally some patients or family members (usually the identified child patient) will be easier for the therapist to understand than others (especially abusive or neglectful parents), it is crucial that the therapist recognize this imbalance and redouble her efforts to appreciate the experience of the less-well-understood person.

With Kate and her parents, I found it much easier to understand and respond to Kate's experience than to her mother's. I had been an adolescent daughter myself at one time, but had not yet been the parent of one. Kate also was very idealizing of me and easygoing, while Mrs. S. was often critical and demanding. As will be seen in the description below, I struggled mightily with this issue and believe that addressing it was crucial to the success of the treatment.

Helping family members better understand themselves and each other: Through the process of empathic inquiry and the establishment of a "therapeutic dialogue" (Ornstein & Ornstein, 1986) with each family member being seen, the therapist helps each one explore, clarify, and make sense of his or her subjective experience, especially the experience of and reactions to other family members. She listens especially for themes that reflect underlying selfobject needs and seeks to highlight and clarify these, especially the experience of more vulnerable affects such as needs and longings, pain, and hurt (Livingston, 2001).

The therapist consistently conveys interest in and curiosity about family members' current experience—especially about how it came to be—and encourages similar curiosity in family members. This process leads to the gradual illumination of the impact of previous relational experience on each member's current experience—or of each one's unconscious organizing principles and implicit patterns of interacting. The therapist can also draw attention to patterns she notices evolving in the room between family members or between herself and family members. "Something important seems to be happening between us," she might say. "I think maybe I hurt your feelings a minute ago, and now you're shutting down like you learned to do as a child?"

Facilitating new relational experience in the family: This process of interested curiosity, exploring and "making sense together" (Buirski & Haglund, 2001) in each other's presence is, in itself, often a new relational experience for family members. Simply translating conflicts into the language of unmet needs and longings and encouraging the expression of more vulnerable affects can lead to a gradual shift in family members' experience of each other and ways of being with each other. So can shared humor and shared experiences of the therapy or the therapist. Finally, just witnessing firsthand the therapist's differing experience of each family member can lead to a shift in family members' experience of each other: the therapist's more positive or more integrated experience can be contagious. For example, I believe that Mrs. S.'s experience of Kate became more positive more through Mrs. S.'s exposure to my more positive experience of Kate than from any verbal interpretations or comments of mine.

The conjoint therapist can also facilitate new experience between family members by gently encouraging, orchestrating, or "coaching" positive interactions between them and empathically limiting negative ones. Such orchestrating or coaching can occur in separate sessions with individual family members or subsystems, such as when anticipating and planning for an impending joint session. It can also occur during joint sessions, as when the therapist cues, reminds, or gently suggests an alternative way of interacting. For example, the therapist might say, "Seems like what your mom needs to hear from you is that you understand what hurt her, Kate, and maybe that you're sorry about it. And I think you do understand and do feel badly, so could you try to tell her?" In this way the therapist can gently encourage new relational behaviors.

When it comes to interrupting or limiting unhelpful behaviors, it is of course important to do so carefully, to reduce the chances of family members feeling criticized, shamed, or narcissistically injured by the limit. It often helps to first highlight the offending person's legitimate feelings and needs and the possible reasons for the problematic behavior before gently limiting it. It is also important to emphasize that the purpose of the limit or suggestion is to help the person be more easily heard and understood. "I know how furious you are, and how much you need to say this, but still, we've got to help you say it in a way that increases your chances of getting what you need here," the therapist might say.

CLINICAL EXAMPLE—TREATMENT DESCRIPTION

Course of treatment prior to session to be presented—individual work with Kate: During the six-month period of weekly individual work preceding the first conjoint session, Kate had developed a positive transference to me with both mirroring and idealizing components. She used the therapy to discuss various "fights" and disappointments with her friends and her mother, as well as anxieties and other feelings about boys she had crushes on. We gradually sketched out a life narrative that began to make sense of how Kate's current difficulties with self-esteem and relationships had developed. This included exploring the contribution of the early medical problems, the loss of a best friend who had moved away at a crucial time, and eventually, her experience of mother as critical, demanding, and disappointed in her.

Little by little, Kate began to recognize the ways her self-doubt was contributing to her difficulties with peers. She became more aware of her need for constant affirmation and reassurance, her hypervigilance to her standing in the peer "pecking order," and her intense reactivity to slights or rejections by peers, all of which made her less appealing to them. She also began to recognize that her angry outbursts and outrage when she felt mistreated or insulted by others reflected these underlying injuries and unmet needs, as well as behavior learned from her mother, but only further alienated others and worsened the relationship problems.

Although initially Kate had strongly resisted joint work with her mother, adamantly insisting that mother would never change and much preferring to focus on self-esteem and peer issues, she became slightly more amenable to the idea as time went on. As she felt more understood and attended to in the individual work, she became slightly less moody and irritable and less pessimistic and negativistic in general. She also began to see a bit of her own contribution to the mother-daughter conflict, and, perhaps most important, had started to see a bit of change in her mother, discussed below.

If it had been left entirely up to Kate, she would probably never have requested a family session; however, she eventually agreed with my suggestion that it she would be more likely to achieve the goals she had for herself (e.g., feel better about herself, decrease her self-doubt and angry outbursts, etc.) if she could get more of what she needed from her parents. She therefore reluctantly accepted my recommendation for some joint sessions, to be held *in addition to* her regular weekly time—not instead of it.

Course of treatment prior to session to be presented—work with Mr. & Mrs. S.: It was clear to me from the initial intake telephone call from Mrs. S. and from the first few minutes of the initial session that conjoint mother-daughter work was not yet appropriate, so I did not propose it. I hesitated to even suggest parenting sessions because I sensed Mrs. S. might well be offended by any implication that Kate's difficulties were not solely a result of poor coping skills. I therefore framed the parent sessions as standard parent-therapist "conferences," similar to parent-teacher conferences. This allowed Mrs. S. to initially view the sessions as an opportunity to convey to me what she felt I should be covering with Kate individually, rather than as an opportunity to explore her own issues, thereby protecting her fragile self-esteem. With Kate's awareness and consent, I also had a number of telephone conversations with Mrs. S. between sessions, contacts in which she was sometimes more able to take in a very carefully phrased idea more easily than she was in person.

As of the time of the session detailed below, six parent sessions had been held, three with both parents and three with Mrs. S. only because Mr. S. was out of town. As noted earlier, I initially experienced Mrs. S. as quite intimidating, difficult, and offensive, especially when I had thoughts or ideas about what she might do differently with Kate (which was constantly!) but felt I couldn't convey them because she wasn't interested in them or would be injured by them. I was very aware of how much more identified I was with Kate than with Mrs. S. and repeatedly struggled to address this imbalance by immersing myself more fully in Mrs. S.'s experience and internal world.

After a great deal of struggle and consultation, I eventually discovered that it helped enormously if, when interacting with Mrs. S., I closed my eyes a minute, forcibly blocked images of Kate from my mind and pretended to myself that Mrs. S. was my individual adult patient whose daughter I had never met. This shifted me out of my other-centered (Fossaghe, 1997) or "Kate-centered" perspective and allowed me to eventually understand Mrs. S.'s demanding, off-putting behaviors as the best way she knew to try to help and reconnect with the daughter she so loved and needed. Focusing on the intensity of Mrs. S.'s love and hopes for her daughter and their relationship led naturally to discussions about Mrs. S.'s childhood experiences with her own mother.

Occasionally, after a moment or period in the session in which Mrs. S. seemed to have felt particularly well understood and supported by me, when I sensed she might be able to take it in without injury, I would tentatively float a brief thought, almost in passing, about Kate's experience or about how Mrs. S.'s childhood experience might be affecting her reactions to Kate, and then quickly revert to a stance more within Mrs. S.'s own perspective. On occasion, I misjudged and had to quickly shift to repairing the resulting empathic rupture between us, but gradually Mrs. S. was able to take in a sound bite or two of my ideas without apparent injury.

Although she still experienced the problem as primarily in Kate, Mrs. S. was agreeable to conjoint sessions, which she saw as an opportunity to show the therapist how horrible Kate could be even when she (mother) was "doing everything right." Approximately six months into the treatment, the first family session was held after both mother and daughter complained about another "huge fight" they had recently had.

Description of family session: Both Kate and Mrs. S. glare at me as they enter the office, accompanied by Mr. S. Kate's body language and expression make it clear that she would rather be anywhere else, while her mother appears visibly enraged and disgusted. Mrs. S. sits down in her usual seat, directly opposite the therapist, which she does not realize is also Kate's usual spot for her individual sessions. Disconcerted, Kate takes the chair next to me, across from her parents, shooting me a look (unseen by Mrs. S.) that says, "See! What did I tell you? She's already taken my chair!"

Mrs. S. begins by reporting that she and Kate had just had a fight during the drive to the session and that she (Mrs. S.) is now questioning whether the therapy is doing any good. Kate angrily responds that just last week mother said things were better and launches into a description of the incident in question. Kate is angry and blaming and portrays mother as the primary villain or cause of the problem. Angrily interrupting, Mrs. S. insists that what "really happened" was quite different: she had not spoken in the hostile manner Kate portrayed, Kate had "started it" and provoked Mrs. S.'s response.

Listening to this exchange, I feel as though I have two adolescent (or preadolescent) girls in my office, rather than an adult and a teen. I can easily grasp Kate's experience as she describes what happened and privately agree that Mrs. S. should not have said what Kate says she did. I feel a rush of sorrow and sympathy for my vulnerable fifteen-year-old patient and a flash of exasperation with Mrs. S. for her limitations. "Not an auspicious beginning," I think to myself wryly. "Five minutes into the session and already you're siding with the child and enraged with the mother."

Aware that my reactions are understandable but still a significant danger sign, I try to force myself back to an empathic, subject-centered perspective (Fosshage, 1997) toward Mrs. S. When Kate pauses, I catch each family member's eye in turn, nod, and hold up a finger to signal, "wait just a second while I think a minute." I close my eyes briefly and deliberately try to call up a visual image of Mrs. S. as a little girl with an extremely critical and largely unavailable mother—a mental "channel change" from my current image of the adult woman who is parenting poorly. My previously developed understanding of Mrs. S., formed in our separate sessions, thankfully comes flooding back to me, rescuing me from my anger at her and over-identification with Kate.

I am then back in touch with my view that Mrs. S.'s early experiences left her with significant deficits in her ability to regulate affect and self-esteem and a natural need to defend against or protect herself from further threats to the self. They also resulted in an unconscious organizing framework of herself as inadequate and of others as often dangerous and unfair. I remember how much Mrs. S. needs her daughter's positive regard to counter these feelings and see that she is naturally experiencing Kate's description of an almost intolerable narcissistic injury that replicates traumatic earlier injuries. Finally, I note that Kate is being quite provocative, blaming, and hostile herself, due to the teen's similar, although less severe, self-deficits and organizing framework.

Having reaccessed an internal sense of equal empathic connection with both of my patients of the moment, I open my eyes. Only a few seconds have passed, but my brief "time out" and obvious thoughtful concentration has slowed things down and altered the pressured and intense mood in the room very slightly. I attempt to summarize the subjective experience of both mother and daughter, trying to match each one's affective tone, saying something like: "Sounds like you felt your mom let you down big-time . . . (Kate nods) . . . you really hated what she said and though it was very wrong (vehement nod) . . . and now you want her to understand how bad you felt so you can begin to fix things (Kate gives me a look that says "you're stretching it a bit here, but I'll go along with you") . . . while you, Mom, know the feeling because you're feeling pretty let down yourself right now, maybe like all the blame's being pinned on you as this terrible mother when you feel your behavior was very justifiable, very provoked?"

Mrs. S. nods vigorously, gives her daughter a pointed glare, and states again (in sum) that she only said what she did because Kate had first said something to deserve it. She adds that it is about time Kate stops blaming everything on mother and starts taking responsibility for her part of things. Kate, outraged, vehemently denies this and accuses, "You're the one who always refuses to see what you do!"

I hold Kate's gaze here, trying to convey my understanding with my eyes and expression and motion to her, "I'm coming to you in a minute." I then try to empathize with and legitimize her mother's experience, saying something like, "Of course you want Kate to see her part in these things, how she hurts you or provokes you or sets you off. We all want our actions to be understood in context. Obviously you react to something," I say emphatically, trying for a slightly toned-down version of Mrs. S.'s outraged tone, "it certainly doesn't come out of the clear blue sky!"

"Exactly! That's just what I've been trying to tell her!" responds Mrs. S. approvingly. I hold her gaze intently and nod, hoping the connection will "hold" her for a minute while I turn to Kate. Aware that she may have felt a bit "sold out" by my previous comment, I add quickly, "And naturally, Kate, you want the same thing, am I right? For your mom to understand how she can hurt you and upset you and trigger you, maybe without meaning to (I nod to Mrs. S., to soften what might be a hurtful message), which then leads to some of what you say or do?"

Kate agrees and elaborates briefly, in a slightly softened but still huffy manner, that she knows they both are part of the problem, she wasn't saying she wasn't. (Note that Kate's ability to make a statement like this is an indication of her readiness for or capacity to participate in conjoint work. She is able to acknowledge and agree with part of her mother's statement, however minimally. She is also able to tolerate my empathic response to her mother without experiencing it as an empathic rupture or selfobject failure by me, a significant change from her abilities at the beginning of treatment.)

I flash Kate an approving look and say that being able to admit to being part of the problem is an important step toward the goal of reconnecting and learning to express anger differently. I continue, "Seems like what we really need to do here is understand what you each say or do that hurts the other, and why something that might seem fairly minor to one of you—like a minor suggestion, criticism, broken rule, or whatever—could be felt by the other to be so big and so hurtful."

After some elaboration on this both Kate and Mrs. S., I gradually say some version of the following, in bits and pieces. To Mrs. S.: "Of course you're hurt—the little girl who used to think you could do no wrong and used to rely on you so much is now in your face, telling you how you're wrong and how you've hurt her and how things are your fault. That's got to be so horrible for you—you heard enough of that as a child, you don't need it from your own daughter now, of all people! Especially since you've so much wanted something so much better than that with her." (Mrs. S. nods and chokes up.) And to Kate: "Here's your own mother, who you've always looked to for support . . . and somewhere along the line you start to feel she's constantly telling you what's wrong with you instead of what's right with you, . . . I can really see how this would be so awful for both of you—you both so much need this relationship to make you feel better, not worse." Here I am trying to empathically appreciate both patients' experience and begin to provide a new view of the problem, shifting from a view of one or the other as at fault to one of mutual underlying needs and narcissistic vulnerabilities.

Once mother and daughter have calmed a bit, I try to address Mr. S.'s role in the family. He has been sitting quietly, listening but somewhat disengaged, consistent with his view of the problem as primarily between his wife and daughter and not something he can do much about. With my encouragement, he talks briefly about how much he wants his wife and daughter to "work this thing out" because he loves them both and knows they love each other. He notes, too, that his efforts to help usually only get him "in trouble" with one or both of them, and make things worse, so he now just tries to "stay out of it." Kate and Mrs. S. respond by expressing considerable resentment about Mr. S.'s "spineless," "chicken" behavior and his refusal to "stand up to" the other.

Again trying to empathically appreciate both perspectives, I say that of course Mrs. S. and Kate would each want Mr. S. to side with them. "People naturally want their partners or parents to defend them, take a stand for them and back them up," I tell them. "On the other hand, Dad," I joke with Mr. S., "having been in your position at times, like today, I certainly know how it feels to care about both of these women and have them both want you to take their side against the other." All three smile, acknowledging the parallel. Mr. S. agrees and elaborates briefly, giving another example of this pattern.

"Of course you want to stay out of the fray if all that happens when you get in it is that they both end up mad at you, too!" I tell him. "I can't blame you for wanting to keep yourself out of trouble" (we smile at each other), "but we all know that's not really what they most need from you when this happens. You only resort to it because you don't know what else to do that would actually help rather than make things worse." (Mr. S.: "That's true.") "Seems to me what they need from you and me both at these times is to feel that we really understand how they feel. Then they need some help figuring out how they are hurting each other or setting something off in each other and maybe some help finding a middle ground where they can each get at least some of what they need when they have opposite needs. Easier said than done, obviously, but that's the goal we'll work toward together."

Here I'm trying to help Mr. S. learn to provide important selfobject experiences for his wife and daughter, especially when they are temporarily unable to access such experience from each other. My goal is mainly to provide an initial framework, enough to interest Mr. S. and set the stage for our future work. Knowing that Mr. S. is somewhat of a therapy skeptic, I am hoping my advice and identification of goals will establish the sessions as a place he can get help with things he struggles with, as opposed to merely a place for his wife and daughter. My use of humorous validating statements is also an effort to help him feel more relaxed and understood.

Course of treatment after session presented: After this session, joint sessions were held approximately every other week for several months, in addition to Kate's weekly individual sessions and intermittent parent sessions. Mrs. S. gradually became more aware of the impact of her mother's criticism on her current reactions to Kate's "attitude" or criticism and how her intense need to feel that her relationship with Kate was very different than her relationship with her own mother made it hard for her to tolerate almost any expression of negative feelings by Kate. She never made the changes she probably could have made if she had been willing to enter an intensive individual treatment (she'd had a bad experience with treatment in the past and adamantly refused to try again). However, she did come to see that despite her intense desire to be different than her mother (and even though she had succeeded in many ways), the hostile, critical patterns of interaction between she and her mother were encoded within her and could be triggered or reactivated in similar situations.

Kate, too, came to see how any criticism from her mom could feel intolerable because she (Kate) was so afraid that there was something wrong with her—so afraid that her difficulties with Mrs. S. and her peers were in fact due to her own inadequacies. Although she understandably did not want her more positive experience of her maternal grandmother "messed with" too much, she did come to understand that her mother's reactivity had to do with Mrs. S.'s own history rather than to a problem within Kate. She also recognized that although she hated the way her mother expressed rage, she could behave in a similar manner when threatened and became determined to change that.

Although initially they simply hated themselves all the more when these dreaded similarities became apparent, Kate and her mother eventually came to see this kind of repetition as understandable and natural, but not inevitable. They began to see the need to convey their anger, disappointment, or negative feedback more carefully, so as to avoid stimulating these negative repetitive processes in each other. We worked particularly hard on the idea of resisting the "magnetic pull" of their old familiar, reactive, impulsive interactions when injured or angry and trying instead for a more reflective, thoughtful dialogue once they had calmed down and the adrenaline had stopped flowing.[3] We agreed that the treatment goals required both of them at times to behave in ways that felt "counterintuitive" or against their gut impulses.

Finally, as the treatment progressed, Mr. S. became better able to express his understanding of "both sides of the story," when his wife and daughter were at odds. Mrs. S. and Kate also became more able to examine, understand, and eventually reduce their insistence that Mr. S. side with them against the other during conflicts.

Case discussion: The case of Kate and her parents illustrates how concepts from self psychology and intersubjective systems theory can inform the treatment of family relationship difficulties, as they do the treatment of couples and groups. In particular, the case illustrates how an emphasis on understanding each person from within his or her own perspective can allow the therapist to stay empathically attuned even to several family members who have very different or conflicting experiences of an incident or of each other. By focusing on clarifying each one's subjective experience, translating or reframing conflicts into the language of underlying emotional needs, and focusing on how each person's experience developed over time—rather than on who is more objectively right or wrong—the therapist can help family members out of the battle over "the facts" and into an understanding of each other's experience and underlying needs.

The session described illustrates the therapist's efforts to respond to the differing selfobject needs of three patients in one session, simultaneously and sequentially. Both mother and daughter needed to feel understood and validated in their opposite accounts of an incident, while Kate's father needed help staying emotionally engaged and in learning a new skill or idea. All needed help reducing their anxiety and hopelessness about ever being able to resolve such incidents, as well as a framework for understanding what they needed from each other and why they experienced each other as they did. By providing a solid theoretical framework for understanding and making sense of family members' behaviors and needs, contemporary self psychology and intersubjective systems theory can assist the family therapist in this challenging task.

SUMMARY AND CONCLUSION

Self psychology and intersubjective systems theory are readily applicable to work with various systems, including families. The concepts of selfobject experience and of the family as a selfobject matrix can help clinicians understand more clearly what family members need and seek from each other and from their family therapist. When family interactions are understood in terms of selfobject needs, narcissistic vulnerabilities, unconscious organizing principles, and implicit relational patterns, even the most chaotic, abusive, resistant, or otherwise challenging families begin to make more sense, and the road to repair and growth becomes clearer.

REFERENCES

Altman, N. (1995). *The analyst in the inner city: Race, class and culture through a psychoanalytic lens. (Relational perspectives book series, Vol. 3).* Hillsdale, NJ: Analytic Press.

Amerongen, M., & Mishna, F. (2004). Learning disabilities and behavior problems: A self psychological and intersubjective approach to working with parents. *Psychoanalytic Social Work, 11*(2), 33–54.

Bacal, H. (1985). Object-relations in the group from the perspective of self psychology. *International Journal of Group Psychotherapy, 35*(4), 483–501.

Bacal, H. (1992). Contributions from self psychology theory. In R. H. Klein & H. S. Bernard (Eds.), *Handbook of contemporary group psychotherapy.* Madison, CT: International Universities Press.

Bacal, H. (1998). Optimal responsiveness and the specificity of selfobject experience. In H. Bacal (Ed.), *Optimal responsiveness: How therapists heal their patients.* New Jersey: Jason Aronson.

Beebe, B. (2003). Brief mother-infant feedback: Psychoanalytically informed video feedback. *Infant Mental Health Journal, 1,* 24–51.

Buirski, P., & Haglund, P. (2001). *Making sense together: The intersubjective approach to psychotherapy.* New Jersey: Jason Aronson.

Bowlby, J. (1979). *The making and breaking of affectional bonds.* London: Tavistock.

Chess, S., & Thomas, A. (1986). *Temperament in clinical practice.* New York: Guilford Press.

Cozzarelli, L., & Silin, M. (1984). Therapeutic interventions with families with young psychotic children. *Clinical Social Work Journal, 12,* 140–151.

Eldridge, A., & Finnican, M. (1985). Applications of self psychology to the problem of child abuse. *Clinical Social Work Journal, 13,* 50–61.

Eldridge, A., & Schmidt, E. (1990). The capacity to parent: A self psychological approach to parent-child psychotherapy. *Clinical Social Work Journal, 18*(4), 339–351.

Fosshage, J. (1997). Listening/experiencing perspectives and the quest for a facilitative responsiveness. In A. Goldberg (Ed.), *Conversations in self psychology: Progress in self psychology, vol. 13* (pp. 33–55). Hillsdale, NJ: Analytic Press.

Gottman, J., & Silver, N. (2000). *Seven principles for making marriage work.* New York: Three Rivers Press.

Harwood, I. (1983). The application of self-psychology concepts to group-psychotherapy. *International Journal of Group Psychotherapy, 33*(4), 469–486.

Harwood, I., & Pines, M. (Eds.). (1998). *Self experiences in group: Intersubjective and self psychological pathways to human understanding.* London: Jessica Kingsley Publishers.

Herzog, B. (2004). Reconsidering the unconscious in template theory: Shifting relational states, activators and the variable unconscious. Presented at the twenty-seventh Annual International Conference on the Psychology of the Self, San Diego, CA.

Howard, S. (2004). An attachment systems perspective treatment of a bicultural couple. In W. Coburn (Ed.), *Transformations in self psychology: Progress in self psychology, vol. 20* (pp. 151–168). Hillsdale, NJ: Analytic Press

Jacobs, E. J. (1991). Self psychology and family therapy. *American Journal of Psychotherapy, 45*(4), 483–498.

Joelson, A. (2005). A girl, her mother and her analyst. Paper presented at the twenty-eighth Annual International Conference on the Psychology of the Self, Baltimore.

Kohut, H. (1972). Thoughts on narcissism and narcissistic rage. In P. Ornstein (Ed.), *The search for the self* (pp. 615–662). New York: International Universities Press, 1978.

Kohut, H. (1984). *How does analysis cure?* Ed. A. Goldberg. Chicago: University of Chicago Press.

Kohut, H. (1985). *Self psychology and the humanities: Reflections on a new psychoanalytic approach.* New York: W. W. Norton & Co.

Lachmann, F. M., & Beebe, B. A. (1996). Three principles of salience in the organization of the patient-analyst interaction. *Psychoanalytic Psychology, 13,* 1–22

Leone, C. (2001). Toward a more optimal selfobject milieu: Family psychotherapy from the perspective of self psychology. *Journal of Clinical Social Work, 29*(3), 269–289.

Leone, C. (2004). Friends or foes: Treating the sibling relationship from the perspective of self psychology. Presented at the twenty-seventh Annual International Conference on the Psychology of the Self, San Diego.

Leone, C. (in press). Couples therapy from the perspective of self psychology and intersubjectivity theory. *Psychoanalytic Psychology.*

Livingston, M. (1995). A self psychologist in couplesland: A multisubjective approach to transference and countertransference-like phenomena in marital relationships. *Family Process, 34*(4), 427–439.

Livingston, M. (1998). Conflict and aggression in coupes therapy. *Family Process, 37*(3), 311–321.

Livingston, M. (1999). Vulnerability, tenderness, and the experience of selfobject relationship: A self-psychological view of deepening curative process in group psychotherapy. *Int. J. Group Psychoth., 49*(1), 1–21.

Livingston, M. (2001). Vulnerability in couples therapy. In M. Livingston (Ed.), *Vulnerable moments: Deepening the therapeutic process.* Northvale, NJ: Jason Aronson Press.

Livingston, M. (2004). Vulnerability, affect and depth in group psychotherapy. *Psychoanalytic Inquiry, 23*(5), 646–677.

Livingston, M., & Livingston, L. (2006). Sustained empathic focus in group psychotherapy. *International Journal of Group Psychotherapy, 56*(1), 67–85.

Lyons-Ruth, K. (1999). The two-person unconscious: Intersubjective dialogue, enactive relational representation, and the emergence of new forms of relational organization. *Psychoanalytic Inquiry, 19,* 516–617.

Mitchell, S. (1988). *Relational concepts in psychoanalysis.* Boston: Harvard University Press.

Mitchell, S. (1997). *Influence and autonomy in psychoanalysis.* Hillsdale, NJ: Analytic Press.

Mitchell, V., & Wilson, D. (1998). Extramarital affairs in mid-life: The splintered mirror. Paper presented at the twenty-first Annual International Conference on the Psychology of the Self, San Diego.

Ornstein, A. (1981). Self-pathology in childhood: Developmental and clinical considerations. *Psychiatric Clinics of North America, 4*(3), 435–453.

Ornstein, A. (1985). The function of play in the process of child psychotherapy: A contemporary perspective. *Annals of Psychoanalysis, 12–13,* 349–366.

Ornstein A., & Ornstein, P. (1986). Empathy and the therapeutic dialogue. In *The Lydia Rappaport lecture series* (pp. 3–16). Northhampton, MA: Smith School of Social Work.

Palombo, J. (1985). The treatment of borderline neurocognitively impaired children: A perspective from self psychology. *Clinical Social Work Journal, 13*, 117–128.

Ringstrom, P. (1994). An intersubjective approach to conjoint therapy. In A. Goldberg (Ed.), *Progress in self psychology, vol. 10*. Hillsdale, NJ: Analytic Press.

Ringstrom, P. (1998). Competing selfobject functions: The bane of the conjoint therapist. *Bulletin of the Menninger Clinic, 62*(3), 314–325.

Rubalcava, L. A., & Waldman, K. M. (2004). Working with intercultural couples: An intersubjective perspective. In W. Coburn (Ed.), *Transformations in self psychology: Progress in self psychology, vol. 20* (pp. 127–150). Hillsdale, NJ: Analytic Press.

Schwartzman, G. (1984). Narcissistic transferences: Implications for the treatment of couples. *Dynamic Psychotherapy, 2*, 5–14.

Shaddock, D. (1997). An intersubjective approach to conjoint family therapy. In A. Goldberg (Ed.), *Progress in self psychology, vol. 23*. Hillsdale, NJ: Analytic Press.

Shaddock, D. (1998). *From impass to intimacy.* Northvale, NJ: Jason Aronson Press.

Shaddock, D. (2000). *Contexts and connections.* New York: Basic Books.

Shaddock, D. (2002). Couples therapy as therapy: Fostering individual growth in conjoint contexts. Paper presented at the twenty-fifth International Conference on the Psychology of the Self, Washington, DC.

Shapiro, E. (1991). Empathy and safety in group: a self psychology perspective. *Group, 15*(4), 219–224.

Solomon, M. (1985). Treatment of narcissistic and borderline disorders in marital therapy: Suggestions toward an enhanced therapeutic approach. *Clinical Social Work Journal, July*, 141–156.

Solomon, M. (1988a). Self psychology and marital relations. *International Journal of Family Psychiatry, 9*, 211–225.

Solomon, M. (1988b). Treatment of narcissistic vulnerability in marital therapy. In A. Goldberg (Ed.), *Progress in self psychology, vol. 4*. Hillsdale, NJ: Analytic Press.

Solomon, M., & Weiss, N. (1992). Integration of Daniel Stern's developmental theory into a model of couples therapy. *Clinical Social Work Journal, 20*(4), 377–393.

Stolorow, R., & Atwood, G. (1992). *Contexts of being: The intersubjective foundations of psychological life.* Hillsdale, NJ: Analytic Press.

Stolorow, R., Brandchaft, B., & Atwood, G. (1987). *Psychoanalytic treatment: An intersubjective approach.* Hillsdale, NJ: Analytic Press.

Stone, W. (1992). The place of self psychology in group psychotherapy: A status report. *International Journal of Group Psychotherapy, 42*, 335–350.

Stone, W. (2001). The role of the therapist's affect in the detection of empathic failures, misunderstandings and injury. *Group, 25*(1), 3–14.

Suskind, D. (1998). *Working with parents: Establishing the essential alliance in child psychotherapy and consultation.* Northvale, NJ: Jason Aronson.

Trop, J. (1994). Conjoint therapy: An intersubjective approach. In A. Goldberg, (Ed.), *Progress in self psychology, vol. 10*. Hillsdale, NJ: Analytic Press.

Trop, J. (1997). An intersubjective perspective on countertransference in couples therapy. In M. Solomon & J. Siegel (Eds.), *Countertransference in couple therapy.* Hillsdale, NJ: Analytic Press.

Unger, M. T., & Levene, J. (1994). Selfobject functions of the family: Implications for family therapy. *Clinical Social Work Journal, 22*(3), 303–316.

Weinstein, D. (1987). Self psychology and group psychotherapy. *Group, 11*, 143–154.

Weinstein, D. (1991). Exhibitionism in group psychotherapy. In A. Goldberg (Ed.), *The evolution of self psychology: Progress in self psychology, vol. 7*. New York: Guilford Press.

Wolf, E. S. (1988). *Treating the self: Elements of clinical self psychology*. New York: Guilford Press.

NOTES

1. Since family systems theory developed largely in opposition to psychoanalytic theory, family work has historically been seen in some circles as "not psychoanalytic" or not the province of psychoanalytically oriented clinicians. I believe this has severely limited exploration of the application of psychoanalytic concepts to family work.

2. The concepts of learned relational patterns or implicit relational procedures as I use them here are generally consistent with the work of Stolorow and his colleagues, discussed above, as well as Herzog's "relational templates" (Herzog, 2004), Lachmann and Beebe's (1996) interaction structures, attachment theory's internal working models (Bowlby, 1979) and the work of Mitchell and other relational theorists on relational patterns (e.g., Mitchell, 1988, 1997). For the purposes of this paper, the distinctions between these concepts are not relevant.

3. Based on his empirical research with couples, Gottman and his colleagues (e.g., Gottman & Silver, 2000) have found that it can take at least twenty to thirty minutes for the physiological effects of adrenaline (increased heart rate, increased respiration, etc.) to return to normal once adrenaline has been released into the blood stream. I have at times shared this finding with conflictual couples and families and encouraged them to wait at least that long after an escalation before trying to discuss the problem more calmly.

7

Psychoanalytic Group Psychotherapy: The Leader, the Individuals, the Process

Arthur A. Gray, PhD

Group therapy is subject to various conceptualizations. Traditionally, psychotherapy and psychoanalysis have been formulated and practiced as a dyadic context, that is, a two-person context in which the focus is on treating the individual. The tradition in group therapy has been to conceptualize and practice treatment with an emphasis on social processes within the group (Agazarian, 1989, 1997; Agazarian & Peters, 1981; Bion, 1974; Foulkes, 1964; Foulkes & Anthony, 1973; Lewin, 1951; Lewin, Lippit, & White, 1939; Rioch, 1970; Scheidlinger, 1974; Schermer, 2005). On the contrary, I propose that group therapy provides a unique context in which the focus remains on the individual. In other words, the analyst treats the individual within the presence of a number of others. This unique conceptualization requires an understanding of both individual psychology and group psychology (Freud, 1921/1964). In this paper I argue that, while the analyst maintains an awareness of group psychology, group therapy is a process for treating the individual, rather than the social context or "the group." Contemporary self psychology provides the theoretical foundation for this alternative perspective.

The debate about whether we treat the individual in group therapy or we treat the group-as-a-whole is an old one (Elias, 1939/2000; Foulkes, 1948; Kibel & Stein, 1981; Scheidlinger, 1997; Stacey, 2005; Wolf, Kutash, & Nattland, 1993). In this debate, those who tend to prefer a group-as-a-whole perspective also make assumptions about treating the individual. They do conceptualize that the group-as-a-whole perspective treats the individual. And, they assume that making social-oriented interpretations about the group-as-a-whole contributes to this treatment. On the other hand, Wolf, et al. (1993) have always proposed treating the individual in group therapy. I, however, found his perspective (A. Wolf, 1988) problematic as well. In his approach the analyst focuses on an individual, while others watched and waited their turn. Such an approach does not exploit the interactive potential of a number of patients being present together in the treatment setting. On the other hand, those who espouse group-as-a-whole seem to be blinded by the social dimension of a group treatment setting. The model I propose maintains a focus on the psychology of the individual patient, while at the same time exploits group psychology to facilitate the individual treatment goals.

In the group therapy literature group-as-a-whole references are often vague, abstract, and misleading (Schermer, 2005, p. 132). For example, in describing a group session many group-as-a-whole authors refer to the group experiencing something. Such a description is made from the leader's perspective. At the moment of the leader's observation, any member might be feeling something different from what the leader is identifying. When the leader attributes the experience to everyone in the room, he obliterates each member's unique, individual perspective. In my early experience with treating patients in group, I found myself using group-as-a-whole interpretations, especially toward the end of a group session. I would often say for example, "You all seem to be feeling that you fear you can't have your needs met in this group." Note that I was never comfortable saying, "The group seems to be. . . ." However, I was implying the same thing. What I implied obliterated individual experience. One of my favorite patients in the group, Richard, would often respond with, "That is not what I am feeling. You shouldn't assume that I am feeling the same as everyone else." At this point I had a choice. Either I could recognize Richard's objection as valid or I could see it as a resistance. I honored Richard's expressed difference. In so doing I encouraged him and others to elaborate on their individual experiences. Richard took intense pride in calling my attention to any time I tended to make a group-as-a-whole interpretation, no matter how deftly I attempted to disguise such an interpretation. By honoring Richard's concern the focus remained on his individual experience. Since the focus returns to his individual perspective, what was the advantage of having made a group-as-a-whole interpretation to begin with?

Those who emphasize group-as-whole tend not to honor the individual's perspective. Richard's opposition would be interpreted usually as some resistance. In the case of Agazarian's (1981, 1997) earlier writings, she insisted that the complaining member's reaction stands for the unexpressed reactions of a smaller group within the overall larger group. Such a formulation is troubling. It robs Richard of his individuality, and continues to cast him only as part of a group. That is, he and others are the subgroup of complainers. Theorists such as Bion (1974) and Rioch (1970) insist that Richard and other complainers are simply resistant to doing the important work that the group is there to do. The complainers are then forced to conform or be identified as resistant to the "work group." When a group leader negates the subjective experience of a group member, this can be considered quite tyrannical. And, if the leader identifies others in a session as supporting his group-as-a-whole position against a complaining member, then such an occurrence represents what Kohut (1978) referred to as the "tyranny of the group."

When the group leader and all members have an agreed on sense of a shared common experience, it usually results from a shared affective state. The shared affect could be in response to several things. For example, the leader or a specific member might capture a common focus through humor. Or, all present could share a common moment of relief as some tension-filled struggle between two members becomes meaningfully understood. But there are those instances where the leader makes an interpretation such as, "The group seems angry tonight." Inherently there is nothing wrong with the accuracy of such an observation—from the leader's perspective. The question is what to do with it. By observing that the members all seem angry might inform them that they are sharing some common experience that they might not be aware of, or might not feel comfortable admitting. In the other example there is a much more direct experience of everyone laughing together, sighing together, sharing humor, or sharing a sense of common relief. And, while the feelings are shared the motives might be very different for each member.

In "the group seems angry tonight" example, the leader herself might not be sharing in this angry feeling. My concern is that in such situations group-as-a-whole proponents tend to interpret the hostility of the whole group. My experience instead is that the leader has frustrated every member of the group in some significant way. While each member might have a unique understanding of the situation, the frustration is so glaring that each member shares a common angry reaction to it. They might even share a common wish not to acknowledge their disappointment in their leader. To interpret the group as hostile and resistant undermines the potentially valid reaction of each of the individual members. Individual experience is sacrificed to some vague theorizing about some social entity, the group. In addition, assumptions are made about the inherent hostile, destructive tendencies of the entity. On the contrary, the common response of the members might instead reflect the leader's frustrating behavior that needs to be explored. Interpreting the group's experience and attributing it to the group's destructive hostility undermines valuable information about the individuals in relationship to each other and the leader as well. Broad group-as-a-whole interpretations tend to simplify complex interactive processes among the group participants, attributing them to formulations about the group as a social entity (Wolf, et al., 1993; Stacey, 2001, 2003, 2005).

In treating the individual within a group context, there really is no such thing as the group. The group does not act, learn, achieve, or master. Only the individuals do these things. Each individual accomplishes these things in the context of being with the analyst and the others in the treatment setting.

The perspective from which I discuss group therapy makes the following assumptions: If one could fly over a group therapy room, that observer would refer to the conglomeration of people present as a group. Subjectively, each member of that conglomeration will to some extent consider themselves to be members of a group. However, as they interact, each member does so with each of the other individuals who are present. This includes the leader as well. But Mary, for example, could address all others present in the group. In so doing she would be telling each of the people something she wants each person to know about her. She would be addressing all the other members present as if they were an audience. She is not addressing the group. It is not the group as she is no longer included in those she is addressing. Mary is a member but she now stands apart from the group that she is addressing. Furthermore, her subjective experience of addressing the remaining members will be different from their subjective experience as listeners. Similarly, for George the group is made up of a different set of members. For him the group now includes Mary, but he is apart from it addressing Mary, others, and the group leader. So, from the perspective of each member there is no such thing as the group. For each member the group is differently constituted. This is true except for the leader. So long as the leader does not consider herself as a member of the group, for her the group remains the same. However, the group that the leader refers to is not the same that the members refer to. Together speaker and audience constitute the group. Any member in the group is referring to a uniquely defined subjective experience, when he or she refers to the group. Only the pilot flying over the conglomeration can talk about a static, concrete entity, the group, as she is not a part of it.

Descriptively any member can refer to what takes place as something that occurred in the group. Here the referent the group symbolizes in shorthand the event of the meeting. For example, Mary might say to others present, "Paul is not saying much, again. What's up?" In this statement Mary might be addressing the leader, indirectly saying, "What are you doing to address my concerns about why Paul keeps being silent?" Or, Mary might be saying to each of the members, "I have a concern about Paul and would like each of you to look at this with me." Mary's reference to the group is a shorthand for "each of us together." So, while the event is the group, the personal experience is subjectively occurring between individual members. The subjective event is always dyadic. As each dyadic interaction occurs, others watch, are affected, respond, and generate new dyadic interactions. The traditional psychoanalytic interest in the dyad and its impact on the individual seeking treatment is maintained in this group therapy model.

Given the group context, one might question triadic configurations. Even in a triad, one person is conceptualizing his relationship with one other person. At the same time he questions how the first relationship affects his connection with a third person. So, even in the concept of a triad the configuration is several simultaneously conceived dyads. Group therapy looks at such questions as, when Richard engages his dyadic experience with Mary, what impact does his dyadic tie to Paul have on his present interaction with Mary? It also considers Mary's situation of addressing the other members as if they were a single participant in a dyadic process with her. Does her approach suggest a sense of alienation from all others present as she lumps them together? Or, might she be saying that the presence of the other members represents for her a new heretofore unarticulated meaningful experience? How can this complex process be defined as therapeutic? If we put together a number of people in a room, something will happen. A number of people together will create something. What process insures that this group of individuals functions therapeutically? And, specifically, how does the process function therapeutically for each of the individuals present?

I propose that the tenets of contemporary self psychology provide a cogent and coherent theoretical basis for treating the individual in a group context. In the contemporary model there remains an appreciation for the formulations of traditional individual self psychology (Rowe & Mac Isaac, 1991; Kohut, 1971, 1977, 1978, 1982, 1984; Goldberg, 1995; Orenstein, 1974; Orenstein & Orenstein, 1993; Siegel, 1996; Tolpin, 2002; E. Wolf, 1988). Traditional formulations emphasize the importance of selfobject experience, and of the analyst immersing herself empathically in the patient's subjective world. Contemporary self psychology (Bacal, 1998; Beebe & Lachmann, 2002; Buirski, 1999; Buirski & Haglund, 2001; Fosshage, 1994; Kindler, 1998; Lachmann, 2000; Lessem, 2005; Shane, Shane, & Gales, 1997) additionally relies on dynamic systems theory, empirical findings from infant research, and a richer understanding of subjectivity, specificity theory, and an understanding of aggression as reactive. These additions lead to the reformulation of clinical approaches to transference, early development, psychic process, and a theory of how change takes place in analysis.

GROUP PSYCHOLOGY

Group therapy is a different modality. It may be used in conjunction with individual therapy or not. While this might be the case, I consider group therapy an adjunct to individual treatment. Understanding an individual is our goal in psychoanalysis. Individual treatment engages that process within the dyad. While group therapy might maintain a focus on the dyad, the process in the group decidedly adds a level of complexity to understanding the individual. Therefore, getting to know a patient, formulate an initial treatment plan, and establish a working alliance (Greenson, 1967, 1971) are best achieved within individual therapy sessions. Yet, many clinicians are drawn to a group therapeutic context. How can this complicating, clinical phenomenon be understood as a contribution to the analytic process?

Freud (1921/1964) attempted to address this question in his paper "Group Psychology and the Analysis of the Ego." He is often misquoted as having stated that the herd instinct is responsible for the tendency of people to belong to a group. On the contrary, Freud was vehemently arguing against this theorizing by Trotter (1916/1985), who proffered the herd instinct as a sense of gregariousness essential for combating a sense of feeling alone. Freud (1921/1964) theorized that in group psychology the members of a group identify with the leader and idealize that person. Kohut (1971, 1977, 1984) clarified that the idealization of a valued other is essential to a vital sense of self. The understanding of how groups form suggests that the leader is crucial in the group process. I propose, therefore, that it is the group leader's responsibility to define the group experience such that it is therapeutic for each member present. Deleterious group experiences serve the leader at the member's expense. Effective psychoanalytic groups serve the therapeutic needs of the individual members. While the leader functions in the service of the therapeutic needs of the patient, she too gains much satisfaction during the process. Her satisfaction emerges from her sense of competence (Lichtenberg, 1988) as an effective group analyst. However, while identifying with the leader defines how groups form, this understanding does not give a rationale for why group treatment should be considered as a valid treatment approach.

CONTEMPORARY SELF PSYCHOLOGY AND PSYCHOANALYTIC GROUP THERAPY

As therapists, we challenge each other on what defines transference and its relationship to early development. We question our various formulations and assumptions about this early development and what it implies about a model of the mind. We still heatedly debate what constitutes change in our work. In the midst of all of these conundrums, one perspective we unequivocally share is an interest in stimulating our patients' curiosity about themselves. An effective theory on group therapy needs to be based on stimulating patients' curiosity about themselves and instituting some hoped-for change.

In a recent group session Kimberly said, "I feel like attacking you." She wanted me to help her to control her angry outbursts in the group. Instead of helping her increase her control, I encouraged her to pursue with me and the others why she felt like attacking me. She became curious, and finally with tears said, "The group has helped me to feel better and more hopeful about myself. But can you promise me that you can really help me to get to my goals. Tell me. Tell me. Sign a contract with me. Promise me you will get me there. You can't. You can't." The goals she aspired to were a better relationship with a man and a more wholehearted pursuit of her professional aspirations.

Kimberly's excitement, curiosity, and hope for her life were stimulated in her group therapy. However, her excitement frightened her. She feared that I would disappoint her as her parents and previous therapy had. She directed her curiosity at the contradiction between avidly aspiring for a particular job and simultaneously avoiding an all-out effort to attain it. Following the session, she pursued more actively and landed the job.

In a previous paper, I (Gray, 2001) clarify that any theory of treatment needs to be based on a rationale, a goal, and technique for clinical intervention. The rationale provides a convincing reason for defining group process as therapy for the individual. The goal clarifies what we strive to accomplish in group treatment and presents this as a valid treatment objective. And the technique for clinical intervention provides guidelines for how the analyst facilitates this therapeutic group process. The focus on stimulating patients' curiosity and hopefulness about themselves defines my approach to group treatment. In group treatment, such curiosity and hope emerges from how one is individually engaged in the process. The group-as-a-whole is the backdrop to be maintained as silently as possible by the group leader. In the foreground the interactive participation among members and leader provides for therapeutic action (Loewald, 1960; Lear, 2004). The gathering of individuals in a therapy group can be described as a social entity. However, given that the purpose of the gathering is to provide therapy in a group context, that social entity functions as a therapeutic agent on behalf of the individual. The context is social; the focus is on therapy for the individual.

Within the group therapy literature, several trends can be identified as defining the goal of group therapy. Some of these are attitude change (Aronson, 1978; Caligor, Fieldsteel, & Brok, 1984; Durkin, 1964; Durkin & Glatzer, 1973; Foulkes, 1975; Rutan & Stone, 1993; Slavson, 1964; Yalom, 1985), spirituality (Porter, 2004; Drescher, et al., 2004), identifying individual differences (Stacey, 2005), increased vulnerability to and acceptance of affective states (Livingston, 2001; Livingston & Livingston, 2006), defining oneself through the nature of the social entity of the group (O'Leary & Wright, 2005), understanding the role of values (Segalla, 2006), intimacy

(Stone & Karterud, 2006), and empathy (Kleinberg, 1990, 1991). An individual's attitudes may change as a result of the group experience. Members may explore their spirituality in a group. Self differentiation may result. Intimacy and empathy may occur. And within the social context members might uniquely define themselves and reevaluate their sense of values. However, when such goals are maintained by a leader, they tend to limit the spontaneity in the group. Members will identify with the leader and restrict themselves to the process of changing attitudes and values, or getting to "deeper feelings," or being spiritual, or identifying differences, or trying to learn empathy and intimacy. In the hands of some group therapists, a lack of compliance with the leader's prescriptions or opposition to it is labeled as resistance. Such resistance is then linked to the pathology that brings the person to group therapy. When such attitudes are maintained, there is the danger that consent is validation, leading to the formulation that conformity defines growth in the group. That conformity is deleterious to understanding the personal world of an individual is a given.

A SELF PSYCHOLOGICAL APPROACH

In order to define a group therapeutic approach that exploits the social context for the specific therapeutic gains of each individual present, I rely on a number of contemporary self psychological formulations. Some of these formulations have been presented by Shapiro (1990). The important conceptual contributions that are relevant to this discussion include empathy (Kohut, 1982), the selfobject experience (Kohut, 1971, 1977, 1984), specificity theory (Bacal, 1998), subjectivity (Stolorow & Atwood, 1992), Lichtenberg's (1988) five motivational systems, a redefinition of transference (Stolorow & Lachmann, 1984/1985; Lachmann & Beebe, 1992), an understanding of the redefinition of narcissism (Stolorow & Lachmann, 1980), an understanding of Stern's (1985) lived episode (see also Gray, 1992), three principles of salience (Beebe & Lachmann, 2002), the concept of implicit and explicit communication (Beebe, Knoblauch, Rustin, & Sorter, 2005), and Lachmann's (2000) elaboration on aggression as reactive. It is my contention that each of these formulations contribute to a patient's sense of curiosity and hopefulness.

In conducting group therapy these constructs provide the analyst with the following tools: Through the selfobject experience, the analyst realizes that his or her presence and responses provide a silent but salient, validating, and vitalizing experience for each member in the group. Neither the therapist nor a given member is aware of this experience until some activity in the session highlights its presence. However, should the patient feel his selfobject experience is disrupted, that patient becomes agitated and has difficulty defining the source of the agitation. The patient's reaction is the result of experiencing an empathic failure between patient and analyst (Kohut, 1984). With an appreciation of the selfobject rupture and repair sequences that can occur in a session, the leader is able to understand certain complex communications in the group. Without an understanding of the selfobject transferences, these complex communications often result in patients being seen as difficult, impossible, and labeled "resistant." Labeling a patient as resistant discourages him. It implies that he is an impediment to the goodwill of the analyst. Understanding the selfobject rupture and repair sequence validates the patient and analyst as jointly sharing goodwill toward one goal—helping the patient. Such goodwill is different from being simply nice to the patient. The sense of a shared goodwill toward helping the patient stimulates the latter's curiosity about the meaning of his own actions. The selfobject rupture and repair sequence is one of Beebe and Lachmann's (2002, p. 188) "three principles of salience in the organization of the patient-analyst interactions." The other two are "ongoing regulation" (p. 187) and "heightened affective moments" (p. 189).

Bacal's (1998) specificity theory informs us that the selfobject needs of each patient are uniquely defined. All interpretations and understanding need to be tailored to the idiosyncratic way that a patient's world is subjectively organized. Bacal calls this "optimal responsiveness" (p. 141). Bacal formulates optimal responsiveness in opposition to Kohut's (1984) notion of optimal frustration. The sense of responding to each patient, understanding how that person uniquely defines all experience, selfobject or relational, garners the patient curiosity about self, other, and self with other. In the group the sense of being understood this way creates an experience of having a personal and private place in the group. This subjectively defined, personal/private space is what Shapiro (1990) refers to as safety in the group.

Subjectivity (Stolorow & Atwood, 1992) is often referred to as intersubjectivity (Stolorow, Brandchaft, & Atwood, 1987). I make a distinction between the two. Intersubjectivity refers to a theoretical system which describes how individuals co-create subjective experiences. Subjectivity refers to an individual's experience within that interactive system. Understanding a patient's subjectivity encourages the group therapist not to see any experience in the group as an objective event to be validated or invalidated. Instead, each member is to be understood in terms of how he or she organizes any experience in a uniquely subjective way. The group leader is to understand the patient's subjective organizing of a particular experience as occurring within the multiple, dyadic contexts that occur during any communication in a group session. The unique way that a person organizes his experience provides the grist for the analytic mill. Within this perspective, whether or not a specific event is real is never questioned (Mitchell, 2000;

Silverman, 2000). The focus always remains on how each person interprets and organizes the experience of a given event. The inherent curiosity in such an approach is self-evident.

Stern's (1985) infant research reveals that perception is one of the mos reliable and consistent, invariant properties of interpersonal experience (Gray, 1992). Therefore, the notion of reality testing in psychoanalysis should be given up in favor of an understanding of why any given patient might organize a particular group experience in any given unique manner. The unique organization must then be understood as a result of the patient's interaction with others in the group. The patient is not seen as transferentially distorting present group experience through the lens of past experience. Instead, the group member is understood as describing how current personal organization is shaped both by the present occurrences in the group as well as expectations resulting from significant past experiences. The leader and other members become interested in how each member with a unique past interprets and engages with each event in the group. Instead of being seen as distorting the present, the patient is to be understood as revealing how present experience intertwines with past expectations. The result is transference expressing how the patient organizes experience of self, other, and self with other. This perspective is referred to as the representational dimension of the transference (Lachmann & Beebe, 1998) as distinct from the selfobject dimension described above. This representational perspective redefines transference (Stolorow & Lachmann, 1984/1985; Lachmann & Beebe, 1992) as an effort to organize experience, as opposed to the traditional classical view of transference as distortion or projection (Stolorow & Lachmann, 1984/1985).

The view of transference as organization relies on the "functional definition of narcissism" (Stolorow & Lachmann, 1980). In order to understand transference as it is redefined, it is also necessary to integrate three crucial constructs from infant research: the lived episode (Stern, 1985; Gray, 1992), heightened affective moments (Beebe & Lachmann, 1994), and the five motivational systems (Lichtenberg, 1988).

Any event in the group is considered a lived episode. Stern (1985, p. 95) defines this as the basic unit of psychic process. From lived episode, or lived experience, each member of the group formulates expectations about themselves, about others, and about themselves with others. When an event is particularly salient for a given patient the group leader can usually identify this salience by the heightened affective moment (Beebe & Lachmann, 2002, p. 189) that occurs for the particular patient. The event is crucial to that group member. To effectively explore this event within the patient's transference communications with others in the group, Lichtenberg's (1988) motivational systems illuminate complex interactions that take place. The five motivations are: 1) the need to fulfill physiological requirements; 2) the need for attachment and affiliation; 3) the need for assertion and exploration; 4) the need to react aversively through antagonism and/or withdrawal; 5) the need for sensual and sexual pleasure (p. 60). None of these needs are hierarchically more important than any other. Lived episodes, heightened affective moments, and the motivational systems all add nuance to understanding the complex interchanges that occur in group therapy. These nuances stimulate both the patients' and the analyst's curiosity about the events that unfold in every group session.

During interactions within the group, communications can take place implicitly or explicitly (Beebe, et al., 2005). Implicit communications are those that occur through behaviors and carry a decided emotional message. Implicit communications tend to be out of awareness. Explicit communications are usually equated with those which are verbal and can be reflected on. These are usually conscious. However, in verbal communication affective nuances and choice of words can often communicate implicit meanings as well. Vigilance about implicit and explicit messages adds color to the richness of how patients communicate in the group.

Attempts to understand all communication can generate angry responses by any patient during a group session. Crucial to contemporary self psychology is that aggression is not a drive that needs to be tamed. Lachmann (2000) demonstrates that any aggressive communication can be understood therapeutically as reactive to some frustration, deprivation, or injury to self-esteem experienced by the patient. The sense of frustration, deprivation, or injury to self-esteem is uniquely and subjectively organized. The analyst's consistent interest in how a patient feels thwarted when angry encourages a group member to be as curious about angry states as about any other affective state.

GROUP AS THERAPY

In the group therapy literature a rationale for group therapy is largely unstated. It is questionable to promote any theory without a clear rationale for doing so. I therefore propose the following rationale for group therapy: we do group therapy because we like it. This rationale might sound surprising and simple. However, if one thinks about it, the implications are vast. If we do group therapy because we like it, then we cannot make the assumption that to put people together in a group is automatically a therapeutic experience. As therapists it is necessary to assess our theoretical formulations to make sure that they in fact contribute to the goal of making group treatment a context which is therapeutic for all of its members (Harwood, 1995).

The proposed rationale for group as therapy and contemporary self psychology contribute to formulating a goal for group therapy. When people are put together in a group, there can arise a sense of curiosity about self with other. This curiosity prompts members to assess themselves and their affiliations. Through the group process a member may seek to increase the complexity of his connection to others present. Or, some members might come to recognize significant limitations in their affiliations. These members often find it necessary to constrict the nature of their involvement with others. I define the goal in group therapy as that of encouraging the curiosity of each member such that he or she can observe the subjectivity of each of the other members and of the group leader as well. Through this interactive exposure each person broadens his or her own expectations of what can be experienced subjectively. The result is a greater sense of understanding self, other, and self with other (Stern, 1985).

The proposed rationale and goal make it possible to consider the procedure of group therapy. I define the procedure as the step-by-step operations that the analyst attends to in order to provide a therapeutic experience that is valid for each patient. I consider the therapeutic experience as valid when it stimulates the patient's curiosity and meets his or her unique needs. Through these specific procedural actions, the leader attends to both his activity as leader as well as the activity of each of the members. The three procedures are participation, membership, and compliance.

The leader facilitates for each member full, consistent participation without criticism from the leader. All criticisms that are experienced from other group members can be explored to promote both the full continued participation of the member who is criticized as well as the member doing the criticizing. That is, while the leader refrains from judging any member in the group, the leader does not require that group members should not challenge each other. Criticism between members is seen as communication to be understood transferentially. All participants involved in the criticism can be understood with a sense of continued acceptance. This is a highly complex process.

The leader facilitates the group process such that each patient is able to define personally his or her own membership in the group (self-delineation). That is, the leader supports each person in his effort to define his experience of what is necessary for a sense of inclusion in the group according to rules, restrictions, and privileges. The rules are that each member is to talk about herself and to give reactions to others. Not talking is also recognized as communication of one's experience of self, other, and self with other, and needs to be actively engaged and interpreted noncritically by the group leader. Restrictions are the mechanics of the meeting time and place, and include the purpose of the group. The purpose is different from social events, where socialization is the aim. And privileges are that the group encounter as a therapeutic experience counts but does not count. That is, the events of the group count toward understanding and therapeutically influencing the experience of self, other, and self with other, but the events that take place in this process are not held against the group member. An additional privilege is that each member is able to pay and in so doing engages the group therapist's availability and expertise.

The third aspect of the procedure is compliance. Compliance is not a procedure initiated by the group leader. It is an action experienced and maintained by the members. When members feel committed to a group, they themselves ascribe to the leader responsibility for the group. They identify with how the group leader functions. According to the first two procedures in this model, the group leader sees each member as fully essential and a crucial participant. Freud (1921/1964) states that members in a group take the leader as their ego ideal. Each member then goes to great length to comply with the leader's formulation. This is an interesting aspect of the group procedures. In its pathological form, members will be observed giving up personal convictions in order to comply with ideals with which the leader is imbued. However, the leader's responsibility to the first two aspects of the procedures of group therapy—participation and membership—insures that this pathological condition is guarded against, brought out, explored, and processed. In so doing, the group leader helps each member curiously pursue his or her unique goals. Each member's participation and personally defined membership outlines the range of expectations to be explored in the group. No single person defines what is expected. And, expectations are not formulated according to consensus. Each member can feel free to define and explore any expectation. The leader therefore recognizes that as each person experiences herself as an integral part of the group, that person goes to great length to comply with the general functioning of the group. The paramount function that a group leader maintains as central is that of exploring whatever is uniquely important for a particular group member. As a member complies with this aspect of the procedure, he or she becomes increasingly confident in expressing what is uniquely important to him or her. These communications are to be explored and understood without criticism from the leader.

PAUL

The treatment of Paul from one of my groups can illustrate this model in action. I had stated above that each person defines his or her membership according to certain rules: "The rules are that each member is to talk about herself and to give reactions to others. Not talking is also recognized as communication of one's experience of self, other, and self with other, and needs to be actively engaged and interpreted noncritically by the group leader."

Paul spent much of his time being silent in the group sessions. My perspective on Paul's silence in the sessions illustrates working with the silent patient in the group. Paul came to treatment at thirty-seven years old. He was a slim man who was about 5′11″ tall. He grew up in Long Island in a Catholic family. His father, an accountant, was detached and browbeaten by my patient's quick-tempered, housewife mother, who had grown up in a wealthy family. She was very attached to Paul. She sexualized their relationship but denied this by dressing him up as a girl when he was a little boy. As he became older she treated sexualizing events as if they were chance encounters—such as leaving her bedroom door slightly ajar as she was dressing in the mornings.

Paul sought treatment because he was suicidal. He was the third child, with all suggestions that the pregnancy resulting in his birth was unplanned. His brother, John, was thirteen years older than Paul, and Ruth, his sister, was eight years older. At thirty-seven, Paul had never had sex. However, sexually he would dress up in women's underwear and would look at himself from behind using a full-length mirror. He would reach his left arm over his right shoulder showing his fingers caressing that shoulder. With his right hand he masturbated himself to orgasm.

Paul's suicidal feelings emerged after he was almost caught in the middle of his masturbatory routine. Often, he had dressed up in his mother's and sister's underwear and had remained relatively safe doing so. Then, a good friend of his mother's had asked him to watch her house while she was away on vacation. Her son who lived at home temporarily was away on business. One morning he went to her house, entered her bedroom, found her underwear, and was about to embark on his sexually exciting routine. Suddenly, he was startled by the rustling in the woman's son's bedroom. Her son had arrived home unexpectedly early from his business trip and was beginning to wake up. Paul made a fast, undetected exit from the woman's bedroom. He became suicidal with the thought of his behavior being discovered, and so he sought treatment.

Prior to beginning group therapy, Paul had been in individual treatment with me. In his individual sessions Paul slowly and carefully gained confidence about us working therapeutically together. Within this increasing confidence he gingerly began to be curious about his desire to dress in women's underwear. He began to explore with me the meaning of this behavior. As his curiosity grew, he came to understand that his dress-up behavior emerged out of his yearning for his mother to have demonstrated her love through accepting him for who he was. That is, as her son he needed her to recognize his sexuality independent of her needs. His viewing himself from behind while dressed in women's underwear had become heir to his desire to be accepted as sexual. This view from behind with the focus on the underwear represented a woman responding to his sexual advances. This understanding led to the ending of his desire to put on women's underwear and led to a model scene (Lichtenberg, Lachmann, & Fosshage, 1992) which has served to guide his treatment since.

The model scene is an action-oriented scene co-created between the therapist and patient. This scene from the analysis describes the patient's pathology and strivings. A model scene emerged through a memory:

> Paul was about five years old. His sister, who tended to be even tempered and noncommittal in her behavior, was thirteen years old. She therefore was beginning to develop secondary sexual characteristics such as budding breasts and pubic hair. His mother, in her covert sexualizing of her relationship with Paul, used to have him bathe with his thirteen-year-old sister. But with her emerging sexuality, his sister began to place a washcloth over her pubic area during these baths. One day Paul could not resist the urge to yank the washcloth from its resting place to explore what was beneath it. His mother, in a fit of disapproval, yanked him out of the tub. Nothing was mentioned ever again about the incident and the joint bathing never occurred again.

The model scene is of five-year-old Paul's outstanding curiosity. However, acting on this curiosity resulted in being shamed and having his curiosity met with disapproval, denial, and ostracism. At the time this model scene unfolded, it was approximately eight months into his twice-weekly treatment. I became increasingly concerned with his isolation, depression, and his yearning for but anxiety about his contact with others. I decided to encourage him to go into group therapy with me. He accepted the invitation to add group therapy to his twice-weekly individual sessions.

In the group Paul was silent but obviously deeply engaged. He and I had agreed that given how ashamed he felt about never having had sex at his age—now thirty-eight—he did not have to reveal his sexual inexperience to the other people in the group. He could wait until, or if, he felt ready to do so.

I facilitated all in the group exploring and understanding his need to not reveal things which would leave him overwhelmed with shame. The first of the three step-by-step operations that I defined as the procedure of a therapeutic group is that of participation. That is, the leader "facilitates for each member full, consistent participation without criticism from the leader." Paul could participate any way he wished. I would understand it. Other members could be critical. Their reactions would be explored and understood in relation to themselves and to Paul.

This is a highly complex process which allowed Paul the opportunity to grow extensively in combined group and individual therapy. In the group experience, I spoke for Paul. He was silent through much of each group session. However, this silence was not characteristic of him during our individual sessions. So, in the group sessions I insured his active participation by closely observing the slightest response he might have to any given event. That is, I relied on his implicit communications. Some of these responses were a slight smile, extra blinking of his eyes, sitting forward in his chair, leaning back ever so slightly in his chair, tightening his lips, staring reflectively, glancing out of the corner of his eyes at me, and turning his head slightly away from me or from someone else.

Informed by the model scene with the washcloth, his sister, the tub, and his mother's reaction, it was clear that I had to co-create with him a mirroring selfobject experience. In that experience I could mirror his curiosity and assertive engagement of others in the group. His silence was not seen by me as resistance or passivity. I saw it as an active effort to express his curiosity without creating overwhelming shame for himself. That is, his experience was one aimed at self-regulation (Lachmann & Beebe, 1992) rather than that of expressing hostility toward me or other group members.

Of course other members often found his silences enraging. Once Mary asked, "Why are you talking for Paul?" I explored how she felt frustrated by my speaking for him. After she had a sense of how she was responding to Paul, he remained silent. I then asked Paul if he wanted to respond to her question, or if he would prefer that I did. He asked me to. I then explained to her that he was not always clear about what he was feeling and was often afraid that his actions could be misunderstood and prove threatening to him. Here I was responding to the transference defined by the model scene of the bath with his sister resulting in shame, disapproval, denial, and ostracism.

Whenever I spoke for him, I would ask him to confirm my experience and understanding of him. He would either confirm or correct me and speak quite movingly and eloquently about the experience I attempted to capture for him. Eventually, after about one year in the group he told the other members that he had never had sex. Now at thirty-nine he was even more ashamed of this fact. All members were extremely sensitive to his predicament. All members began to explore curiously their own struggle with being sexual. After another four months in the group therapy, Paul arrived with a twinkle in his eye and a slight smile on his face. He announced that he had had sex with a nice girl from Washington, D.C., while there for a graphic arts exhibit representing his company.

Through my understanding of the process of group therapy influenced by the findings of infant research, Paul's implicit communications were relied on as his unique tone of effectively participating in the group. Through my understanding of his transference, the way he defined his membership, all members complied with my leadership that implied that each person could uniquely define how he or she wanted to function. Paul's difficulty talking was—for me—talking. He simply did it implicitly. Through this process Paul revived his curiosity about his inhibited sexual assertiveness. He went on to explore more explicitly his sexual and loving feelings for the women in the group. In a symphony of further curiosity, and exploration he, the other men, and the women additionally investigated significant issues around closeness, sex, and love.

CONCLUSION

In this chapter, I clarify how the tenets of contemporary self psychology can be used to understand the group therapy process. In this process patients and analyst define together what is necessary for the psychological growth of each member. Contemporary self psychology describes this growth as a greater degree of flexibility in how one can experience and define a sense of self, a sense of other, and a sense of self with other (Stern, 1985). These definitions need to be formulated uniquely for each individual according to the nature of past experience, innate capabilities, aspirations, and limitations.

A model of group therapy is presented that views group treatment as a unique context for treating an individual. This model challenges group-as-a-whole formulations, and more specifically it challenges the value placed on group consensus. In fact, I contend that the emphasis on group-as-a-whole formulations give group consensus an inordinate role in group treatment. Rather, I propose an approach where each member's subjective perspective is understood in a way that promotes curiosity among members. The group therapist fosters this atmosphere of curiosity by relying on the three interrelated procedures of participation, membership, and compliance. Through these procedures, the leader allows the social context of the group setting to be exploited on behalf of each individual present. While attitude change, intimacy, spirituality, empathy, a sense of values, or experiencing vulnerable moments can be meaningful pursuits in any group treatment, these pursuits do not define the goal of the group process. In this model the goal is to promote curiosity. Each individual deems what is important to pursue. Furthermore, despite the social nature of the context, the therapeutic process still relies on a series of dyadic interactions that promote therapeutic growth for each member.

The case of Paul demonstrated how this model works. Paul spoke very little in the group for a long time. Contemporary self psychology relies on implicit as well as explicit communication. Implicit communications can be particularly helpful to the analyst when a patient finds it difficult to talk. Paul progressed in group therapy despite his taciturn tendencies. Nonverbal cues were relied on as effective, implicit communication. And, in time, part of his progress was evaluated by the extent to which he was able to increasingly express himself verbally and explicitly in the group.

In the group sessions with Paul, there were often intense reactions to his silences. During such occurrences, members compared how they reacted to him. Each person sought to understand himself or herself through these reactions and comparisons. No other patient reacted to him as angrily as did Mary. She and the others embraced her intense reactions as an opportunity to get to know more about her. Her responses to Paul were uniquely her own, and were relied on to contribute to her development. Her curiosity about herself in relationship to Paul and others grew. Through these experiences both she and Paul developed increased self-confidence. All members flourished through this and other similar interactive experiences in the sessions.

Sometimes a group member might make comments and observations that seem to represent the group-as-a-whole. These comments can be explored and understood to explicate that person's personal experience. However, when the group therapist makes group-as-a-whole assumptions which assimilate or dilute individual differences, such assumptions work against the individual experience of each of the members. Any action that subverts any member's individual experience attenuates that member's curiosity about a sense of self, or a sense of other, and/or a sense of self with other.

REFERENCES

Aronson, M. L. (1978). The unique advantages of analytic group therapy in the middle and later phases of the therapeutic process. In L. R. Wolberg, M. L. Aronson, & A. R. Wolberg (Eds.), *Group therapy: An overview* (pp. 35–45). New York: Stratton International Medical Book Corporation.

Agazarian, Y. M. (1989). Group-as-a-whole systems theory and practice. *Group, 13,* 131–154.

Agazarian, Y. M. (1997). *Systems-centered therapy for groups.* New York: Guilford.

Agazarian, Y. M., & Peters, R. (1981). *The visible and invisible group.* London: Routledge & Kegan Paul.

Bacal, H. (1998). Optimal responsiveness and the specificity of selfobject experience. In H. Bacal (Ed.), *Optimal responsiveness: How therapists heal their patient.* Northvale, NJ: Jason Aronson.

Beebe, B., & Lachmann, F. M. (1994). Representations and internalizations in infants: Three principles of salience. *Psychoanalytic Psychology, 11,* 127–165.

Beebe, B., & Lachmann, F. M. (2002). *Infant research and adult treatment.* Hillsdale, NJ: Analytic Press.

Beebe, B., Knoblauch, S., Rustin, J., & Sorter, D. (2005). *Forms of intersubjectivity in infant research and adult treatment.* New York: Other Press.

Bion, W. R. (1974). *Experiences in group.* New York: Ballantine. (Original work published 1959.)

Buirski, P. (1999). The selfobject function of interpretation. In A. Goldberg (Ed.), *Pluralism in self psychology: Progress in self psychology, vol. 15* (pp. 31–49). Hillsdale, NJ: Analytic Press.

Buirski, P., & Haglund, P. (2001). *Making sense together: The intersubjective approach to psychotherapy.* Northvale, NJ: Jason Aronson.

Caligor, J., Fieldsteel, N. D., & Brok, A. J. (1984). *Individual and group therapy: Combining psychoanalytic treatments.* New York: Basic Books.

Drescher K., Ramirez, G., Leoni, J., Romesser J., Sornborger, J., & Foy, D. (2004). Spirituality and trauma: Development of a group therapy module. *Group, 28*(4), 71–87.

Durkin, H. (1964). *The group in depth.* New York: International University Press.

Durkin, H., & Glatzer, H. T. (1973). Transference neurosis in group psychotherapy: The concept and the reality. In L. R. Wolberg & E. Schwartz (Eds.), *Group therapy* (pp. 129–143). New York: Intercontinental Medical Book Corp.

Elias, N. (2000). *The civilizing process.* Oxford: Blackwell. (Original work published 1939.)

Fosshage, J. (1994). Towards reconceptualizing transference: Theoretical and clinical considerations. *International Journal of Psychoanalysis, 75*(2), 265–280.

Foulkes, S. H. (1948). *Introduction to group-analytic psychotherapy.* London: Midway Press.

Foulkes, S. H. (1964). *Therapeutic group analysis.* New York: International Universities Press.

Foulkes, S. H. (1975). *Group analytic psychotherapy: Methods and principles.* London: Gordon & Breach.

Foulkes, S. H., & Anthony, E. J. (1973). *Group psychotherapy: The psychoanalytic approach.* Harmondsworth: Penguin.

Freud, S. (1964). Group psychology and the analysis of the ego. In J. Strachey (Ed. & Trans.), *The standard edition of the complete psychological works of Sigmund Freud* (Vol. 18, pp. 67–145). London: Hogarth Press. (Original work published 1921.)

Glatzer, H. T. (1959). Notes on the preoedipal phantasy. *Amer. J. Orthopsychiatry, 24,* 383–390.

Goldberg, A. (1995). *The problem of perversion: The view from self psychology.* New Haven: Yale University Press.

Gray, A. A. (1992). Book review (Stern, D. L. [1985], The interpersonal world of the infant: A view from psychoanalysis and developmental psychology. New York: Basic Books). *International Forum of Psychoanalysis, 1*(2), 119–120.

Gray, A. A. (2001). Difficult terminations in group therapy: A self psychologically informed perspective. *Group, 25*(1/2), 27–39.

Greenson, R. (1967). *The technique and practice of psychoanalysis, vol. 1.* New York: International Universities Press.

Greenson, R. (1971). The "real" relationship between the patient and the psychoanalyst. In *Explorations in Psychoanalysis.* New York: International Universities Press, 1978.

Harwood, I. H. (1995). Toward optimum group placement from the perspective of the self or self-experience. *Group, 19,* 140–162.

Kibel, H. D., & Stein A. (1981). The group as a whole approach: An appraisal. *International Journal of Group Psychotherapy, 31,* 409–427.

Kindler, A. R. (1998). Optimal responsiveness and psychoanalytic supervision. In H. A. Bacal (Ed.), *Optimal responsiveness: How therapists heal their patients*. Northvale, NJ: Jason Aronson.

Kleinberg, J. (1990). Working with the fragile patient in the initial phase of group therapy. *Psychoanalysis and Psychotherapy, 7*(1), 31–40.

Kleinberg, J. (1991). Teaching beginning group therapists to incorporate a patient's empathic capacity in treatment planning. *Group, 14*, 141–155.

Kohut, H. (1971). *The analysis of the self.* Madison, CT: IUP.

Kohut, H. (1977). *The restoration of the self.* Madison, CT: IUP.

Kohut, H. (1978). Creativeness, charisma, group psychology. In P. Ornstein (Ed.), *The search for the self, vol. 2*. Madison, CT: IUP.

Kohut, H. (1982). Introspection, empathy, and the semi-circle of mental health. *International Journal of Psycho-Analysis, 63*, 395–407.

Kohut, H. (1984). *How does analysis cure?* Ed. A. Goldberg. Chicago: University of Chicago Press.

Lachmann, F. M. (2000). *Transforming aggression: Psychotherapy with the difficult-to-treat patient.* Northvale, NJ: Jason Aronson.

Lachmann, F. M., & Beebe, B. (1992). Reformulations of early development and transference: Implications for psychic structure formation. In J. W. Barron, M. N. Eagle, & D. Wolitsky (Eds.), *The interface of psychoanalysis and psychology* (pp. 133–153). Washington, DC: American Psychological Association.

Lachmann, F. M., & Beebe, B. (1998). Optimal responsiveness in a systems approach to representational and selfobject transferences. In H. Bacal (Ed.), *Optimal responsiveness* (pp. 305–326). Northvale, NJ: Jason Aronson.

Lear, J. (2004). *Therapeutic action: An earnest plea for irony*. New York: Other Press.

Lessem, P. A. (2005). *Self psychology: An introduction.* Lanham, MD: Rowman & Littlefield Publishers.

Lewin, K. (1951). *Field theory in social science.* New York: Harper and Row.

Lewin, K., Lippit, R., & White, R. K. (1939). Patterns of aggressive behavior in experimentally created "social climates." *Journal of Social Psychology, 10*, 271–299.

Lichtenberg, J. D. (1988). A theory of motivational-functional systems as psychic structures. *Journal of American Psychoanalytic Association, 36*(Suppl.), 57–72.

Lichtenberg, J. D., Lachmann, F. M., & Fosshage, J. L. (1992). *Self and motivational systems: Toward a theory of psychoanalytic technique.* Hillsdale, NJ: Analytic Press.

Livingston, M. (2001). *Vulnerable moments: Deepening the therapeutic process.* New York: Jason Aronson.

Livingston, M., & Livingston, L. (2006). Sustained empathic focus and the clinical application of self-psychological theory in group psychotherapy. *International Journal of Group Psychotherapy, 56*(1), 67–85.

Loewald, H. (1960). On the therapeutic action of psychoanalysis. In *Papers on Psychoanalysis* (pp. 221–256). New Haven, CT: Yale University Press.

Mitchell, S. (2000). Response to Silverman (2000). *Psychoanalytic Psychology, 17*, 153–159.

O'Leary, J., & Wright, F. (2005). Social constructivism and the group-as-a-whole. *Group, 29*(2), 257–276.

Orenstein, A. (1974). The dread to repeat and the new beginning: A contribution to the psychoanalysis of narcissistic personality disorders. In *Annual of Psychoanalysis* (pp. 231–248). Madison, CT: International Universities Press.

Ornstein, P. H., & Ornstein, A. (1993). Assertiveness and destructive aggression: a perspective from the treatment process. In R. A. Glick & S. P. Roose (Eds.), *Rage, power, and aggression* (2nd ed., pp. 102–117). New Haven, CT: Yale University Press.

Porter, K. (2004). Who we really are: Buddhist approaches to psychotherapy and group psychotherapy. *Group, 28*(4), 53–69.

Rioch, M. J. (1970). The work of Wilfred Bion on groups. *Psychiatry, 5*, 573–596.

Rowe, C. E., & Mac Isaac, D. (1991). *Empathic attunement: The technique of psychoanalytic self psychology.* Northvale, NJ: Jason Aronson.

Rutan, J. S., & Stone, W. N. (1993). *Psychodynamic group psychotherapy* (2nd ed.). New York: Guilford Press.

Scheidlinger, S. (1974). On the concept of the mother-group. *International journal of group psychotherapy 24*, 417–428.

Scheidlinger, S. (1997). Group dynamics and group psychotherapy revised: Four decades later. *Journal of Group Psychotherapy, 47*, 141–159.

Schermer, V. L. (2005). An orientation to the two-volume special edition: The group-as-a-whole: An update. *Group, 29*(1), 109–137.

Segalla, R. (2006). Selfish and unselfish behavior: Scene stealing and scene sharing in group psychotherapy. *International Journal of Group Psychotherapy, 56*(1), 33–46.

Shane, M., Shane, E., & Gales, M. (1997). *Intimate attachments: Toward a new self psychology.* New York: Guilford.

Shapiro, E. (1990), Self psychology, intersubjectivity, and group psychotherapy. *Group, 14*(3), 177–182.

Siegel, A. M. (1996). *Heinz Kohut and the psychology of the self.* London: Routledge.

Silverman, D. (2000). An interrogation of the relational turn: A discussion with Stephen Mitchell. *Psychoanalytic Psychology, 17*, 146–152.

Slavson, S. R. (1964). *A textbook in analytic group psychotherapy.* Madison, CT: International University Press.

Stacey, R. (2001). *Complex responsive processes in organizations: Learning and knowledge creation.* London: Routledge.

Stacey, R. (2003). *Complexity and group processes: A radically social understanding of individuals.* London: Brunner-Routledge.

Stacey, R. (2005). Social selves and the notion of the "group-as-a-whole." *Group, 29* (1), 187–209.

Stern, D. (1985). *The interpersonal world of the infant.* New York: Basic Books.

Stolorow, R., & Atwood, G. (1992). *Contexts of being: The intersubjective foundations of psychological life.* Hillsdale, NJ: Analytic Press.

Stolorow, R., & Lachmann, F. M. (1980). *Psychoanalysis of development arrests: Theory and treatment.* New York: International University Press.

Stolorow, R., & Lachmann, F. M. (1984/1985). Transference: The future of an illusion. In *The Annual of Psychoanalysis* (pp. 19–38). Madison, CT: IUP.

Stolorow, R., Brandchaft, B., & Atwood, G. (1987). *Psychoanalytic treatment: An intersubjective approach.* Hillsdale, NJ: Analytic Press.

Stone, W. N., & Karterud, S. (2006). Dreams as portraits of self and group interactions. *International Journal of Group Psychotherapy, 56*(1), 47–62.

Tolpin, M. (2002). Doing psychoanalysis of normal development: Forward edge transferences. In A. Goldberg (Ed.), *Postmodern self psychology: Progress in self psychology* (pp. 167–190). Hillsdale, NJ: Analytic Press.

Trotter, W. (1985). *Instinct of the herd in peace and war 1916–1919.* London: Keynes Press. (Original work published 1916.)

Wolf, E. (1988). *Treating the self.* New York: Guilford.

Wolf, A. (1988). Personal Communication. New York.

Wolf, A., Kutash, I. L., & Nattland, C. (1993). *The primacy of the individual in psychoanalysis in groups.* Northvale, NJ: Jason Aronson.

Yalom, I. D. (1985). *The theory and practice of group psychotherapy* (3rd ed.). New York: Basic Books.

8

A Radical Self Psychological Model of Supervision

Judith Teicholz, Ed.D.

"Your voice is like a pitcher of something that is being poured into me. Without it I feel so sad and empty. I realize now how much I've had to see something of me in your eyes, before I could feel it in myself. Without the flashlight of your eyes, your voice, there's nothing in me but harshness and cold." These were the words of the patient Jasmine, whose previous communications in treatment had been dominated by images of abandoned carcasses and frozen landscapes. Jasmine's new and different words—for the first time expressing selfobject longings in the transference—were music to my ears and to the ears of Dr. Helen, her analyst and my supervisee, who for two years had been in a gentle tug-of-war with me about how best to help this patient.

Until Jasmine spoke these words, Dr. Helen had begun most of her supervisory sessions by expressing a wish that she could feel something other than anger and a cold heart toward this patient whom she found numbingly superficial and maddeningly devaluing. Now, Dr. Helen was able to speak more positively of Jasmine in supervision: "There's a new clarity in her communication. There's been such a struggle between us. Now I wonder how much the struggle was necessary." Jasmine was becoming more coherent, more in touch with and expressive of her feelings in the transference, and less dysphoric. But not surprisingly, in the months just before these changes, Dr. Helen had also been able, for the first time, to view the world from Jasmine's vantage point.

Dr. Helen was an intellectually curious analytic candidate, simultaneously in supervision with me and a neo-Kleinian analyst. Initially, she argued with my self psychological communications concerning Jasmine. Fueled by chronic resentment toward her patient, Dr. Helen wanted to interpret Jasmine's devaluing behavior in terms of the patient's aggressive feelings toward her analyst and the defenses against these. She was perturbed by my suggestions that she try to understand and resonate with Jasmine's past and present experience, convinced that this approach would perpetuate the status quo.

Dr. Helen also had trouble acting on my suggestions that she explore with Jasmine how Dr. Helen, herself, might be contributing to Jasmine's experience of the treatment. She was often unable to link the analytic couple's transference-countertransference experience to the formative relationships of Jasmine's childhood, in which, it seemed, a well-meaning but anxious mother had been unable to attend to her child's basic needs, while an apparently "empty" father had intruded upon his daughter's every attempt at engagement in life outside the family. Although Dr. Helen "got" all this at a cognitive level, she could lose it in interaction with her patient because of anger stirred up in her by Jasmine's devaluing attitude toward the treatment.

I gave voice to my sympathy with Dr. Helen's frustrations but also repeatedly told her a story of how Jasmine might have come to feel, behave, and affect her analyst in the ways that she did, hoping to help Dr. Helen get more on the "inside" of her patient's experience. I told Dr. Helen that I thought she often missed the veiled declarations of love and need that were hidden in the heart of Jasmine's seemingly dismissive communications.

Although I would like to tell more of this particular story—the story of Jasmine, Dr. Helen, and me—I will instead try to extract from it a theory of supervision that might have application beyond the specifics of the three of us and the two dyads that we comprised. Thus, the model of supervision that I shall present is an abstraction of the story of how this supervisee and I moved toward each other from an initial standoff and how the patient moved from an initial sense of deadness to the point that she was able to speak the powerfully poetic words with which I have begun.

PSYCHOANALYTIC TRAINING GOALS AND THE CHALLENGE OF INTERSUBJECTIVITY IN THE TREATMENT AND SUPERVISORY RELATIONSHIPS

To provide psychoanalytic supervision is to engage in one of the most challenging and rewarding activities available to the seasoned analyst, a task made even more challenging when the supervision is part of a formal training program. Most psychoanalytic programs aim to facilitate in their trainees mastery of a multifaceted and controversy-laden body of knowledge—the history of psychoanalytic ideas—along with a set of ineffably complex "skills." The programs also seek ways to enhance in their trainees the ability to transform these skills and knowledge into everyday language in the context of a psychotherapeutic relationship: a setting where the trainee's every move, at innumerable choice-points, will be contingent on an indeterminate array of factors, largely unknowable in advance.

This unpredictability of psychoanalytic treatment devolves, in part, from the intersubjectivity of influence inherent to all human relationships, and it is a double-edged sword: its open-endedness may leave room for a healing creativity to expand and grow, but also, on occasion, for a spiraling destructiveness to be set in motion. Psychoanalytic supervision, itself, can enhance, inhibit, or derail the best efforts of even the most gifted supervisee; at the same time, a supervisor may on occasion be powerless to prevent an emotionally or professionally inept analyst-in-training from doing harm.

The double-edged sword of intersubjectivity, in both the treatment and supervisory relationships, places the supervisor's own emotional capacities at the center of the competencies needed to do the job well, and leads to a further goal of most analytic training programs: the goal of personal emotional growth for trainees, especially the enhancement of their capacities to bear and regulate intensities of painful affect in themselves and their patients. The question I raise in this chapter, then—and will try to answer—is: what kind of supervisory relationship might serve to facilitate all of these goals?

In tentative response to this question, I have developed what I am calling a radical self psychological model of psychoanalytic supervision, labeling it "radical" because, in spite of the explicit educational goals of the supervisory situation, the model comes close to matching self psychological treatment in placing the supervisee's experience at the center of its practice. The model itself does not delineate the richness and multiplicity of interactions and relatedness that are possible in a powerfully effective supervision, but it suggests an initial approach to supervision intended to lay the groundwork for these greater riches and multiplicities to emerge.

By presenting a "model," I run the risk of overschematization and reductionism. I will therefore preface my presentation with a brief description of some of the many kinds of interactions that might occur in any analytic supervision, regardless of the supervisor's approach. Although these activities are not exclusive to my model, all of them, and others as well, could become part of a supervisory relationship conducted in accordance with it. Indeed, the model's very purpose is to facilitate the development of a relationship in which the broadest range of supervisory activities can be effectively engaged.

Included in my "list" of supervisory activities and goals would be all those suggested by Buirski and Haglund (2001) who, in presenting their own intersubjective model, have highlighted such activities as promoting the unfolding and illuminating of the patient's affective experience as part of a general process of "making sense together" across the treatment and supervisory dyads. Other activities that the supervisory and treatment dyads may have in common, according to Buirski and Haglund, are the articulation and reorganization of meanings, the regulation of affect, and conveying or modeling an appreciation for contextualism.

THE COLLABORATIVE NATURE OF THE SUPERVISORY RELATIONSHIP AND ITS MULTIFACETED INTERACTIONS

In any supervision, a preliminary goal is to develop a collaborative relationship based on mutual trust, in which there is a constant genuine exchange between supervisor and supervisee, and in which a spirit of curiosity, improvisation, and creativity may prevail on behalf of the patient whose treatment is being presented. Once such trust and collaboration are established, supervisor and trainee alike can enjoy free imaginative range to explore both the patient's and the trainee's experience of the treatment, with the supervisory dyad able conjointly to conjure up a universe of ways to engage the patient, resolve relational impasses, diminish the patient's suffering, and facilitate psychic growth in both treater and treated.

There are innumerable ways that supervisee and supervisor might interact in pursuit of these goals—regardless of theory—while working together to further the trainee's learning and the patient's treatment. Either supervisor or trainee might raise questions about the patient's early experience, or generate hypotheses concerning the relationship between the patient's early experience and here-and-now transference-countertransference phenomena. Supervisor and supervisee might also explore how the patient's residual issues might be intermingling with the trainee's own. They might discuss the patient's dreams and, hearing the associative material, the supervisor might offer her own interpretations of the dreams, bringing to bear the supervisory dyad's understanding of the patient's history and current life, any "day residue" of which they are aware, and the prevailing affective themes in the analytic treatment dyad. Supervisor and supervisee might also ask each other how the patient might have responded differently had the trainee taken a different tack in a session already past. And they might brainstorm together or conduct role-plays, the better to imagine how a patient might respond to various approaches the trainee might try in future sessions.

Effective psychoanalytic treatment is an emotionally demanding endeavor for patient and analyst alike, and occasional supervisory sessions are taken up with the trainee's expression or "venting" of intense feelings toward the patient being treated—feelings of anger, resentment, lust, admiration, or love. Sometimes simply the opportunity for such expression, in the accepting presence of an admired supervisor, is enough to free the supervisee to do further self-analysis, independently or with his analyst, and to go back to the patient, able to use his feelings more constructively in the clinical encounter. But at other times such feelings generate in the trainee a conviction that he must somehow convey them directly to the patient, as was the case with Dr. Helen and her angry feelings toward her patient Jasmine.

As in any clinical situation, the supervisory dyad can explore the wisdom of such plans; they can help each other toward a deepening understanding of the patient, the analyst-in-training, and the treatment dyad around the issue under discussion. But if even such collaborative effort leaves supervisor and supervisee in conflict, the supervisor can either support or try to dissuade the trainee from his intention, explaining as fully as possible the reasons for the recommended stance.

As a supervisor, I tend to explore such situations with my supervisee, to express my thoughts and feelings as clearly as I can, and then try to support whatever the trainee goes on to do until either I am proven wrong by subsequent events or the trainee learns from his mistakes. But even in making recommendations, I may risk undermining a supervisee's learning process, because for some trainees a supervisor's advice—no matter how lightly offered—may leave little sense of choice. On the other hand, if I do not speak my mind when we disagree, the supervisee might end up feeling betrayed by me anyway, when he discovers that I left him free to act on his own instincts but that the treatment has come to grief.

If a supervisory dyad agrees that certain clinical action is called for, the supervisor might work to "shore up" the trainee—even role-playing and rehearsing possible scenarios with him—working toward increasing his readiness for a confrontation with his patient, a confrontation that the supervisor nevertheless recognizes will take place only if and when the clinical moment feels right to the supervisee. Supervisor and trainee work toward cognitive-affective understanding of the patient and the treatment dyad, they work toward emotional and practical preparedness on the part of the trainee but they leave up to the supervisee the question of when and whether he will use what has been in some way prepared. Any supervisory preparation is acknowledged to be incomplete and on somewhat shaky ground, due to the recognition that the patient's part of the equation, both affectively and behaviorally, remains unknown until the "now moment" between patient and analyst-in-training. Whatever the issue at stake, the conversation in supervision is usually in terms of ways to think about the patient and analytic relationship, possible ways of engaging in that relationship, and only rarely a demand for the trainee to speak to his patient in a prespecified way.

The exception to this open-ended exploration of possibilities, of course, is when a treatment is not going well, in the view of patient, supervisor, or supervisee. In such cases, the supervisor might bring to the trainee's attention some point at which the supervisor would probably have done something different from what the trainee did, explaining why. But supervisors are also, on occasion, able to say that although they might have spoken differently to a patient, they can see that the patient seemed to deepen his material after the intervention, connect more affectively with the analyst, or move toward greater effectiveness or intimacy in his extratransference relationships. Since the patient's subsequent behavior, along with the quality of the evolving analytic relationship, is the only criterion by which to judge the analyst-in-training's performance, the supervisor must conclude in such cases that the trainee's approach was "good enough." Future events might shed light on whether the therapeutic effectiveness was manifest because the trainee was more attuned to his patient than the supervisor believed, or because human beings—including our patients—are able to extract what they need, even from a less-than-perfect selfobject surround (Ornstein, 2004).

There are also times when the relationship between supervisor and supervisee itself may transiently take center stage in the supervisory dialogue. Processes may emerge, in the supervisory exchange, that run parallel to transference-countertransference enactments in the treatment, or there may be discomfort in the supervisory dyad around residual theoretical and clinical differences, even after extensive discussion. But the radical self psychological model tends to offset the potentially destructive aspects of such conflict, because of its supervisee-centered approach.

THE DIALECTICS OF THE SUPERVISORY RELATIONSHIP

There are many complexities in the supervisory project, and the analytic supervisor holds in dialectical tension the potentially opposing values of providing the best possible learning environment for a particular supervisee and working to diminish the possibly negative impact on the patient of being in treatment with an inexperienced analyst. There are other internal tensions for the supervisor, such as between the value of providing "expert" clinical guidance to the supervisee and the value of allowing a trainee to exercise her judgment and learn from her own experiences of trial and error. We often ask ourselves where to draw the line between a felt need to rescue a patient from what seems to be a less-than-optimal treatment and a commitment to fostering confidence in the trainee by respecting the integrity of a treatment that may have been underway long before we came on the supervisory scene. As supervisors we may feel tension as well between the value of imparting a set of general treatment guidelines and the value of fostering in the supervisee an appreciation for the absolute uniqueness of every individual and dyadic pair, which renders essential the capacities for spontaneity and improvisation. There may be tension between the didactic mission of the supervision and an interest in exploring aspects of the supervisory relationship itself, and tension between the need to focus on the patient's transference and affect combined with a need to focus on the trainee's countertransference and blind spots. Finally, for me, there is always a tension in my supervisory role, between the wish to convey my own passion about psychoanalysis and how it works and my openness to learning from others, including from my supervisees and their patients.

THE SUPERVISOR'S NONJUDGMENTAL STANCE AND THE SUPERVISEE'S OPENNESS

With all these many concerns, I still begin with the goal of developing a mutually trusting and collaborative supervisory relationship, because the value of the supervisor's contribution is dependent on the supervisee's openness, while the trainee's openness is a measure of the supervisor's nonjudgmental stance. These facilitative, mutually influencing attitudes in the supervisory dyad make it possible for the trainee's countertransference feelings or errors to be openly expressed or "vented," relationally held, and over time processed intersubjectively and intrapsychically. I believe that these processes are at the heart of analytic supervision, and it was in thinking about what might further a nonjudgmental stance in supervisors and a responding openness in supervisees that I developed what I am calling my radical self psychological model of supervision.

RATIONALE FOR THE MODEL AND SOME REMAINING PROBLEMS

I see my model as being largely compatible with Buirski and Haglund's (2001) earlier-mentioned intersubjective model of supervision. Since my model, like theirs, also relies on Stolorow, Brandchaft, and Atwood's (1987) outline of psychoanalytic intersubjectivity and later elaborations (Stolorow & Atwood, 1992; Orange, Atwood, & Stolorow, 1997), one might well ask, why offer yet another supervisory model? I think, to a greater degree, my model makes central the selfobject aspects of the supervisory relationship. But since I have written elsewhere (Teicholz, 1999) that Kohut's (1971, 1977, 1984) selfobject concept holds within it the seeds for Stolorow, et al.'s (1987) intersubjectivity theory, perhaps I need to clarify some differences I see between the selfobject and intersubjectivity concepts.

Both the selfobject and intersubjectivity concepts refer to an ongoing exchange of influence and constitutive psychic experience between the two parties to a dyad (Kohut, 1984; Stolorow, et al., 1987; Teicholz, 2001, in press). There are still important ways, however, in which the two terms differ. Intersubjectivity explicitly includes mutuality in the core of its meaning, whereas in the selfobject concept mutuality may be more or less central. The selfobject term refers to the constructive and growth-promoting aspects of relationship, implicitly leaving destructive relational experience outside its realm, except as "selfobject failures" (Teicholz, in press). By contrast, Stolorow, et al.'s (1987) expansion of the selfobject concept, into a general theory of intersubjectivity, gives us a single term and a unified concept for referring to the ongoing, two-way exchange of influence—whether constructive or destructive—between any two people in a relationship. Buirski and Haglund's (2001) intersubjective model of supervision explicitly includes the supervisor in this mutual exchange of influence, raising the number of interacting "influencers" to three, across the treatment and supervisory dyads. Buirski and Haglund also alert supervisors to both the constructive and destructive potential of their influence in the supervisory role, a point which cannot be overemphasized.

One further difference between the concepts of selfobject relating and intersubjectivity lies in the greater specificity of the selfobject term, through its reference to particular developmental needs and how they are met in the primary relationships of childhood. Because of these two areas of difference—having to do with the destructiveness as well as constructiveness that can be included in the more general intersubjectivity concept, and with the specificity of the essential developmental needs included under the selfobject concept—I see a value in preserving the terminology of both intersubjectivity and selfobject relating, as well as a rationale for an additional intersubjective model of supervision, which distinctively emphasizes the selfobject functions of the supervisor.

Laying the groundwork for later intersubjectivity theories, Kohut (1984) saw no true autonomy in psychic health, only primitive and more mature forms of selfobject relating. Kohut's qualified view of human autonomy was part of his belief that throughout the life cycle we need and are sustained through our close ties with others, in which experiences of affirmation, belonging, and idealization are constantly and mutually exchanged. Initially we are literally constituted through these exchanges; after we have developed a rudimentary sense of self, we are enhanced and sustained by them. Stolorow, et al. (1987) embraced Kohut's selfobject concept but proposed an open-ended field of selfobject functions, beyond the few Kohut identified. Today the selfobject concept may include self-delineation (Trop & Stolorow, 1992), aversive motivations (Lichtenberg, 1989), and other growth-promoting experiences.

With the radical self psychological model of supervision, I propose that a professional identity, along with a sense of professional belonging and "internalized" psychoanalytic ideals, can emerge only through the same kinds of exchanges, in the learning environment, that serve to forge the initial emergence of subjectivity—or the earliest sense of personal self—in childhood. To this end, the model proposes that we apply the central self psychological principles of development—especially the selfobject concept—to the supervisory relationship, in which the supervisee is allowed professional experiences of mirroring, twinship, and idealization as well as theoretical/clinical self-delineation. There is room as well for constructive supervisory conflict, when the supervisor's clinical understanding or recommendations feel aversive to the trainee.

Most beginning therapists suffer a legitimate sense of anxiety—either directly felt or subtly defended against. Trainees are asked to take on therapeutic responsibility for patients—sometimes with even a human life on the line—knowing that they are going to be evaluated. Although psychotherapy supervision holds a potential to diminish beginners' anxieties, it can also exacerbate them. Supervisors can thus enhance the learning process if they can find ways to minimize their trainees' anxieties. But expectable differences among trainees can mean that no matter what supervisory approach we take, there will be some who are not well-matched to work with us. Some supervisees arrive in training hoping to be told what to do and when to do it: to be saved from their "mistakes." Others come determined to try things for themselves, with a high tolerance for learning from their own experience. Some have an interest in and talent for theorizing, while others feel overwhelmed by too many choices and at first do better when they are able to act largely on the basis of more procedural and relational kinds of "knowing."

Beyond these differences in the interests, talents, and learning styles of our trainees there are differences, as well, in how a supervisor can approach the training situation. These differences may transcend both form and content, to constitute a basic stance toward the trainee. One such stance on the part of the supervisor coincides with selected principles of self psychology, relying less on a didactic approach than on careful listening and ongoing attunement to the supervisee, about both himself and his patient.

Whether in treatment or in supervision, the person seeking help must begin with a sense of safety which can be either enhanced or destroyed by the analyst or supervisor. When a sense of safety is lacking, it is the responsibility of analyst or supervisor to figure out how he is contributing to the problem and to fix his part in it. Whether in treatment or supervision, the help-seeker needs to be proffered an environment and process conducive to the development of an identity or a functionally cohesive sense of self, either personal or professional. Psychoanalytic therapy aims explicitly to facilitate emotional growth and integration in its patients, but these goals are no less important for the analyst-in-training.

Psychoanalysts engage in a life-long struggle toward levels of affective openness and psychic integration that will enable them to withstand the assaults of their patients' suffering. Intensive treatments may involve analysts in painful relational entanglements that they must find ways to leverage therapeutically; they must find ways to extract themselves without doing harm to either member of the dyad, and in ways that generate new understanding and integration in both partners. Beyond the teaching of theory and technique, the affective holding environment that a supervisor can provide goes a long way toward enabling the trainee to bring her better self to these entanglements, and creatively to seek intersubjective resolutions.

A RADICAL SELF PSYCHOLOGICAL MODEL OF PSYCHOANALYTIC SUPERVISION

Self psychology teaches us that affective integration, leading to an empowering sense of cohesion, will be enhanced by the experience of empathic listening and responsiveness on the part of another (Kohut, 1971, 1977, 1982, 1984). But what can such a stance accomplish when the help-seeker is learning a concrete set of skills and a discrete task, however complex? In psychoanalysis, the empathic stance can facilitate in the patient an opening to psychic experience and an ability to articulate this newly-accessed experience in interaction with the understanding and engaged analyst. Once directly experienced and articulated in the analytic relationship, the previously repressed or split-off thoughts and feelings of the patient can be integrated for the first time into more highly differentiated sectors of his personality and functioning. By virtue of such integration the patient may become emotionally richer and more deeply resonant with the experience of both self and others. He will be able to express himself more fully and to live in accordance with a wider range of his feelings, skills, and talents, as well as to seek others with whom he can sustain satisfying intimate relationships.

Empathic listening and responsiveness in supervision can similarly render the trainee more likely to communicate about those aspects of her professional experience that have raised questions or caused her to feel confusion, embarrassment, or shame. Problems or mistakes that can be shared, and opened to examination are less likely to be repeated than ones that remain hidden and unexplored. Once a supervisee has been able to discuss these more troubling clinical experiences with a nonjudgmental supervisor, there is a better chance that she will feel emotionally prepared when she returns to her patient, or when similar challenges arise with others.

Through empathic listening, the supervisor models for the trainee how to listen to his patient. The empathic listener tries to understand what the communicator is thinking and feeling, and to convey both understanding and acceptance. But since human empathy is fallible, it includes an expectation of error. As supervisors, we acknowledge our empathic failures. We extend ongoing invitations to our supervisees to correct us, and hope that they will do the same with their patients.

There is usually a chance to "right" things for the patient and the analytic relationship, after mistakes or failures on the analyst's part, except in suicidal cases. No matter what the supervisee has already said to her patient, the supervisor can help the supervisee listen retrospectively to how the patient has responded, and to learn from that. By helping our trainees attend to how the session progressed after a particular interaction, we can avoid becoming critics ourselves and instead foster development of our supervisees' independent, critical faculties and self-monitoring.

The supervisor should initially try to identify things that feel *right,* in how the trainee is going about her work, finding ways to support the trainee's fledgling attempts at being an analyst, much as the mother embraces the spontaneous gesture of her child (Winnicott, 1958). I do not place the trainee's independent clinical functioning above the therapeutic well-being of patients but I believe that the supervisor's reliable support of the supervisee's early analytic attempts is more likely than other approaches to help the trainee remain open to her own affect, her independent thought-processes, and her patients' reactions to her interventions. The supervisor's psychic embrace is what is most likely to keep the trainee learning from her patients and from her own mistakes—sources of learning as important as what can be learned from supervisors. As supervisors, little harm will be done if we speak first about what pleases us, giving voice to our discomforts only with tact and careful timing, aware that such communications can make-or-break the effort to help both patient and therapist attain their goals.

Self psychology suggests that initially, people learn and grow psychologically when they are given an opportunity to feel more positively about both themselves and significant others. It suggests that positive self-feeling might contribute to increasing psychic strength and cohesion, which in turn make possible greater openness to learning from all sources, intrapsychic and interpersonal. We are more likely to achieve our dual goals—of helping the patient get better and helping the trainee to learn—if we can calmly support the trainee to think about how he has intervened, how the patient has responded, and how the rest of the session (and subsequent sessions) seemed to evolve. We can encourage our supervisees to note changes in the patient's affect, disruptions of communication, uncharacteristic cancellations, no-shows, or lateness, and any self-destructive behavior and to wonder about the analyst's role in these—especially when these are not convincingly explained by other events in the patient's life.

The radical self psychological supervisor believes that empathic listening and responsiveness are among the initial conditions for psychic grow and change whether that growth is to occur in the personal or the professional realm. If we are going to convert a supervisee to our way of thinking, it usually happens only slowly and in small increments. Most trainees need time to absorb new ideas and try them on for size. We can ask them how they have been thinking about their work or what they learned from prior supervisors. Most contemporary theories recognize relational and experiential curative factors and these may figure in any treatment conducted in a humanely respectful, responsible, thoughtful, and (moderately) feeling-ful manner, regardless of theory. Sometimes the most challenging supervisory task is just to stay out of the way of a supervisee whose treatments are going well. Teaching a point of view is an important function of analytic supervision, but for some supervisees—especially advanced candidates—the opportunity to articulate their own viewpoint is a priority. My model of supervision proposes that Kohut's theory has relevance for the development of either a personal or professional self. Kohut (1984) believed that a healthy sense of self develops only in a "self-selfobject milieu" by way of a normative period of grandiosity and attribution of omnipotence to parental figures (Kohut, 1971). Perhaps because he recognized the world's terrors and attendant human vulnerabilities, Kohut reasoned that no individual could set forth without an initial overestimation of both self and others. Early aggrandizement enables the young individual to acquire interests, develop skills and talents, and begin to make her way through a tough and competitive world without being totally crippled by universal, existential anxieties. At first the parents accept and even affirm the young child's sense of grandiosity, protecting him from discovering that it has little basis in "external reality." The transition from overvaluation to a more reality-based assessment of both self and others is facilitated by the parents' increasingly accurate mirroring of the child's actual abilities as they gradually replace the earlier grandiosity, and by the child's increasing capacity to perceive and tolerate his parents' inevitable imperfections and limitations, as well as his own.

If we now apply this theory of normal development to the emergence of a professional sense of self in the supervisory situation, we might say that initially the trainee needs a period in which she is permitted the fantasy that she can "do no harm:" a brief period in which supervisor and supervisee collude to "suspend disbelief" in the supervisee's clinical abilities. At the outset the supervisor holds the reality of the trainee's lack of experience, at the same time as seeking ways to mirror back to the supervisee whatever seems somewhat useful in what she is doing. Meanwhile the supervisor is both modeling and teaching a different approach as they go along, but without necessarily drawing attention to what has been clinically less than optimal.

This process is similar in some ways to what happens when the novice toddler takes her first steps. Of course she is toddling and not walking, and she is going to bump into things and fall. Parents try to remove obstacles in the new toddler's path; they soften the edges of obstacles that cannot be removed. They show not anxiety and censure in response to the toddler's inevitable wrong steps, but rather calmness and pride. When they pick up the toddler after a fall, their affirming expression makes all the difference as to whether or not the toddler will try walking, again and again, until she becomes steadier on her feet.

As with the parents' need to contain their fears for the toddler who is newly learning to walk, the supervisor must contain her fears for the well-being of the patient who is in treatment with a beginning analyst. Better to provide an atmosphere in which the trainee can talk about and learn from her clinical bumps and bruises than an atmosphere in which the supervisee is "taught" what to say in any number of situations, but never gets to establish her own analytic footing or develop her own analytic voice. This way of approaching the work with new supervisees usually evolves into a collaborative working relationship, in which both partners openly and spontaneously share their thoughts and feelings about the work being presented. Such a process helps the trainee to make uniquely his, the best that the supervisory couple is able jointly to generate. The supervisee feels held and supported in his psychoanalytic work while gradually developing confidence in his own psychoanalytic radar, conceptualizing capacities, and unique analytic self-expression.

SOME FURTHER LIMITS AND CAVEATS THAT PERTAIN TO THIS MODEL

I would certainly understand if at this point some of my readers were to feel uncomfortable that I have placed such emphasis on providing a facilitative learning environment for the supervisee at what may seem to be the expense of the patient in treatment. But I place this emphasis because I believe the patient will ultimately be best served by having an analyst who is given the vital opportunity to learn in an optimal environment. Of course an optimal learning environment can encompass a wide range of needs across supervisees, and the approach I present may be more suited to some than to others—it might even feel aversive, for those who start with an authoritarian approach to learning. My model is best used, then, as a starting point that can be changed or fine-tuned in ongoing negotiation between every supervisor and her individual trainees.

Any new supervision might begin with a discussion of how the supervisor usually approaches her task, as well as a discussion of what has worked and not worked for the trainee up to this point. With these two sets of starting points, the supervisor can forge a way of working with the individual trainee that is most likely to facilitate his learning. In my own initial supervisory conversations with new trainees, I convey my willingness to "teach" a coherent approach but also my sense of how richly complex is every analytic dyad, and how important are the analyst-in-training's own affective experiences and observations toward developing a feel for what is going on in a treatment. However the supervisory work begins, our interactions tend to move toward a more collaborative exchange.

It is deeply rewarding for a supervisor to work toward enhancing a trainee's clinical effectiveness while increasing the chances that his patients will get better. When these dual processes go well, the supervisor has a lasting impact on both the supervisees he has trained and the patients that were treated by them. Similarly, the admiration and delight that a supervisor may feel, toward both those she has trained and those who have made creative use of their analytic treatments under supervision, are pleasures that can last a lifetime.

REFERENCES

Buirski, P., & Haglund, P. (2001). *Making sense together: The intersubjective approach to psychotherapy.* Lanham, MD: Rowman & Littlefield.

Kohut, H. (1971). *The analysis of the self.* New York: International Universities Press.

Kohut, H. (1977). *The restoration of the self.* New York: International Universities Press.

Kohut, H. (1982). Introspection, empathy, and the semi-circle of mental health. *Internat. J. Psycho-Anal., 63,* 395–407.

Kohut, H. (1984). *How does analysis cure?* Ed. A. Goldberg. Chicago: University of Chicago Press.

Lichtenberg, J. (1989). *Psychoanalysis and motivation.* Hillsdale, NJ: Analytic Press.

Orange, D., Atwood, G., & Stolorow, R. (1997). *Working intersubjectively: Contextualism in psychoanalytic practice.* Hillsdale, NJ: Analytic Press.

Ornstein, P. (2002). Informal discussion at MAPP meeting, May 12.

Stolorow, R., & Atwood, G. (1992). *Contexts of being.* Hillsdale, NJ: Analytic Press.

Stolorow, R., Brandchaft, B., & Atwood, G. (1987). *Psychoanalytic treatment: An intersubjective approach.* Hillsdale, NJ: Analytic Press.

Teicholz, J. G. (1999). *Kohut, Loewald, & the postmoderns.* Hillsdale, NJ: Analytic Press.

Teicholz, J. G. (2001). The many meanings of intersubjectivity and their implications for analyst self-expression and self-disclosure. In A. Goldberg (Ed.), *The Narcissistic Patient Revisited: Progress in Self Psychology, vol. 17* (pp. 9–42). Hillsdale, NJ: Analytic Press.

Teicholz, J. G. (2006). Negative identifications, messy complexity, and windows of hope: Response to Pickles' discussion of "Qualities of engagement and the analyst's theory" by Judith Guss Teicholz. *IJPSP*, Vol. 1, No. 4, 435–44.

Trop, J., & Stolorow, R. (1992). Defense analysis in self psychology: A developmental view. *Psychoanal. Dial.*, *2*, 427–441.

Winnicott, D. (1958). The capacity to be alone. In *The maturational processes and the facilitating environment: Studies in the theory of emotional development* (pp. 29–36). New York: International Universities Press.

IV

CONTRIBUTIONS TO THERAPEUTIC PROCESS

9

Shame: A Major Instigator of Secrets

Andrew P. Morrison, MD

A shorter version of this paper was presented at the conference in New York, "Hide and Seek: When Secrets Haunt the Treatment," presented by the National Membership Committee on Psychoanalysis in Clinical Social Work (NMCOP) and the Psychoanalytic Psychotherapy Study Center (APSC) in February, 2006.

Shame remains the most painful of dysphoric affects, reflecting harsh judgments by ourselves about ourselves. We find ourselves to be defective, inferior, flawed, tiny, insignificant, dirty, unworthy—feelings of shame are the result of these self-denigrating judgments. Shame had previously been considered to be strictly social and external—the judgment about oneself by another. It was thought that where there is shame, there must be a shamer—an external observer, an accuser, an audience. This vision of shame has been challenged by a small band of psychoanalytic renegades—the group that Helen Block Lewis referred to as "the shameniks." It is now accepted, I believe, that shame takes its place in the pantheon of intrapsychic psychoanalytic phenomena (along with its sibling guilt, forming the "moral" emotions), equally worthy of study and treatment. It can suffice that I alone find myself wanting, make the shaming condemnation against myself. I don't need the help of outside others. A testimony to this change in the place of shame is the fact that a major conference in New York of the psychoanalytic journals—Symposium 2006—was titled, simply, "Shame."

Shame reflects the conviction of a gap between ideal self (the self as I would want to be, toward which I aspire) and actual self (the self as I really am, the self that I am "stuck with") (Sandler, Holder, & Mears, 1963). Since this definition of shame relates to states of self, shame is, I have argued, the principal affect underlying narcissism and narcissistic phenomena (Morrison,

1989). I refer to a set of phrases that depicts this gap, representing shame and narcissistic vulnerability, as "the language of shame" (Morrison, 1996). Such words as "worthless," "loser," "different," "insignificant," "invisible," "pathetic," and "ridiculous" constitute this language of shame. When they appear in the therapeutic dialogue, the therapist is well-advised to think about, look for, and articulate hidden shame. It most frequently is present, and, when identified with tact and skill, characteristically elicits the surprised "aha" response from the patient, indicating a feeling of being truly understood.

One feature of shame is, then, its tendency to be concealed, disguised, hidden. A recent paper by Lansky (2005), entitled "Hidden Shame," explores both the theoretical and clinical-phenomenological reasons for shame remaining hidden. In theory, Freud was initially interested in shame, which at first he saw as a noxious affect—the "incompatible idea" as judged by conscience (Lansky, 2005). He then shifted his view to one of shame as a defense, a "moral dam" holding back from awareness unbidden and disallowed sexual and aggressive thoughts (Freud, 1905). With Freud's attention shifting to the structural hypothesis (1923), guilt and the Oedipus complex predominated, and shame (whether affect or defense) receded to the sidelines. This meant, of course, that shame was marginalized by Freud's immediate disciples. Only in the second half of the previous century did shame reappear as a consequential psychoanalytic phenomena, this in conjunction with renewed interest in narcissism (e.g., Hartmann, 1950; Kohut, 1966, 1971; Lewis, 1971).

Before exploring the relationship between shame and secrets, it will be helpful to examine a developmental sequence of shame as affect. When shame is considered in terms of ideals, and the failure of the self (or "selves") to attain them, we are approaching the affect from a more highly delineated position than is the case with the scowl or cry of an infant rebuked by her caretaker. I have suggested a developmental line for shame that begins as inborn affect for the newborn and infant (Tomkins, 1960). The characteristic facial expression of shame (down-turned head, eyes, and lips) can be seen in response to a rebuff or turning away by the caretaker, suggesting, perhaps, a sense of subjective inefficacy or an unexpected response. This proto-shame response can also be viewed, from the perspective of self psychology, as the result of selfobject failure or rupture.

The next level in the developmental progression of shame occurs with the appearance of differentiation of self from the other, or "objective self-awareness" (Broucek, 1982). It is at this point that the individual recognizes that she or he stands alone (for the bad as well as the good of it). Since we are separate from everyone else, we become capable of experiencing difference, comparison, and competition. With these distinctions, shame becomes an affect imposed by an external other, even as it remains an internal, subjective experience.

Finally, at a point developmentally analogous to Freud's oedipal stage, the child becomes able to conceptualize, and thus to imagine, to create goals, ideals, aspirations. Clearly the formation of ideals involves internalization of the ideals and standards of others—parents, society—but these others needn't be physically present for their representations to be forged. Thus, with the formation of ideals, the capacity emerges for the internalization of shame. Before our own eyes alone we make judgments about successes and failures, about our superiorities and inferiorities (Morrison, 1987). It is particularly with regard to failure in attaining ideals that our most glaring deficits are hidden, our most intricate secrets crafted.

In phenomenological-clinical terms, it is the searing pain of shame as affect that induces concealment, secrets. Lansky (1997) speaks of the fantasy of shame's bearability or unbearability as the factor determining the patient's need to conceal shame. I have written about the defenses against shame that lead to its concealment, including anger and rage, contempt, envy, withdrawal, and forms of depression (Morrison, 1999). These defenses against shame are true for analyst as well as patient, and it is our own shame sensitivity that has contributed for so long to its remaining hidden, both in theory and in treatment. Shame is an acutely contagious affect, as our patients' shame reverberates with our own feelings. There has been, I believe, an intersubjective tendency toward collusion between analyst and patient to avoid examining or exploring shame, for the sake and comfort of both parties (beginning, perhaps, with Freud in his own treatment of Dora). There is much to suggest that Freud himself was particularly shame-sensitive, and that this factor may well have played a part in his turning from shame to guilt as his principle affective concern. In fact, it is not uncommon for analysts after Freud to "dissociate" entire shame-based aspects of their patients' self-experience because of this contagion.

One further element in understanding the connection between shame and secrets is the relationship between shame and narcissistic phenomena. I have suggested elsewhere (Morrison, 1989, 1994) that there exists a tension between two poles of narcissism—the expansive and the contracted poles—with shame a resultant response to failure in either one. I refer to this tension as the "dialectic of narcissism," in which there is internal tension within each of us, to achieve grandiose yearnings (for power, autonomy, independence), as well as yearnings for merger (dependency, union, attachment). These poles can also be described as the large and small elements of narcissism.

Each pole leads, inevitably, to a sense of failure, and hence to shame. In the expansive pole, we either fail to achieve our grandiose aspirations, or our grandiosity and ambitions spill over and we feel exposed (Kohut's [1971] view of shame). In the contracted pole, we feel small, insignificant, invisible—this, the experience of narcissistic vulnerability. Or, we feel unworthy of merger with the idealized other. There tends to be an oscillation between these two poles in each of us, with one dominating for a given individual, or at a given moment. Shame is frequently the dominant affective response to the unsuccessful outcome in either of these realms of narcissism.

This brief pastiche on shame brings us to the matter of secrets—the "hide and seek" of work with shame. The devastating pain that accompanies shame explains why it is driven underground, through repression, disavowal, or dissociation. Of course, our private concern about a shamed sense of self, in addition to the jolt inflicted on our self-esteem, generates the wish to hide the self-deficit from the observing other. Here, audience or perpetrator must be prevented from bearing witness to the shaming event or quality embodied in what is concealed, or kept private. When we are aware of specific attributes or qualities that cause shame, we seek to mask these entities or retreat from those others who might "see" it. We create and maintain a secret—of our unworthiness, our defect, our insignificance.

In a paper on secrets in group therapy, I wrote, "This [need to conceal] often leads to the generation of personal secrets, both conscious and unconscious, which may represent the most important sources of individual shame and self-loathing. Not infrequently shame will be hidden behind manifest defenses" (Morrison, 1990). Sometimes, therefore, the secret itself may be out of awareness, an unconscious decision reflecting repression or dissociation. In these instances, we may hide a secret from ourselves as well as from another. Dramatic examples of recovered memories (e.g., of childhood trauma, of humiliating origins) illustrate these secrets, usually accompanied by shame.

For example, a woman in treatment for overwhelming anxiety in social as well as sexual contexts was angry whenever I tried to investigate her childhood and relationships to her parents. She recalled, with great sadness, the many instances in which her parents left her alone with a cruel housekeeper when they went out to many dinner parties and social events. It was relatively easy for her to speak of the sadness of her childhood, but she balked at talking of other than angry hatred for her cold, absent father. We both acknowledged that there must be something more to explain her sexual remoteness with a husband whom she loved. After many years of circling around her childhood memories, she eventually was able to remember—or, perhaps, reconstruct—events with her father when he called to her and begged her to get into bed next to him, always after her mother had fallen deeply asleep. Her memories were of herself as a girl of about five or six, and his holding her with a tight grip so that she couldn't pull away. Eventually she remembered, she thought, that she didn't always want to pull away, that she enjoyed being so close to him. Expectable feelings of fear and terror accompanied recollection of these events, but the feeling most striking to both of us was that of shame and revulsion—at first that he would do such a thing, but ultimately that she might have induced, and actually might have enjoyed her father's sexualized embrace.

How could she be such a person as would enjoy this activity? It was disgusting of her. She felt that she must never reveal to her parents, or even to her husband, that she had remembered, retrieved, these childhood memories of revulsion and desire. Trauma, yes, but also overwhelming shame, at having participated, and perhaps even enjoyed, this "kind of contact" with her father. Such trauma, as embellished by memory, frequently causes overwhelming, unbearable shame leading to dissociation, not simply to repression. In sexual and some relational situations, my patient became so overwhelmed that she "absented" herself from her body and from connection with the other—her husband (or her therapist).

This is, of course, an extreme example of a shame-generated secret, one that took years of therapeutic connection and supportive acceptance before she gained access to such trauma- and shame-soaked memories. Other examples of secrets and their relationship to shame need not be so startling and dramatic. Some come, not from the consulting room, but from literature, and I shall look at one recent example from the novels of Philip Roth. Certainly, his early *Portnoy's Complaint* is famous for its scatological allusions reflecting the pain and shame-drenched torment of its secretive hero, but I want to examine the shame-based secrets that emerge in his more recent book, *The Human Stain*. This tells the tale, through the eyes of Roth's Nathan Zuckerman, of Coleman Silk, former dean of Athena College, who has been forced to resign from the college because he gave an ambiguously worded critique of some students frequently absent from class—"spooks" in the classroom—which was interpreted as a racial slur. As the novel unfolds, Silk becomes more of a mysterious figure, compounded by his unlikely love affair with a young custodian at the college and their sudden death in a car crash.

The book's cover states the issue clearly. "Coleman Silk has a secret. But it's not the secret of his affair, at seventy-one, with Faunia Farley, a woman half his age with a savagely wrecked past. . . . And it's not the secret of misogyny, despite the efforts of his ambitious young colleague at the college. . . . Nor is it the secret of Coleman's alleged racism. . . . Coleman's secret has been kept for fifty years: from his wife, his four children, his colleagues, and his friends." Silk's secret is that he had been born black, but, being light-skinned, had spent his life and marriage passing as a Jew. Zuckerman had learned this about his friend only after Silk's funeral, when he met and spoke with Silk's sister, Ernestine. In Zuckerman's words,

> I couldn't imagine anything that could have made Coleman more of a mystery to me than this unmasking. Now that I knew everything, it was as though I knew nothing, and instead of what I learned from Ernestine unifying my idea

> of him, he became not just an unknown but an uncohesive person. In what proportion, to what degree, had his secret determined his daily life and permeated his everyday thinking? Did it alter over the years from being a hot secret to being a cool secret to being a forgotten secret of no importance, something having to do with a dare he'd taken, a wager made to himself way back when? Did he get, from his decision, the adventure he was after, or was the decision in itself the adventure? Was it the misleading that provided his pleasure, the carrying off of the stunt that he liked best, the traveling through life incognito, or had he simply been closing the door to a past, to people, to a whole race that he wanted nothing intimate or official to do with? . . . By the time I met him, was the secret merely the tincture barely tinting the coloration of the man's total being or was the totality of his being nothing but a tincture in the shoreless sea of a life-long secret? Did he ever relax his vigilance, or was it like being a fugitive forever?

These questions about Silk's secret, raised so eloquently by Roth, provide us with many issues to ponder about secrets, shame, and hide and seek. To what degree does one's secret dominate the shape and course of a life? How crucial is it that a particular secret be uncovered, in therapy as in life? Where does shame—implied, but never explicitly identified by Roth—fit in to the fabric of Silk's secret identity? What might be the dangers inherent in probing too forcefully into the privacy that Silk maintained about his origins and childhood?

In the novel, Silk approaches his neighbor Zuckerman, mad with anxiety and anger immediately after the death of his wife. He requests that Zuckerman write the tale of his downfall at Athena for the "absurd" charge of being a racist, with the whole plot unfolding from this premise. Let us suppose that Zuckerman was, instead of a writer, the town psychoanalyst, and Silk was coming to sort out the trauma of the charges that ruined his professional career and led, he believed, to the death of his wife. In your meetings with him you learned of his very private relationship with Faunia, a young woman who was a custodian for the college and was separated from, though still married to, an abusive husband. You learned that Coleman was soothed and revitalized through this relationship, inappropriate though it seemed on the surface.

Let us suppose as well that you came to suspect, unlike Zuckerman, that there was something a bit strange about the intensity of his reaction to the charge of racism, and somewhat suspicious about his use of the term "spook," especially given your conviction that he must have been aware of its colloquial usage. Wearing your detective hat, you suspected that he was hiding something, and you set out to seek for it. Let's assume, further, that you came to suspect that Coleman was hiding his genetic racial identity. Your tentative, speculative questions had yielded nothing—what would you do? I am raising, here, questions implied in Roth's fiction. What function does the secret serve in maintaining the cohesion and integrity of your patient's personality and the warp of his life? To what degree is the secret driven by shame, and how do you assess whether that shame is bearable (i.e., nameable) or unbearable (must remain hidden)? How much patience, time, and acceptance must be committed to the "project" of winning the patient's confidence in sharing a secret so searing and character-determining as Coleman's? What about moral questions—at what point does a secret become a lie?

To me, the beauty of Roth's fiction is the degree to which he maintains ambiguity in assessing Silk's motives and experience, in the finest convention of postmodern thinking, and as ambiguity might inform contemporary analytic therapy. As Silk's therapist, you might wonder whether the structure of his whole character might crumble if he were confronted with his perfidy. On the other hand, might he respond with relief, as suggested earlier, at the articulation and normalization at last of his great fear and shame—his African American origins? The extent of danger from exposing his secret would rest on the intensity of shame and/or fear attached to it, and the assessment of this intensity becomes one of the major challenges of analytic work with shame. Alternatively, was Coleman immersed in shame because of his deception, and would relieving himself of his secret provide liberation from shame (which frequently serves as both the trigger and response to a secret)? These are among the questions raised by this novel that might not seem so alien in our clinical practices, reflecting as they do the ambiguity that is the true challenge to our skill and art.

In other, perhaps more familiar, scenarios, consider the patient who comes ready to share with you, his potential analyst, the long-held secret kept from others—the affair that is concealed from her husband, the demotion at work that will mean less income and status among friends, an abrupt outburst of previously dormant herpes, the failing grade in college that must, at all costs, be kept hidden from ambitious parents. We might imagine that Coleman Silk comes to his analyst with the dilemma that he has kept from his children—details of their African American heritage. Let us suppose that he feels guilty and ashamed about this deception, and he wants help with this dilemma and its consequent feelings. How can we best work with these problems?

I recently heard details of a patient who came to his therapist with the quandary of whether to tell his wife of his lifelong homosexuality. Rob had grown up Catholic in a Midwestern town and had known since childhood that he was gay, but was convinced both that this was a sin and also that he would indeed be the target of taunting and torment were he to acknowledge his sexual orientation. He had created an existence of heterosexual dating and ultimately marriage, not unlike the secret maintained by Coleman Silk about his racial identity, and not at all uncommon among homosexual men who grew up in homophobic environments of a decade or more ago. Rob maintained secret homosexual contacts throughout his marriage, and currently is engaged in a gratifying, sustaining homosexual relationship that he wants to acknowledge and maintain publicly. His desire to "come out" reflects his particular fear that his children might eventually discover his secret identity and come to feel that he has been false, a sham to them. Work with Rob focused on his fears of being discovered—"outed"—as well as the admixture of guilt toward his wife, for the hurt and rejection that his disclosure would cause, fear of being seen as a fraud in the eyes of his children; and remnants of his Catholicism which reminded him that he was a "sinner." It was shame, however, that bracketed his secret homosexuality.

Let's look in greater detail at Rob's shame. Growing up as he did in an environment particularly antagonistic to homosexuality, he came to feel that this attribute of his personality symbolized his whole identity. He was different, a loser, a wimp. There was something the matter with him, even perverse, especially in the eyes of the all-seeing church. His parents, were they to know, could never accept him. These self-excoriations are excellent examples of what I have referred to as the language of shame, and it is clear that Rob's childhood was shame-saturated because of his homosexuality. His shame, unbearable were its source to be known, instigated his development of a false identity—that of a heterosexual man. He married, developed a dual identity that worked well enough for him until he realized that he wanted to live an open existence with his current lover, and came for treatment with a conflict over his secrecy. At this point, Rob was feeling ashamed about the false identity that he had generated, wanted to "out" himself to all concerned, but was severely frightened of the consequences.

Rob provides an example in which a secret is kept from the outside world, not from the therapist. Therefore, it is less a challenge involving "seeking" by the therapist (as it might have been with Coleman Silk) than in providing help and acceptance to deal with the consequences and shame from the long-kept "hiding," his secret. Rob is asking for help in giving up his secret, in going public with the information that he had sequestered for a lifetime—at first generated out of shame, but now maintained from fear over the consequences. His current shame may well be for having kept secret something so basic to his very existence. But how can we as therapists be helpful? We must start by accepting the reality for Rob of his feelings—related to his secret and to the thought of "outing" himself. Gently, we might help him accept the turbulence of his predicament, face into it (as into any painful feeling), and then begin to think about his alternatives.

Ultimately, Rob will have to make decisions and choices—whether or not to face the guilt of hurting his wife and the shame of letting his children and the world know; whether to relinquish his attachment to his lover in exchange for the pain of lost intimacy and self-cohesion; or whether to hold on to his secret and maintain a false, shame-ridden existence and self-image. These are among the conflicts Rob will have to face. I believe the analyst's task is not to seek for the best pathway for Rob to take but, rather, to help him brace himself and face into the pain of engaging his options and his choices, and to make that decision which ultimately feels most palatable to him, that is, to accept the inevitability of ambiguity and of conflict in choosing his life course at this time in his life.

In summary, I am suggesting that shame is a major instigator and ingredient in the secrets people create for themselves. In approaching the treatment of secrets, we therapists often best utilize methods developed in the treatment of shame itself. These include patience, empathy, acceptance of the conviction of alleged shortcomings generating the patient's shame, and, finally, a gentle questioning of the assumptions about self that have caused the secret, and about the consequences anticipated when the secret is exposed. These principles were implied in the vignette of Rob's treatment. The issues are different when the secret isn't known by the patient (i.e., remains unconscious, denied, or dissociated), or when it is concealed from the therapist as well as from the outside world (as in our illusory treatment of Coleman Silk). In the latter situation, much greater caution and sensitivity must be exerted in trying to define or bring forth the secret, and we must ask, "For whose benefit are we trying to 'out' the secret?" The title of the panel for which a version of this paper was first written implies this issue, by coupling "hide" (the hidden, the concealed) with "seek." There are times, as with Coleman, when it may be deleterious or destructive for us to seek, especially if it reflects more distinctly our own agenda or curiosity. Sometimes the patient may be better served if we don't seek. Frequently this decision remains unclear, and we must use our best judgment (or intuition) in managing the ambiguity.

For example, a colleague spoke in detail about her patient Anthony, where issues of "difference," isolation, and shame were prominent in the treatment. Unlike Rob, Anthony was not clear—in his own mind, and certainly in what he shared with his therapist—whether he was or was not gay. What he was clear about, however, was that he bitterly resented those who asked or implied that he might be gay. The therapist observed that Anthony was uncomfortable in thinking about, or facing, many aspects, fears, about himself, including especially matters of his gender identity. One session that my colleague discussed with me went something like this: "Anthony came into the office in a fussy mood." (I noted the word and sense implied by the term "fussy"). "He was annoyed that the other men, like him in junior faculty positions at the community college where he taught, seemed interested in talking only about the attractive women in their classes, or about the Red Sox. He wasn't even slightly interested in these matters, nor did he want to join the 'local elk hunters,' as he had named them. He spoke of his great disdain for these guys, and then associated to childhood experiences when he went exploring in the local woods with a 'gaggle' of guys in his elementary school class. Apparently as part of a ritual initiation, they all pulled down their pants and touched each other's penises. Anthony recalled this experience with great disgust, and didn't play with this group of boys again." (I noted the "gag" in gaggle.)

The therapist went on to describe Anthony's close friendship with a senior member of his department, and of their mutual respect for each other's writings. Often Anthony would speak longingly of his friend, yearning for an even closer, more intimate friendship, but he spoke disparagingly about Rene's involvement with the "elk hunters," his enjoyment at talking sports with the other guys, and his apparent preference for going with the "hunters" for a beer rather than taking good wine with Anthony. He found Rene's choices hard to understand, but he wondered whether his friend was wary of being tagged gay if he got too close to Anthony. This, apparently, was the closest that Anthony came to thinking of, or calling, himself gay in the vignette that the therapist told to me.

"I mean, it was right there—Tony's distaste for anything that smacked of homosexuality, for any allusions that anyone made to his manner or to his lifestyle, his own critique of the preoccupations of the 'elk hunters.' Yet at the same time, something very strongly tells me to stay away from it, at least for now, that it would be a big mistake to confront him with his apparent homosexual urges." I strongly agreed with her intuition, as we talked about the ways in which this "evasion to confront" runs counter to the interpretive dictates of traditional analytic theory. Clearly, the matter of timing is essential, but mightn't it also be that there would never be a "right" time to confront him with his homosexual fears?

Again, I found myself in agreement with my consultee, and was impressed with her sensitivity. It seemed likely that Anthony was tenuously maintaining his sense of self through his denial (or dissociation) of what he considered to be a grievous fault in his character—the matter of gender identity. It sounded as though he felt shame and humiliation over what he sensed as a serious flaw in his persona. He also appeared unable to articulate his concern, suggesting an experience of shame that is unbearable. His shameful secret is, in essence, being kept from himself, as well as from his therapist and from the world in general. Inquiry about Anthony's secretive gender preferences should await a firmer experience through therapy of self and of relational attachments.

Anthony's predilection for self-shaming was supported by information during a subsequent consultation with his therapist, who presented his great humiliation over his modest sociocultural background. His mother had left his father, taking Anthony and his sisters to live near her parents in

the south. Thus, he grew up in a one-parent household, with infrequent visits from his drug-addicted father, in a suburban community dominated by intact families and family life. Also, his mother and his family were among the poorest in the community, and Anthony recalled feeling very self-conscious (another shame designator) in school with other, more affluent kids.

He discussed his mother's criticisms of him as being selfish, thoughtless, and not very masculine. He envied the boys in the neighborhood who played happily with their fathers, recalling particularly informal softball games with the kids and their fathers. His own father would visit very occasionally, and he remembers him as a swaggering, bragging "ladies' man" who didn't pay much attention to Anthony or to his siblings. As Anthony developed, he recalls feeling embarrassed by his mother's attacks on him, by their economic poverty, and particularly by the absence of a loving, supportive father.

I suggested that the therapist explore with Anthony his feelings of shame around those matters about which he was aware and able to acknowledge—his loneliness, his feeling of having different tastes and interests from those of Rene and the "elk hunters," his family background. This might at least enable him to accept and become familiar with the affective experience surrounding his deeply held secret, and to associate it with aspects of his life that he is able to acknowledge. I have found that efforts to work with—to gain acceptance and understanding of—shame often leads to an expanding capacity to face the various convictions of deficits, failures, and flaws that have generated shame. When shame itself moves from the unbearable (unconscious, disavowed) to the bearable (aware, accepted), those instigating circumstances that generate it may also come to the surface.

From a self psychological perspective, we might conceptualize the therapist's task with Anthony to be that of providing selfobject support to help him consolidate a firmer sense of self. With this support and more cohesive self-state, he might become able to tolerate exploration of his ambivalent and ambiguous gender preferences. This task clearly requires time and patience by both therapist and patient. Relational theory might conceptualize the task in terms of developing a sense of trust in the benevolence and acceptance from the other, who might—as exemplified by the interacting therapist—find Anthony's self-assumptions tolerable (in contrast with the accusations of his early mother). A more traditional analytic posture would emphasize the superego, and might speak of a softening of the harshness of superego injunctions (Wurmser's [2000] "inner judge").

Exploration of shame indicates that it may exist in primary or secondary forms (Morrison, 1983, 1984). Primary shame represents the penetration of this affect to the deepest layers of self-experience, and hence is frequently unconscious, unbearable, and hidden. This quality of shame I have referred to as narcissistic shame—narcissistic, in that it refers to all manners of the sense of self, to its very core. Anthony's shame is experienced as relating to who, at base, he is, and may not be consciously experienced so long as he can avoid thinking about its deepest source (his gender identity). With primary, unbearable shame the therapy must move very slowly, tactfully. Anthony's secret must be respected, not ruthlessly bludgeoned. With primary shame, characteristic defenses are utilized to protect and maintain its hidden nature. For example, Anthony employs anger toward Rene and contempt for the "hunters" to protect concealment of his shame about his sense of himself.

Secondary shame is bearable, not hidden, and is related to a specific action or quality that can be readily examined. Sometimes secondary shame itself can serve as a defense against underlying rage or guilt, the opposite of the sequence in primary (narcissistic) shame. For example, Anthony overslept one morning and failed to be present for a discussion section in one of the classes that he taught. His first reaction was one of shame—nothing hidden or secretive about the source of his embarrassment/shame in this instance. He had failed to fulfill one of the expectations of his teaching job. It was easy enough for his therapist to explore his shame over his dereliction of responsibility, and fairly readily she got to his underlying anger at this discussion group for their disinterest in the literature that he was teaching. In this instance, Anthony's shame covered, defended against, guilt over his anger at the group that he was teaching. Secondary shame, then, represents a conscious, acceptable feeling that is more bearable than the other underlying affect, and thus itself serves as a defense. Also, secondary shame is about an action, not about the state of the self.

Secrets that are fashioned out of shame, then, generally reflect that shame which is primary, narcissistically fundamental, and essentially unbearable and hidden. By bringing the shame into consciousness and a state of bearability, the secret's content comes into awareness, and the affect becomes what I have designated as secondary shame. In this way, we might hope that, as Anthony becomes more familiar with, and accepting of his shame, he might eventually become aware of his fear of homo- (or bi-) sexuality, and this anxiety might be brought into the treatment.

In conclusion, I am suggesting that shame has been the instigator of the patient's resorting to secrecy. Our therapeutic inquiry into secrets may at times itself be shaming, as it would have been had Anthony's therapist pushed her observations of homosexuality on him. On the other hand, the delicate and subtle naming and exploration of shame (and the self-assessment that engenders it) can lead to understanding, and sometimes even to the selective dismantling, of our patients' secrets.

REFERENCES

Broucek, F. J. (1982). Shame and its relationship to early narcissistic developments. *Int. J. Psycho-Anal, 63*, 369–378.

Broucek, F. J. (1991). *Shame and the self.* New York: Guilford Press.

Freud, S. (1905). Three essays on the theory of sexuality. *SE, 7*, 135–243.

Freud, S. (1923). The ego and the id. *SE, 19*, 12–66.

Hartmann, H. (1950). Comments on the psychoanalytic theory of the ego. *Psychoanalytic Study of the Child, 5*, 74–96.

Kohut, H. (1966). Forms and transformations of narcissism. *JAPA, 14*, 243–272.

Kohut, H. (1971). *The analysis of the self.* New York: International Universities Press.

Lansky, M. R. (1997). Envy as process. In M. R. Lansky & A. P. Morrison (Eds.), *The widening scope of shame* (pp. 327–338). Hillsdale, NJ: Analytic Press.

Lansky, M. R. (2005). Hidden shame. *JAPA, 53*, 865–890.

Lewis, H. B. (1971). *Shame and guilt in neurosis.* New York: International Universities Press.

Morrison, A. P. (1983). Shame, the ideal self, and narcissism. *Contemp. Psychoanal., 19*, 295–318.

Morrison, A. P. (1984). Working with shame in psychoanalytic treatment. *JAPA, 32*, 479–505.

Morrison, A. P. (1987). The eye turned inward: Shame and the self. In S. Nathanson (Ed.), *The many faces of shame.* Baltimore: Johns Hopkins University Press.

Morrison, A. P. (1989). *Shame, the underside of narcissism.* Hillsdale, NJ: Analytic Press.

Morrison, A. P. (1990). Secrets: A self-psychological view of shame in group psychotherapy. In B. Roth, W. Stone, & H. Kibel (Eds.), *The difficult patient in group: Group psychotherapy with borderline and narcissistic disorders.* New York: International Universities Press.

Morrison, A. P. (1994). The breadth and boundaries of a self psychological immersion in shame: A one-and-a-half person perspective. *Psychoanl. Dial., 4*, 19–35.

Morrison, A. P. (1999). Shame on either side of defense. *Contemp. Psychoanal., 35*, 91–105.

Roth, P. (1969). *Portnoy's Complaint.* London: Cape.

Roth, P. (2000). *The Human Stain.* Boston: Houghton Mifflin.

Sandler, J., Holder, A., & Meers, D. (1963). The ego ideal and the ideal self. *Psychoanal. Study Child, 18*, 139–158.

Tomkins, S. (1987). Shame. In D. L. Nathanson (Ed.), *The many faces of shame* (pp. 133–161). New York: Guilford Press.

Wurmser, L. (2000). *The power of the inner judge.* New York: Springer.

10

Our First Fight: Reflections on the Psychoanalytic Concept of Enactment

Ellen Shumsky, CSW, and Donna Orange, PhD, PsyD

We begin with a clinical story: I (ES) have been seeing Joan for psychotherapy for years—once a week. Over time, the flavor of our being together has evolved from very formal and constricted, to informal and considerably more relaxed. However, Joan continues to live a relatively narrow and isolated existence and still feels quite stuck in her life. Perhaps the biggest risk she has taken in the time we have been working together has been to give up a hated, demeaning, demanding, and consuming full-time job to become a freelancer in her field. She has managed to sustain herself in this less lucrative, but more importantly, less stressful lifestyle for a number of years—in part because she is one of the few New Yorkers fortunate enough to be living in a rent-controlled apartment. Her overhead is a fraction of current real estate market realities. Her apartment, located in the heart of the city, is a small, one-room studio in an old, increasingly run-down building. She can't afford to continue her freelance lifestyle and move to a more desirable living situation which would quadruple her overhead, but she feels perpetually deprived, trapped, and angry—the run-down, too-small apartment a potent metaphor for her experience of deprivation and self-constriction. She has been talking for a long time about wanting to improve some of the shabbiness of her personal space, but has avoided dealing with the landlord about making repairs because he is so resistant. She starts the session by telling me she finally got herself to call the landlord to tell him she wanted him to replace broken floor tiles.

Joan: "I'm so angry with him. He's so disgusting. He doesn't say 'of course I'll fix it.' He starts to give me a hard time. Why does it have to be like that?" (We have been over this ground so many times. She is always angry with service providers who aren't politely responsive. I usually respond with an empathic appreciation of the pain of dismissal or negation, sometimes followed by a genetic interpretation about how it evokes early experience in her family of origin. But today I feel conflicted. I can certainly empathize with the frustration of dealing with a New York City landlord, but I find myself feeling annoyed by her contemptuous tone. I want her to take responsibility for her "unrealistic" expectations in this situation).

Ellen: "He is not being a caring parent." (I deal with my conflict by making an interpretation dripping with criticism).

Joan: "I hate that. He's not a parent. He's a landlord and he's not doing his job. It's his job to manage his building. And now I'm angry at you." (She has heard the annoyance behind my "interpretation.")

Ellen: "He is the landlord of a rent-controlled apartment. It is unlikely that he is going to be pleased as punch to improve an apartment he is dying for you to vacate." (I won't back down).

Joan: "You're taking his side."

Ellen: "Yes, I guess I am. . . . I want you to see the hypersensitivity that you bring to this kind of interaction. . . . But look! We are having our first real fight."

She is momentarily stunned into silence, then says with a smile, "Yes, we are."

The tension has broken. We go on talking easily about her feelings of frustration, helplessness, and the trapped and childlike position she is in because she doesn't have the ultimate power to leave the neglectful, abusive parent/landlord. At some point she says, "I guess I am thin-skinned about things like this." And I point out to her that although the interaction with the landlord didn't go as she wished, in the end, after she put up with his "rudeness" and was assertively insistent, he had in fact agreed to make the requested repair. I say, "Things don't always have to be nice, but you can keep standing up for yourself." Incremental changes in her entitlement to self-assertion have been the reward for her years of work in therapy.

This interaction can be seen as an Enactment. It can also be understood through the lenses of rupture and repair, intersubjective disjunction (Atwood, Stolorour, & Trop, 1989), "now" moments (Stern, 2004), or dyadic development (Preston & Shumsky, 2000). We will compare two contemporary views of such clinical stories. On the one hand we will consider the Enactment interpretation popular in the Relational tradition that has emerged from interpersonal psychoanalysis, feminist thinking, and British object relations. We will contrast this with the clinical thinking of contemporary relational self psychology and of intersubjective systems theorists. Our intention is to clarify the differences between the theoretical presuppositions and clinical sensibilities underlying both approaches.

ENACTMENT

Enactment appears to be a psychoanalytic concept whose time has come. She is enjoying her turn at fifteen minutes of fame as the spotlight holds and illuminates her on the center stage of therapeutic action. An entire volume of *Psychoanalytic Dialogues* was devoted to this subject (vol. 13, no. 5, 2003) and contemporary Relational writings (theoretical and clinical material) frequently emphasize the centrality of enactment. For the sake of clarity, we will use Fosshage's (2003) distinction between lowercase "r" "relational psychoanalysis" which refers to the broad umbrella holding all analytic approaches that are essentially relational, and uppercase "R" "Relational psychoanalysis" which refers to the somewhat cohesive group of American psychoanalysts, mentioned above, influenced primarily by interpersonal, object relations and feminist theories (p. 412).

The emergence of enactment as a pivotal aspect of therapeutic action is in large part a result of the application of postmodern epistemology to psychoanalytic theory and practice—a perspectival, post-Cartesian reconceptualization in which the authoritarian stance of analytic interpretation has lost its privileged status. Contemporary relationalists recognize the analytic partnership as a framed relational engagement with the potential to facilitate new or expanded life for the patient. In this new paradigm, the analyst, instead of relying on superior or privileged knowledge and interpretation, understands that everything she does or doesn't do—including interpretation—weaves the fabric of analytic engagement. In its broadest sense the term enactment speaks to this understanding that therapy is perhaps more about the implicitly laden moment-to-moment living together of the analytic dyad than it is about one person interpreting, explaining, or shedding light on another person's deep motivations.

In the ongoing conversation about the ubiquity and importance of psychoanalytic enactment, distinctions have been made about the appropriate use of the label. Many Relationalists use the term enactment only when referring to dramatic engagements "constituted by their unique qualities of mutually unconscious influence between patient and analyst" (Aron, 2003, p. 627). Donnel Stern (2003) for example, reserves the term "enactment" for naming those interactions in which there is what he calls a "dynamic necessity," which is heralded by the analyst's loss of his ability to think (p. 12). Aron suggests using the word "interaction" to refer to the ordinary and ever-present dimension of relational engagement and to speak of "enactment" only when referring to "unique" events codetermined by bidirectional unconscious influence. Bass prefers to distinguish between lowercase "e" enactments which refer to ordinary interacting and capital "E" Enactments which refer to co-created dramatic engagements (Aron, 2003, p. 626). We will embrace a broad and inclusive definition of enactment, using Bass's convention, speaking of lowercase "e" enactments to refer to the continual interactive dimension of experience and capital "E" Enactments to denote dramatic entanglements fueled by unconscious influences.

We have been interested in the question of why it is that Enactment is so central to discussions of therapeutic action for Relationalists and so absent from much clinical literature rooted in the relational theories of self psychology or intersubjective systems theory. Surely all psychotherapists experience heightened or "dramatic engagements" with at least some patients. Do contemporary self psychologists and intersubjectivists call them by a different name? Do we engage with our patients in ways that minimize rather than highlight charged interactions? Is there a different perspective and emphasis shaping what we look for and therefore what we see in ourselves, our clients, and our interactions? Do we not view dramatic engagements as pivotally mutative? Do we build our clinical narratives in some other way?

Capital "E" Enactments have long been the cornerstone of therapeutic change for analysts from the Sullivanian interpersonal tradition. An interpersonalist understanding of the psychoanalytic endeavor is expressed by Hirsch (1998) as follows: "Analysis is not only a 'talking about' experience but a 'living out' experience, with the analyst as unwitting partner in the mutual reenactment of core transference themes. The mutative factor in analysis is the evolution of a new relationship that leads to different internalized configurations" (p. 95). Most contemporary relationalists would agree with the latter part of this description—that the mutative power of psychoanalysis resides in the evolution of a new relationship. Indeed, we can see the movement toward the acceptance of the curative role of relationship by considering the following two statements: Kohut's defensive confession in 1984, "I have openly admitted that—*horrible dictu*—we are indeed providing 'corrective emotional experiences' for our patients. . . . So be it!" (Kohut, 1984, p. 153) and Black's (2003) matter-of-fact statement almost two decades later, "We have become increasingly aware that psychoanalysis is indeed a corrective emotional experience" (p. 635).

However, the first part of Hirsch's description—that analysis is a "living out experience, with the analyst as unwitting partner in the mutual reenactment of core transference themes"—seems to us to be incomplete and controversial. This statement fails to do justice to the bidirectional nature of psychoanalytic dyadic influence. It overweights the impact of the patient's unconscious on the "unwitting" analyst, without also recognizing the codetermining influence of the analyst's unconscious on the "unwitting" patient and on the interactive field. In a not so subtle way, it attributes unconscious agency solely to the patient and suggests an immaculate analyst devoid of an unconscious agenda.

In 1992, a panel of the American Psychoanalytic Association described countertransference enactment as "the patient's unconscious efforts to persuade or force the analyst into a reciprocal action: a two-party playing out of the patient's most fundamental internalized configurations" (Hirsch, 1998, p. 78). Here, in addition to a unidirectional conceptualization, the idea of the patient's coercive intentionality is introduced. The patient, like the aggressive infant of the Kleinians, must draw the analyst into the patient's own drama. We think of coercion as a relational phenomenon. One feels "forced" if one's need is to resist in the service of self-protection or theoretical correctness. An analyst who feels comfortable in the role of facilitating needed developmental experience may not feel coerced by the patient's healing intentions.

As the idea of analysis as a "corrective emotional experience" has gained gradual acceptance, so too have Relational understandings about the nature and place of Enactment in the therapeutic process evolved in the past decade. For example, in 1993, Mitchell conceptualized Enactment as a pull for the sacrifice of someone's subjectivity. He described a clinical situation in which the patient creates an either/or demand—join me and give yourself up/don't give yourself up and abandon me. Here we see the "unwitting" analyst besieged by the patient's manipulative entreaties. The analyst, in Mitchell's view, refusing the pathological option of sacrificial inauthenticity, has to search for another alternative—a creative "outburst"—a movement "out of the confines of options that all seem unacceptable" (p. 184). In some clinical situations this struggle to make a place for the analyst's authentic participation may well succeed in generating vital new relational experience. But, with other patients needing validation and mirroring it might just as easily create a power struggle leading to an unyielding impasse or a treatment destroying negative therapeutic spiral. In the latter situation, Mitchell's refusal to join the patient could plausibly be conceived of as a unidirectional morality play in which the patient is seen as holding the pathology, while the analyst defends and champions healthy authenticity. This conceptualization neither considers the patient's developmental needs and readiness, nor holds the analyst accountable for his difficulty with participating in an archaic or merged relationship. It presupposes that the patient is bringing a "dread of a new beginning" and "a hope to repeat" some dysfunctional or infantile (and therefore inappropriate or pathological) unconscious agenda that the analyst must resist (Mitchell, 1993). It does not allow for the possibility that the patient's unconscious agenda is the need for a healing relational experience—the hope for a new beginning (Ornstein, 1974).

Five years later, Mitchell (1998) addressed these limitations. He asked, "How do you decide when a potentially constructive countertransference experience has become self-absorption or self-indulgence? It seems to us that the patient's developmental readiness is crucial" (p. 191). By this time he had acknowledged the developmental dimension in therapeutic action and had recognized that countertransference experience is neither necessarily privileged, nor always intended by the patient, nor always therapeutically useful. By 2000 he went still further. He devised a four-part schema for "housing and comparing different perspectives on and accounts of 'relationality'" and noted that three of these four modes (implicit relational knowing, "affective permeability," and "self-other configurations") might be understood as Kohutian selfobject experiences in which others are not "organized and experienced as others in their own right" (Mitchell, 2000, pp. 59–63). Here, he has embraced the existence, meaningfulness, and clinical validity of oftentimes working with selfobject or environmental (Davies, 2002) transferences. In these situations, the healing dimension of psychoanalytic interaction does not depend on the patient's recognition of the analyst's subjectivity, but on the analyst's resonance with, or recognition of the patient's implicit developmental longings.

Relationalists, relying on Mitchell's (1993) early critique of the "developmental tilt" have tended to emphasize the collaborative nature of the analytic process. As a generalization, there has been more focus on issues of the patient's aggression and the analyst's role in identifying and challenging repetitive patterns. Relationalists often give more weight to the patient's influence on the analyst's process. The rules of the game allow for, indeed encourage, the patient's regression into disorganization and primary process. The patient's responsibility is to struggle to make a place safe enough to express her most primitive self. The analyst's professional maturity is in his capacity to "bridge primary and secondary process, self and other, past and present, reality and fantasy" (Mitchell, 2000, p. 52). The patient is allowed to be messy and this messiness has tremendous influencing power over the field. The patient is encouraged to include the irrational and unprocessed, while the analyst is reined in by the responsibility to be thoughtful.

In fact, for many contemporary Relationalists a major defining feature of Enactment is the analyst's experience of the splitting apart of analytic observation and emotional participation. The analyst is either caught up in the "swirl" of the interaction, unable to think or observe, or can think only by becoming detached and cerebrally analytic, unable to feel (Aron, 2003, p. 628), (Stern, 2003, p. 10). This drama/Enactment is variously described as "rigid," "unyielding," "irresistible," and "blinding." The analyst is "in the grip" of the transference/countertransference field and his successful emergence will give birth to new relational experience. This conceptualization of enactment underscores the analyst's experienced inability to perform the analytic functions of both emotionally participating in the interactional dance and observing it. Here, at least theoretically, the patient's unconscious intentionality is not necessarily assumed. We don't know what is contributing to the disruption of the analyst's optimal performance. Contemporary relational understandings assume the inseparability of the patient's and analyst's co-influence so that the extent to which the analyst's derailment is attributable to the patient's unconscious agenda, or is fueled by the analyst's own idiosyncratic experience of the moment derived from her unique world of meanings, remains indeterminate.

When the analyst loses the ability to think, it is of course necessary to move through this. One thing that often distinguishes a Relational from a self psychological approach to an impasse is the answer to the question, Is the content of the analyst's countertransference always a carrier of the patient's vital unconscious communication in the treatment? Is it always providing essential information about the patient? From an intersubjective systems perspective it is understood that in a system of mutual influence, the analyst's response is of course influenced by the patient's conscious and unconscious participation, as the patient's experience is influenced by the analyst's conscious and unconscious participation. Influence always lands in a fertile and influencing field of otherness. It is an intersubjective process. From this perspective, the loosening of a countertransference-generated impasse moves a stuck treatment forward, not necessarily because the patient is owning projected material, but because a newly emergent interpersonal experience has been co-generated.

In the current vibrant cross-fertilization of relational perspectives different lineages borrow, modify, and relanguage each other's constructs and ideas. Aron (2004) recently commented that today the study of comparative psychoanalysis might more fruitfully investigate differences within lineages (e.g., across a spectrum from classical self psychology to contemporary relational self psychology) than the differences between schools, so much has been bridged under the relational umbrella. To a considerable extent we agree. Yet, when a case is presented, we can usually hear and recognize the theoretical influences guiding the treatment process, certainly in the language, but also in the flavor of analytic participation. In Relational clinical narratives we recognize a ghostly remnant of an adherence to a belief in the unidirectional influence of the patient's intentionality on the "unwitting" analyst and an overweighting of the healing power of the analyst's authenticity. Likewise, narratives influenced by the theories of self psychology and intersubjective systems theory pay particular (some critics say too much) attention to the developmental dimension of the transference and to the analyst's responsibility to be sensitive to this. Like the very particular flavorings and aromas that distinguish different ethnic cuisines, these nuanced valorizations lend a distinctive theoretical/idiomatic sensibility to the relational clinical narratives.

Someone (our reference is lost) once used a gardening metaphor to capture the difference between the therapeutic action of relational self psychologists and other Relationalists. The former emphasize the watering aspect of the growth process and the latter the weeding aspect. Kohut-influenced clinical work tends to focus on the patient's narcissistic vulnerability. In striving to create the balance of challenge and safety necessary for change, there is an explicit value placed on the analyst's responsibility in co-creating a safe enough relationship for defenses to be brought to awareness. Whereas Relationalists have aggression radar, relational self psychologists are especially vigilant for indications of the patient's pathological accommodation and sensitivity to shame. They emphasize the powerful impact of the analyst's participation, conscious and unconscious, on the vulnerable patient. The patient's developmental longings, embedded in traumatic early experience, render her exquisitely delicate and defended. The analyst, protected by a professional role that calls for mature functioning, has a responsibility to be sensitive to this naked fragility and to guide a developmental process that will lead to more nuance, complexity, and resilience. Like a parent with a young child, the analyst has tremendous power in this situation, which must be recognized and responsibly handled.

Therapies conducted in such a developmental framework underscore the healing potential of small "e" enactments—ordinary, ongoing, emotionally sensitive therapeutic responsiveness that incrementally weaves a fabric of trust, capable over time of sustaining more robust interactions. Intersubjective systems theory, a developmentally oriented approach, is described in the following paragraph.

From a clinical point of view, intersubjectivity is not so much a theory as it is a sensibility. It is an attitude of continuing sensitivity to the inescapable interplay of observer and observed. It assumes that instead of entering and immersing ourselves in the experience of another, we join the other in the intersubjective space. Each participant in the psychoanalytic field brings an organized and organizing emotional history to the process. This means that although the analysis is always for the patient, the emotional history and psychological organization of patient and analyst are equally important to the understanding of any clinical exchange. What we inquire about or interpret or leave alone depends upon who we are (Orange, et al., 1997, p. 9). From this theoretical perspective, accounting for what the analyst brings to the process is essential to an understanding of any clinical exchange, including those called Enactments.

In the case of Joan and Ellen, this clinical narrative might be understood through the organizing lens of the idea of a rupture and repair of a developmentally needed bond. This particular analytic moment was indeed a rupture, but not just any rupture. What gives it dramatic Enactment-like qualities is that this breach was "our first real fight"—that is, the first time the analyst held her ground and didn't make a repair by shifting into an empathic appreciation of the meaning of the rupture for the patient.

To understand the dynamics of this clinical Enactment, it is first necessary to contextualize it, because it is embedded in the years of trust building that led to this moment. There were myriad strands—some developmental and some situational—that were unconsciously influencing the therapist's participation in this interaction. Some of these include the years of attuned responsiveness that resulted in Joan and Ellen feeling more relaxed with each other; the repeated little unintentional ruptures, repaired through empathic understanding that built safety and trust; Ellen's implicit relational sense of the consolidation of the dyadic bond and Joan's growing capacity to tolerate conflict; the fact that it was the last session of a long and trying day; Ellen's lived experience of having been a "landlord" and her identification with that role; the particularly toxic meaning contempt has for Ellen as a result of her early formative experiences. This therapeutic dyad has been evolving and developing for some time toward the moment of "our first fight" and the space it opens up for continuing expanded self-expression and more robust relating for both therapist and patient.

In a narrative sensitive to developmental considerations, we could say that in this moment of intersubjective disjunction (conflict), Ellen reaches for a metacommunication, an "us" statement—"it's our first fight"—in order to restore selfobject connectedness. Aron (2000) might describe this as reaching for the analytic third. By joining Joan to celebrate "our" process, Ellen repairs the rupture and the interaction becomes relaxed and collaborative. The implicit message is that self assertion and conflict negotiation are pride-worthy achievements. This is echoed when Ellen affirms Joan for having gotten her way with the "rude" landlord.

From a Relational perspective, one can organize this same clinical exchange very differently. In this narrative, the Enactment is a "living out" of Joan's core transference theme with the therapist as unwitting partner. Joan inhabits a world in which her self-assertiveness and aggression have been dissociated. Her "internal part-objects" include a "nice" dependent one for whom feistiness is taboo, and a contemptible, self-serving, powerful one organized around aggression. Ellen has been influenced by the field (in collusion with her theory) to stay in the role of "nice" therapist, who defers to Joan when there is a misunderstanding, lest she become the selfish, disregarding other. She has been the politely responsive service provider. Seen through this lens, this clinical moment captures a healing "outburst" in which the therapist refuses to limit herself to the polarized sadomasochistic role options that are defining the field. Instead she becomes the self-assertive other who has a point of view to be heard, but who is also interested in and concerned about Joan's feelings. In so doing she models a new relational option for Joan and cogenerates new relational experience. This is a very cogent story that offers another way of organizing the same clinical material.

What might intersubjective systems theorists or relational self psychologists find valuable in Relational conceptions of enactment? One possibility is Lew Aron's idea of role flexibility. Maybe impasses occur when analyst and patient become locked into role rigidity, like actors who cannot exit their roles between performances, or like teachers, police officers, or analysts who continue in these roles at home with their families. Their range of possibilities become fixed and paralysis results. Aron (2000, 2003) suggests that one partner—and knowing his concept of asymmetry, we can guess which one this will usually be—must have the capacity to keep two roles (subject and object) going at once, and thus create a triangular space in which role reversals can be enacted and the patient can develop a similar self-reflexivity or role flexibility. This account of Enactment places it inside larger Relational themes of thirdness, recognition, multiple selves, and dialectics. Enactment, thus, is a theoretical idea that gains its meaning, Wittgenstein-style, from its functions within a larger theoretical discourse or language game. It is not, therefore susceptible to any easy translation.

The closest translation in the discourse of relational self psychology would be rupture-and-repair processes, but this formulation takes its sense from the whole Weltanschauung of self psychology with its selfobject transferences, the centrality of empathic ways of knowing, and so on. In developmental and intersubjective systems theories, it might be possible to speak of malattunements seeking reattunement through mutually regulatory processes, or of intersubjective conjunctions and disjunctions that lead to impasses that must be resolved by the analyst's reflective self-awareness. But these again are different language games involving larger theoretical systems and carrying few of the presuppositions of contemporary Relational psychoanalysis. So translation is really difficult, and the search for understanding by those who do not speak the language can seem clumsy or pointless to those who do.

In addition, intersubjective systems theorists and relational self psychologists do not subscribe to the Kleinian doctrines of part-objects nor to the view of aggression as psychological bedrock. So we tend to share with self psychologists the priority placed on developmental processes, seeing them, again in Aron's terms, as always mutual but also asymmetrical. Rather than highlighting the mutative value of a particular impasse or dramatic moment (the capital "E" Enactment), we emphasize the healing power of sustained, ongoing, attuned mutual regulation (little "e" enactments) that over time builds a trustworthy relational vessel capable of weathering the inevitable storms at sea.

REFERENCES

Aron, L. (2000). Self reflexivity and the therapeutic action of psychoanalysis. *Psychoanalytic Psychology, 17,* 667–689.

Aron, L. (2003). The paradoxical place of enactment in psychoanalysis: Introduction. *Psychoanalytic Dialogues, 13*(5), 623–631.

Aron, L. (2004). Dialogue with Jim Fosshage, APSP, New York.

Atwood, G. E., Stolorow, R. D., & Trop, J. L. (1989). Impasses in psychoanalytic therapy: A royal road. *Contemporary Psychoanalysis, 25,* 554–574.

Black, M. (2003). Enactment: analytic musings on energy, language, and personal growth. *Psychoanalytic Dialogues, 13*(5), 633–655.

Davies, J. (2004). Whose bad objects are we anyway: Repetition and our elusive love affair with evil. *Psychoanalytic Dialogues, 14*(6), 711–732.

Fosshage, J. L. (2003). Contextualizing self psychology and relational psychoanalysis: Bidirectional influence and proposed syntheses. *Contemporary Psychoanalysis, 39*(3), 411–448.

Hirsch, I. (1998). The concept of enactment and theoretical convergence. *Psychoanalytic Quarterly, 67,* 78–101.

Mitchell, S. (1993). *Hope and dread in psychoanalysis.* New York: Basic Books.

Mitchell, S. (1996). When interpretations fail: A new look at the therapeutic action of psychoanalysis. In L. E. Lifson (Ed.), *Understanding therapeutic action: Psychodynamic concepts of cure* (pp. 165–186). Hillsdale, NJ: Analytic Press.

Mitchell, S. (1998). The emergence of features of the analyst's life. *Psychoanalytic Dialogues, 8*(2), 187–194.

Mitchell, S. (2000). *Relationality: From attachment to intersubjectivity.* Hillsdale, NJ: Analytic Press.

Orange, D., Atwood, G., et al. (1997). *Working intersubjectively: Contextualism in the psychoanalytic practice.* Hillsdale, NJ: Analytic Press.

Ornstein, A. (1974). The dread to repeat and the new beginning: A contribution to the psychoanalysis of the narcissistic personality disorders. *Ann Psa, 2,* 231–248.

Preston, L., & Shumsky, E. (2000). The development of the dyad: A bidirectional revisioning of some self psychological constructs. In A. Goldberg (Ed.), *Progress in self psychology, vol. 16* (pp. 67–84). Hillsdale, NJ: Analytic Press.

Stern, D. (2003). Theories of therapeutic action in self psychology and relational theory. Presented for APSP in New York, April.

Stern, D. N. (2004). *The present moment in psychotherapy and everyday life.* New York: W. W. Norton.

11

Kafka's Window and Kohut's Mirror: A Dialogic Journey to the Center of Traumatic Worlds

Maxwell S. Sucharov, PhD

STANDING ON THE SHOULDERS OF GIANTS

This chapter considers the overlapping worlds of Heinz Kohut and Franz Kafka, who were born twenty years apart as German-speaking Jews in two of the major cities of the widespread Austro-Hungarian Empire, which collapsed in the trenches of the Great War shortly after Kohut's birth. They became giants in their respective fields, joined in their search to evoke the deepest layers of man's suffering. They provide me with two pairs of shoulders on which to stand, a position from which I will engage their work through the lens of a dialogic process sensibility, an engagement that will take us into the ineffable world of human trauma.

What will emerge is a relational dialogic view of trauma and its impact on the psychoanalytic encounter. My central thesis is that an important dimension to the traumatic experience is the freezing of the victim in nondialogic space, thereby shattering his/her capacity to generate meaning. Where trauma has been prolonged, the survivor may be left with large chunks of endured experience with no meaning, creating disquieting gaps and discontinuities in the experience of one's life history. An important therapeutic vehicle is the therapist's provision of a window function, whereby the therapist uses his presence to supply a framework of orientation that can initiate a meaning-generating dialogic process. The yearning for a window—the authentic presence of a dialogic other—will be shown to constitute an important relational striving that includes but is not restricted to a more dialogic view of mirror yearnings.

DIALOGUE, MEANING, AND TRAUMA

We are born into a world of dialogue.

Beginning with the protoconversation between mother and infant and continuing throughout our lifetime, dialogue is the relational vehicle that transforms the buzz and confusion of our existence into digestible packages of personal meaning. Furthermore, the dialogic creation of meaning is not an impersonal outcome of our human encounters but constitutes the motivational glue that forms and sustains our relationships. How and if we make sense of our world bears the indelible stamp of our unique dialogic history.

If we have been blessed with a series of dialogic partners who have fully met us with empathy, compassion, and wisdom, our personal worlds can become exciting dialogic playgrounds where the horizons of possibility seem endless. Life becomes infused with a rich tapestry of fluid and multilayered meanings. The above reflects an idyllic extreme and it is more likely that most of us harbor some wounds that reflect those moments when dialogic partners have been either absent, preoccupied, and/or closed off to our distress. These moments of dialogic failure may coalesce into those shadows of self-doubt, fear, and mistrust that restrict our horizons. Life becomes informed by personal meanings of guarded optimism, meanings that confine us within the secure parameters of a narrow safety zone.

And then there are those of us who have been most unlucky. Our history of dialogic failures was not restricted to isolated moments but constituted the defining feature of a pervasive and traumatizing emotional landscape that persisted for years. Furthermore the quality of dialogic breakdown may have assumed a particularly malignant dimension whereby a malevolent intentionality to abort dialogue was accompanied by an exploitive takeover of our mind and body by the very persons we counted on for protection and support. We have become "prisoners of the soul" (Fogel, 1993) where the very possibility of making sense of our world has been shattered. Life becomes a zombie-like domain of no meaning, a vacuum of haunting absence.

I am therefore suggesting that the dialogic creation of meaning is not a given but is contingent on the presence of a particular relational context, one where there is an attitude of genuine openness and acceptance, hopefully mutual, but at least held by the more powerful member (parent/therapist) of the dyad. I will use the term dialogic other to denote a dyadic member holding such an attitude. It follows that, from the perspective of child/client, the absence of a dialogic other would preclude or seriously disrupt those relational processes necessary for the generation of meaning.

In foregrounding the traumatizing quality of extreme dialogic failure, I am imputing important links between trauma, dialogue, and the creation of meaning. In that context, a major problem I have found in working with survivors of severe trauma is the enormous obstacle both my clients and I have encountered in our struggle to make sense of the horrors of their nightmare world. Trauma eludes and resists meaning.

Viewed through the lens of a dialogic systems sensibility, the traumatic world's slipping away from the categories of meaning can be seen as a severe disruption of those relational processes by which meaning is formed. From the perspective of the traumatized individual, one's capacity to generate meaning has been shattered and one has become a prisoner of the soul, one who is frozen in nondialogic space. From the perspective of the perpetrator the dialogic creation of meaning is actively aborted and replaced with an imposed rigid reality that is not open for discussion. The perversion of a dialogic other, the perpetrator of abuse is motivated to destroy meaning.

When a relationship of sadistic control is perpetuated for a long duration, often for years, the consequences for the survivor can be severe, leaving one with giant gaps in the continuity of life experience. Descriptive terms such as "gaping psychic holes" (Spero, 1998), "experiential black holes" (Brothers, 1995), "space of permanent insensibility," and "dark vacuum of terror" (Gampel, 1998) all speak to the indescribable horror of being trapped in a senseless void, a situation that can threaten one's psychological survival.

PRIMING THE DIALOGIC PUMP: ANALYST AS WINDOW

With respect to the challenge of reinstating a dialogic process with a survivor of trauma, I have encountered at least two obstacles. I have needed not only to earn the trust of my clients but also to introduce him or her to the very notion of a dialogue. In other words we have had to grapple with both fear of retraumatization and the dialogic incapacity of someone who has been frozen for so much of his or her life that the very notion of collaborative dialogue is quite foreign. I have therefore been called upon to include an empathic witnessing approach with a form of relational intervention I will call "priming the dialogic pump." I do this by providing a framework of orientation, a fresh way of looking at the traumatic experience that facilitates the initiation of collaborative dialogue—the first line in a game of piggle. Because this framework often involves the provision of a window into the complexities of relationships including the psychological life of the perpetrator (i.e., the abuse reflected the problems of the victimizer), I will use the term "window relational function" as an umbrella term to depict this experiential dimension of analytic process.

A window relational function is not just a cognitive reframing but more importantly specifies a therapist who is felt to be fully emotionally present as an authentic dialogic other. The provision of a framework of orientation can be seen as a preliminary general organizing function that expands the horizons of interpretive possibilities for both client and therapist. While the provision of a framework will inevitably bear the unique stamp of the therapist's subjectivity, room is left for the client to form his or her own meaning. A window relational function therefore constitutes a particular form of intersubjective relatedness that Strenger calls "critical pluralism," whereby the therapist's "voice is strongly present, but it is a voice which fosters the presence of others instead of drowning it" (Strenger, 2002, p. 552).

The metaphor of window also fits well with a post-Cartesian view of the analytic process that questions the sharp bifurcation of internal/external as well as therapist/client. Windows can be open or closed and therefore constitute a fluid and ambiguous boundary that both separate and join inside to outside, therapist to client. This ambiguity of boundaries contributes to what I have called "quantum relational holism," whereby the contribution of each member of the dyad to the dialogic process is in principle indeterminate (Sucharov, 2002).

In my use of window as a metaphor for priming the dialogic pump, I am indebted to Kafka. My discovery of his use of window as a relational metaphor in his personal correspondence has constituted the inspiration for this paper. So Kafka has served as a window for me, priming my dialogic pump.

KAFKA'S WINDOW: FROM RECLUSE TO RELATIONALITY

In 1903 a youthful Franz Kafka was in the midst of an intense and passionate friendship with Oskar Pollak, a young man whose poise, maturity, and wide-ranging talents and interests constituted a sharp contrast to the awkward and shy demeanor of the budding writer. In a letter to Pollak on November 9, 1903, Kafka described the vitalizing impact of his friend: "For me, you were, along with much else, also something like a window through which I could see the streets. I could not do that by myself, for tall though I am I do not yet reach to the windowsill" (in Pawel, 1985, p. 92).

Upon reading the above in Ernst Pawel's biography of Kafka, I found myself surprisingly moved by the power of Kafka's evocative description as I reflected on persons in my own life who had served as a window for me. I became intrigued with the idea of a window as a metaphor for expansive and vitalizing relational experience both inside and outside the psychoanalytic encounter and how this metaphor compared and contrasted with Kohut's use of the mirror concept to capture essential self-enhancing human responsiveness.

Kafka's use of the window metaphor to depict the meaning to him of his friend also brings forth Pollak as a dialogic other. Around the time of this correspondence Pollak became the first "other" requested to be a reader of Kafka's emerging works. In a second letter to Pollak, Kafka, as only Kafka can, expressed this move from reclusivity to relationality: "[I can] do nothing without others; but I now record, with emphasis and ornate syntax: the life of a recluse is repulsive; lay your eggs honestly in front of everyone and let the sun hatch them out; it is better to bite into life than to bite one's tongue; honor the mole and his kind, but don't make them your patron saint" (Pawel, 1985, p. 92).

The use of window as metaphor for relationality is not restricted to Kafka's correspondence. A perusal of Kafka's works revealed the following short fragment entitled *The Street Window*: "Whoever leads a solitary life and yet now and then wants to attach himself somewhere . . . he will not be able to manage for long without a window looking on to the street. And if he is in the mood of not desiring anything and only goes to his window sill a tired man . . . even then the horses below will draw him down into their train of wagons and tumult, and so at last into the human harmony" (Kafka, 1971, p. 384).

Window as a metaphor for relational contact also plays a key role in *The Metamorphosis*, arguably Kafka's most haunting piece. The protagonist Gregor Samsa is transformed into a giant cockroach, a transformation that punctuates and accentuates his isolation within a family devoid of any empathic responsiveness. Within Kafka's gripping narrative, the window in Gregor's room appears a number of times as a poignant symbol for Gregor's rapidly fading hope for some human relational experience.

While Kafka's window represents the possibility of human contact, much of Kafka's work depicts its stark absence. In *The Trial* and *The Castle* the protagonists search endlessly and hopelessly for some communication with the authorities, a communication which in principle is barred from them. The absolute impossibility of any dialogue between the protagonist and the persons with power contributes to the haunting quality of the two texts that portray the foreclosure of any possibility to make sense of one's world.

I would suggest that the Kafkaesque world is a traumatic world and that a defining feature of this world is the absence of a dialogic other. This absence freezes the protagonists in nondialogic space, thereby shattering their capacity to generate meaning. They are prisoners of the soul, trapped in a world of senseless void. They yearn for the presence of a human window to reinstate a meaning-generating dialogue.

In the midst of my thinking about traumatic worlds, nondialogic spaces, and window yearnings, one of my clients reported a fortuitous dream in which all of the above played a central role. Let us turn to the case of Ann.

ANN AND THE SEALED-OFF WINDOWS

Ann is an adult survivor of repetitive and horrific sexual abuse of a predatorial and demeaning nature at the hands of her foster father (B). B was a psychopathic multiple abuser who exerted a powerful sadistic control not only over Ann's body but also over her mind. In the third year of treatment with me she reported the following dream:

> I am in a room in the house. It is B's house but it seems to be shaped like a cathedral with windows in the ceiling that look out onto trees, sky, and sun. I am not able to leave the room. I am trapped. But I achieve some relief by looking out the ceiling windows as they offer me some connection with the sky and sun. But B begins to board the windows up segment by segment until there is only a tiny opening left and I am no longer able to see out any more.

By the end of her recounting of the dream Ann is shaking with tears. The dream reflected yet one more of a series of retellings that imprinted our therapeutic space with the relentless domination and control by B that characterized her years of enslavement and isolation. What is interesting about this dream is the metaphor of windows representing hope for connection with the outside world (and presumably the hopes mobilized in the analytic process) and the systematic sealing off of this hope by Ann's tormentor.

In the following, Ann's words describe well her status as a "prisoner of the soul," ruthlessly deprived of a dialogic other by a sadist who needed absolute control over the rules by which reality was formed, a reality rigidly imposed and not open for discussion: "There was no one to turn to, no one to talk to, nowhere to go. . . . It was an impossibility to have an authentic conversation with anybody . . . he made sure I couldn't go into the world . . . he controlled everything and everybody."

The protracted duration of being frozen in nondialogic space has also left Ann with large gaps in her sense of temporal continuity, again expressed poignantly in her own words: "Yes, I still can't think . . . he systematically disabled me . . . he dismantled something inside me. . . . I'm like a piece of Swiss cheese with huge gaping holes in my being. The current can't carry through, it's interrupted constantly. . . . I have no solid center."

My therapeutic strategy for Ann combined empathic validation and witnessing with the distinct presence of my own personhood. In retrospect I might say that I used my presence as a dialogic other to provide a window function, thereby reinstating a dialogic process that generated new meanings to Ann's experience, especially in identifying the nature of B's pathological world in which total domination over Ann's mind and body constituted, for him, an emotional imperative. Our work continues, and Ann has shown considerable growth. In a recent session she stated, "The shackles of humiliation and shame are beginning to fall away. . . . I'm not this despicable person that B made me believe. . . . He put all his distortions on me."

The use of Kafka's window as a vitalizing relational metaphor for the healing process of traumatized clients like Ann invites interesting comparison to Kohut's use of the mirror as a central metaphor in his psychology of the self. As it turns out, both the work of Kafka and the clinical challenge of engaging survivors of traumatizing sadistic control were of central interest to Kohut.

KOHUT AND KAFKA: PARTNERS IN THE EXPLORATION OF TRAUMATIC WORLDS

Kafka's literary genius in evoking the torments of relational deprivation had an important influence on Kohut. In the last decade of his life Kohut drew on the literary masters of the century to further refine his ideas on the nature of human suffering. Kafka was his favorite, being quoted more often than any other writer in the 1970s (Strozier, 2001). Kohut felt that Kafka captured in his art the essence of man's most horrific psychic pain. In his last public address in Berkeley, Kohut paid homage to his literary hero: "the worst suffering I've seen in adult patients is in those . . . difficult to uncover, absences of the mother—because her personality is absent . . . It is the hidden psychosis of the mother . . . that Kafka described so well in *The Castle*—the attempt to come close and yet there is absolutely no response" (Kohut, 1991, p. 532). Although Kohut used the term "disintegration anxiety" to denote the above "worst suffering," he was aware that its precise nature eluded any simplistic verbal account: "Disintegration anxiety is the deepest anxiety man can experience . . . the attempt to describe [it] is the attempt to describe the indescribable . . . it is not an exact verbal definition that is called for, but rather an attempt to evoke a taste of the experience in question" (Kohut, 1984, p. 16).

The attempt to transcend the limits of words to capture the depths of human torment is one shared by Kafka. In a letter to Milena Jesenka, Kafka's most passionate but unrequited attachment, he states, "I am constantly trying to communicate something incommunicable, to explain something inexplicable, to tell about something I only feel in my bones and which can only be experienced in those bones. Basically it is nothing other than this fear we have so often talked about" (in Pawel, 1985, p. 96).

Kafka and Kohut are therefore bound up in a common cause, the search for a means to describe the indescribable: the core of man's suffering. Kafka's effort consists in his remarkable prose. Kohut's search took the form of his clinical work, a task deeply informed by both his empathic powers and his lively conceptual mind. In *How Does Analysis Cure,* Kohut's attempt to "evoke a taste of this experience" includes an account of a dream from *The Two Analyses of Mr. Z,* the one where Mr. Z sees his mother from the back. We will now revisit the *The Two Analyses of Mr. Z* as a central example of Kohut's concerns with the core of human suffering. Viewing the work through the lens of a dialogic process sensibility will allow new meanings to emerge that will further our understanding of traumatic worlds.

THE TWO ANALYSES OF MR. Z: A DIALOGIC VIEW

Among Kohut's writings, *The Two Analyses of Mr. Z* is arguably his most enigmatic text. Purported to be a clinical case history to demonstrate the effectiveness of a psychoanalysis informed by a psychology of the self compared to classical theory, his biographer Charles Strozier has presented a powerful argument for the conjecture that Mr. Z is not a real analysand but is a disguised autobiographical proxy. The accepting of such a conclusion could, from one perspective, relegate the text to the status of a hoax and disqualify it from any relevance in illustrating and extending the theory of self psychology (Strozier does not take this position).

I believe that such disqualification would not only be a sad mistake, but would also reflect the thinking of a Cartesian mind that would judge the truth value of a case report with respect to its accurate representation or correspondence to "real" historical events. Such a view would exclude the invaluable dialogic nature of Kohut's text. In this context, I am suggesting that *The Two Analyses of Mr. Z* is much more than a case report and much more than a disguised autobiography. It is also a gripping aesthetic narrative, the protagonist of which takes on a life that transcends the original intentions of the author.

In assigning an artistic aesthetic dimension to Kohut's paper I am trying to bring forward a more fluid dialogic view of the text where ambiguity, playfulness, and undecideability reign. I am, in this perspective, drawing upon two conceptions of literary prose. The first is Miller's depiction of an artistic text as a shared potential space between author and reader (Miller, 1992). Within this view, in accordance with Winnicott's rule of play, the question whether Mr. Z is a real patient or a disguised autobiographical construction should not be asked. Answering it would collapse the dialogic play space between reader and author. Mr. Z lives in potential space.

The second conception is Bakhtin's dialogic theory of the novel, where a superficial structure of linear narrative sits alongside a more fluid structure whereby the reader encounters a number of voices, none of which are authoritative, a "dialogized heteroglossia that reaches no finality" (Harrison, 2005). In the language of contemporary relationality the text interweaves the "scripted" with the "improvisational" (Ringstrom, 2001).

In this duplex structure model, the scripted dimension constitutes the predetermined linear unfolding of the author's intentional design—the demonstration of the superior effectiveness of an analysis informed by Kohut's then new psychology of the self compared to one informed by classical theory. By contrast the improvisational dimension emerges in nonlinear fashion from the dialogic tensions of multiple voices, forming the basis for ongoing debate, both within the text and between author and reader. It is this latter dimension that forms the organic and creative substratum of the text by which its meaning and clinical/conceptual utility can evolve in the context of new conceptual and clinical developments in the psychoanalytic world.

This expanded dialogic view of Kohut's text is grounded in the assumption that any theory of complex human experience, however elegant, will contain internal contradictions, ambiguities, and tension points. These do not invalidate the theory but contribute to its evolution and/or creative transformation. Kohut himself acknowledged the importance of retaining a certain ambiguity in concepts, reflecting "vagueness at the growing points." For Kohut, sets of concepts' optimal creative potential lay not in their enduring aspect but rather in their "pointing into the future, their ability to be, by their very shortcomings, a spur to further thought" (1991, p. 469). In that context, the subtext of *The Two Analyses of Mr. Z* contains a number of ambiguities, or in Bakhtinian terms, multiple voices in dialogic tension that can serve as a base, a shared potential space for further thought through the ongoing creative dialogue between Kohut and his readers, a dialogue that takes his work in directions he could not have known.

In this rich paper one can find a multiplicity of interweaving dialogic tensions and it is beyond the scope of this paper to develop all of these. I will be confining myself primarily to the first half of the second analysis where the reader is introduced to Kohut's new understanding of Mr. Z's narcissistic phenomena and the impact of this understanding on the ensuing analytic process. This portion of the text constitutes a pivotal shift in the narrative, a heightened dramatic moment where Kohut's fresh perspective allowed for new insights to emerge (concerning the mother's pathology) that paved the way to the inevitable successful resolution of the drama.

Heightened dramatic moments can also be seen as highly unstable junctures in the linear narrative, a dynamic flash point where the dialogic agitations of the improvisational subtext impinge on the smooth unfolding of the scripted narrative. In that context, the principal dialogic tension I will focus on is that between the conceptual voice of static intrapsychic structure and the improvisational relational voice of fluid dialogic emergence, where self-definition is continuously formed and re-formed in shifting relational contexts. The former voice is exemplified in the author's account of the appearance of a mirror transference of the merger type early in the second analysis "in accordance with the spontaneously unrolling sequences of transferences that is *determined by endospsychic factors*—i.e., by the structure of the patient's personality and psychopathology" (p. 414). These words, describing a decontextualized isolated transference, evoke a linear determinism of the very classical paradigm Kohut was attempting to transcend.

The above voice of static intrapsychic structure contradicts the improvisational relational voice as reflected in the stated shift in attitude in the second analysis: "I was now able to set aside any goal directed therapeutic ambitions." This statement heralds a letting go of the secure waters of programmed outcomes in favor of the playful uncertainties of dialogic emergence where the "I confronted the patient many times" in the first analysis shifts to "we came to understand" in the second analysis.

This contradiction between the static intrapsychic and the fluid relational voices forms the framing dialogic tension for a number of ambiguities with respect to the meaning of selfobject transferences. In the second analysis we are told that Mr. Z's mirror selfobject transference of the merger type is understood by Kohut as a "replica of an early childhood reality" in which his client's self is struggling to "disentangle itself from the noxious selfobject." This understanding would seem to suggest that pathological past relational experiences inform the current mirror selfobject transference experience—in traditional terms, leading to a "distortion" of the analyst. Yet Kohut later states that with Mr. Z as with other similar cases there is a minimum of transference distortion and that this is a sign of progress: "In order to be able to proceed with the task of perceiving the serious pathology of the selfobject of childhood, the patient has to be certain that the *current selfobject*, the analyst, is not again exposing him to the pathological milieu of early life" (Kohut, 1991, p. 418–9, italics my own).

In the above we are led to understand current selfobject transference as a referent for a mode of experience in which he (the analyst) is felt to be quite different from the traumatizing reality of childhood. Selfobject is also used to denote both a person (the noxious mother or the analyst) and a mode of transference (archaic mirror).

There would therefore seem to be a dialogic tension between selfobject transference as a replay of the traumatic past and selfobject transference as a new and presumably healthier developmental experience than the toxic reality of childhood. There is also a tension between selfobject as a form of transference and selfobject as a person.

It should be kept in mind that it is Kohut himself who is speaking in more than one voice, and that the multiplicity of apparently contradictory voices may serve as clues that the selfobject concept, however powerfully it served as a vehicle to lift the problem of narcissism out of the shackles of classical theory (and this is well articulated in the scripted linear structure of the narrative) is now, in the murkier waters of the dialogic subtext, imposing its own shackles on the achievement of a complex understanding of the relational contextual shifts that is reported to be happening in the second analysis.

It is here that one can imagine that the text has slipped away from the original scripted design of the author and that the dialogic tension constitutes a debate within the text concerning the problem of relating past to present, and of integrating considerations of stable intrapsychic structure with its fluid and continuous reorganization within shifting relational contexts. In hindsight, the contemporary reader can see that the selfobject concept is caught with one leg in the classical world of the intrapsychic and one leg in the emerging relational world. If we playfully anthropomorphize the selfobject concept we might hear it saying: "Ouch! You are overstretching me. I cannot by myself encompass all that is going on in this story. I need some help!" The help that was needed was a contextual language of dialogic systems, one that was only in its infancy at the time of the paper's creation.[1]

That which was going on in the story, awaiting a new conceptual language, was a momentous shift in the quality of the analytic conversation whereby Mr. Z, "*feeling supported by the analyst* [begins] to question the formerly unquestionable" (p. 418, italics my own). What they begin to question is the psychological health of the mother, who is now seen as a highly controlling and invasive individual; her "emotional gifts were bestowed on him under the unalterable . . . condition that he submit to total domination by her." This pivotal shift in the narrative is accompanied by an acceleration of dramatic momentum that pulls reader and author/analyst into the vortex of Mr. Z's traumatic world. I found this portion of the narrative to be especially gripping. I was moved by both the pathos of Mr. Z's childhood helplessness in the face of his ruthlessly controlling and invasive mother and by his touching relationship with Kohut, one in which they worked together in mutual respect as dialogic partners to unravel the nature of Mr. Z's traumatizing relationship with his mother, an unraveling that allowed Mr. Z to make sense of his overwhelming childhood predicament.

Viewed through the lens of a dialogic systems sensibility, Kohut's gripping narrative captures a central dimension of traumatic relational experience from Mr. Z's childhood history of being hopelessly trapped within the domineering relationship with his mother. Within this traumatizing dynamic system, Mr. Z was frozen in nondialogic space where meaning was destroyed and replaced with a unilaterally imposed reality not open for conversation. However, beneath his empty despair, he harbored a lifelong yearning for a dialogic other, a yearning he realized in the second analysis. By being fully present as a dialogic other, Kohut was able to prime the dialogic pump, thereby initiating a dialogic process that provided a window into the heretofore hidden pathology of the mother. It is noteworthy to notice the similarity between the mother's ruthless imposition of reality on her overwhelmed and helpless son and the psychopathic predator in the case of Ann, in his sadistic and relentless control and enslavement of his terrified victim.

WINDOWS, MIRRORS, AND THE ANALYST'S PRESENCE

A comparison between window and mirror as metaphors for vitalizing relational functions is worthy of a full paper (and more), and I will therefore restrict myself to a preliminary conjecture. In that context, I find it interesting that in Kohut's showcase clinical paper, which demonstrates the effectiveness of his new theory, the merger mirror transference of Mr. Z is understood by Kohut (in the second analysis) not as a reinstatement of developmental mirroring needs but as a replica of the past, the child trying to disentangle himself from the "noxious selfobject," that is, the mother's web of enslavement. It would seem that a feature of Mr. Z's mirror transference consists of blotting out the invasive subjectivity of the mother/analyst, suggesting that beneath the mirror transference lies the core of traumatic worlds—a hopelessly enslaving relationship that forecloses dialogue and destroys meaning. One might say that Mr. Z's mirror transference constituted a special form of window, a Lewis Caroll looking glass, through which the analytic dyad stepped to discover the psychotic world of the mother.

By contrast I have suggested that a window relational function involves the vitalizing experience of a therapist who is felt to be fully present as an authentic dialogic other. The therapist's provision of a framework of orientation serves as a dialogic pump that kick-starts a meaning-generating dialogic process. Windows may also reflect and window function can include a mirror aspect, but one with an altered meaning in the sense that the mirror experience is in the context of a therapist providing affirming, reflecting, validating responsiveness but not at the cost of relinquishing his own voice. At every moment of the exchange the unique humanity of the therapist is palpably present in an attitude of full recognition of the patient as "oriented to the good" (see Jacobs, 2006). Including the mirror transference within the more encompassing window transference alters its meaning in a small but important way that allows this important transference experience to live more comfortably inside current relational and dialogic thinking.

A FINAL WORD ON KOHUT'S PRESENCE AND KAFKA'S EGGS

I am suggesting that Kohut's full presence as a dialogic other was a crucial ingredient in the second analysis of Mr. Z. Given the ambiguous nature of Mr. Z's identity, *The Two Analyses of Mr. Z* stands as Kohut's most self-disclosing work, where presence can be seen to have a double meaning. It specifies both the presence of the analyst to Mr. Z in the second analysis and the presence of the author to the reader in his writing of a paper that bears such a personal stamp. Drawing again from Kafka's words, Kohut "lay [his] eggs honestly in front of everyone and let the sun hatch them out."

And our world is all the richer.

REFERENCES

Fogel, A. (1993). *Developing through relationships: Origins of communication, self, and culture.* Chicago, IL: University of Chicago Press.

Gampel, Y. (1998). Reflections on countertransference in psychoanalytic work with child survivors of the shoah. *J. Amer. Acad. Psa., 26,* 343–368.

Harrison, K. (2005). "And as Imagination Bodies Forth": Bakhtin and the filming of Shakespeare's Images. Presented at the Shakespeare Association of America Conference, Bermuda, 2005.

Jacobs, L. (2006). Dialogue, confirmation, and the good. In press.

Kafka, F. (1971). *The complete stories.* Ed. N. Glatzer. New York: Schocken Books.

Kohut, H. (1984). *How does analysis cure?* Ed. A. Goldberg. Chicago: University of Chicago Press.

Kohut, H. (1991a). Four basic concepts in self psychology. In *The search for the self: Selected writings of Heinz Kohut, 1978–1981*. Ed. P. Ornstein. Madison, CT: International Universities Press.

Kohut, H. (1991b). The two analyses of Mr. Z. In *The search for the self: Selected writings of Heinz Kohut, 1978–1981*. Ed. P. Ornstein. Madison, CT: International Universities Press.

Kohut, H. (1991c). On empathy. In *The search for the self: Selected writings of Heinz Kohut, 1978–1981*. Ed. P. Ornstein. Madison, CT: International Universities Press.

Laub, D., and Podell, D. (1995). Art and trauma. *Int. J. Psycho-Anal., 76,* 995–1005.

Miller, M. C. (1992). Winnicott unbound: The fiction of Philip Roth and the sharing of potential space. *Int. R. Psycho-Anal., 19,* 445–456.

Pawel, E. (1985). *The nightmare of reason: A life of Franz Kafka.* New York: Vintage Books.

Ringstrom, P. A. (2001). Cultivating the improvisational in psychoanalytic treatment. *Psychoanal. Dial., 11,* 727–754.

Spero, M. H. (1998). Book review essay: Mentalizing negative spaces in the wake of the holocaust. *Psychoanal Q., 67,* 698–713.

Stolorow, R. D. (1999). The phenomenology of trauma and the absolutisms of everyday life. *Psychoanal. Psychol., 16,* 464–468.

Stolorow, R. (2004). Autobiographical reflections on the history of an intersubjective approach in psychoanalysis. *Psychoanalytic Inquiry, 24,* 542–555.

Strenger, C. (2002). From yeshiva to critical pluralism. *Psychoanal. Inq., 22,* 534–558.

Strozier, C. (2001). *Heinz Kohut: The making of a psychoanalyst.* New York: Farrar, Straus, and Giroux.

Sucharov, M. (2002). Representation and the intrapsychic: Cartesian barriers to empathic contact. *Psychoanal. Inq., 22,* 686–707.

NOTES

1. Kohut's paper was written around the time Atwood and Stolorow were joining the self psychology community. Their theory of intersubjectivity provided the major impetus for the integration of Kohut's self psychology within a contextual systems approach. (See Stolorow, [2004] for a historical account).

12

Twinship and "Otherness": A Self Psychological, Intersubjective Approach to "Difference"

Amanda Kottler, MA

Contemporary self psychologists and relational theorists are currently saying much more than ever before about countertransference and its impact on the work of psychoanalytic psychotherapists. Innovative, creative, and courageous papers have appeared in the literature in which authors disclose aspects of themselves and their selfobject needs in an attempt to demonstrate the effects that their own dynamics have on the way in which therapies unfold. This has also been true of psychotherapists using intersubjectivity theory, who note the significance of the broader context in which each therapy takes place. Those of us who have been able to recognize, in these papers, needs similar to our own will know how they have provided us with a great deal of affirming twinship selfobject experiences that are immensely important to our work.

There is in this literature a conspicuous gap. Few of these pioneering authors have focused on the influence that their own "difference," and therefore their membership of what I shall refer to as a "disadvantaged (supposedly minority) group" against which prejudice is directed, has on their work as therapists. Acknowledging this gap is particularly vital in a country like South Africa, from which this chapter originates, but it also needs addressing globally.

The absence of literature of this kind is not surprising. To engage at this level requires authors to be relatively resolved and comfortable not only with their particular brand of "difference," per se but also with admitting that it is a site of struggle in their professional lives. Nevertheless, the fact is that the paucity deprives colleagues who can identify with this kind of marginalized status of a range of sorely needed mirroring and twinship selfobject experiences. Said differently, the scarcity deprives therapists of important reciprocal exchanges with fellow professionals (Abramowitz, 2001).

The absence is partly what motivated this chapter. While living and working in South Africa, where one is aware of marginalized groups more acutely, should perhaps encourage us to use this idea to reflect on working with issues of race, I decided to focus elsewhere—on another of my own sites of "difference," that of being a lesbian therapist. This should not detract from the fact that much of what I say does not only relate to difficulties that homosexual therapists encounter, but also to problems that straight therapists encounter.[1]

My choice to come out of the closet, so to speak, does not mean that such exposure is comfortable. It is noteworthy that the material used relates to work with a gay male patient rather than a lesbian and that some of the material was first presented at a self psychology conference in North America two years before presenting it to colleagues at home. Certainly, this has to do with a relatively widespread naïve understanding of homosexuality. Attitudes remain largely unchanged, even though South Africa is the only country in the world whose constitution gives homosexuals rights equal to any other citizen in the country and it is fast becoming internationally recognized as a lesbian and gay center. "Homo-prejudice"[2] nevertheless continues to be alive and well. In South Africa, for example, shared membership of medical aid schemes and reduced university fees for partners require an outing process, which is potentially shaming and therefore not necessarily a choice that the member partner would ordinarily want to make. It also shares the following with the United States, where "basic adult relationship affirming rituals—family celebrated dating . . . weddings . . . shared retirement benefits and assumed rights of survivorship either are still not considered normative, or occur with extra hardship" (Abramowitz, 2001, p. 1).

This chapter illustrates how the invisibility gives rise to the multiple and contradictory ways in which each of us can inhabit our gender and sexuality and how and why some of these shifts, at least in relation to gender and sexuality, occur. In so doing, I draw on Mitchell's (1993) idea of multiple selves, but more specifically on the postmodern concepts of "discourses" and "discursive practices."

Used in this context, a discourse reflects a set of attitudes, meanings, and beliefs that play a part in influencing the way in which individuals behave in a range of contexts. Discourses therefore make available varied behavior, or discursive practices, which, in turn, shape subjectivity. This is achieved by foregrounding some areas of experience or knowledge, and by creating gaps or silences in others (Davies & Harre, 1990, in Kottler and Swartz, 1995, p. 184). In a slightly more simplified way, discursive practices are similar to Brandchaft's (2001) patterns of attachment behavior or what the intersubjectivists refer to as "organizing principles" (Brandchaft, 1995, p. 94).

Whatever terminology is used, an individual's subjectivity, his or her behavior and beliefs about how the world works is a product of: 1) his or her history; 2) the positions each has taken up in particular discourses; and 3) the psychological investment each has had and still has, in taking up these particular positions (Hollway, 1984, p. 238). Individuals, having identified themselves with a particular subject position, "inevitably see the world from the vantage point of that position" (Davies and Harre, 1990, in Kottler and Swartz, 1995, p. 184). A gay, black, Muslim, Jewish, or disabled person then would see the world from the vantage point of being gay, black, Muslim, Jewish, or disabled and a straight or nongay person will see the world from the vantage point of being straight or not gay. An individual may, however, be positioned within multiple discourses in unpredictable and often contradictory ways. For example, as the clinical material will illustrate, being gay might have different meanings within the discursive practices of heterosexuality, masculinity, or femininity. Our sense of self is elaborated in terms of a series of dichotomous categories, which serve to include us in some groups, for example, as homosexuals, and exclude us "automatically" from others, for example, for a gay man, from being masculine. Gender, sexuality, race, religion, and disability are five such categories, and whether we like it or not, the complex discursive practices surrounding our gender, sexuality, race, religion, or disability shape every social encounter, including our therapeutic encounters.

Complicating things further, it is noteworthy that the positions we occupy in discourses are not simply determined in any rational, conscious, or unitary way, for example, because of biological sex. Discursive practices associated with discourses play a part in influencing which position may be filled by which gender or which sexuality at any particular time. Choices are therefore largely socially constructed and the ways in which they are given expression vary depending on the individual's emotional commitment in being there, for whatever reason. There is always some payoff or protection for the choice and a reason for taking up the chosen position (Hollway, 1984). This is true even though the take-up position might seem irrational and, in terms of other consequences, satisfaction might seem inexplicable. This is evident in the material presented, which draws attention to the effects of the shame involved in being homosexual and how psychologically debilitating it can be to have to try to "pass" as heterosexual to one's sense of (homosexual) self, one's (homosexual) sense of reality, integrity, and self-cohesion. The material also points to the psychologically damaging effects of the need to "pass" in an attempt to accommodate to what I shall refer to as society's pathology. I am referring to the dominant discourse that endorses heterosexuality as the norm.[3]

Briefly, before going on to the clinical material, I shall contextualize the theories used in this chapter. I come from a very rigid background where ideas or concepts were black or white, true or not true. I was expected to either like or dislike something. There was no room for uncertainty and even less for changing my mind. In my fourth year at university (which was my sixth in therapy), as a mature student and following a change in career from being an accountant with a multinational oil company, I discovered social constructionism, postmodernism, and feminist theories. These theories radically destabilized all that I had believed about the way in which the world and everyone in it, worked. I recognized myself in them and realized that other possibilities were open to me and the way I could live my life. The theories changed my experience of, and consequently, the nature of, my own personal therapy and they each inform my daily practice with my own patients. This is illustrated in the material presented.

At the time of these discoveries, I was drawing on object relations and Kleinian psychoanalytic theory, which had begun to feel inadequate and wrong for me. At around this time a prominent self psychologist (the late Peter Thompson) visited relatives in South Africa and gave a few public lectures. Discovering self psychology significantly shifted my understanding of my own and my patients' struggles both in relating to and being in the world. It, together with the theories mentioned above made me realize that different views or perspectives were possible. And, finally, my discovery of intersubjectivity theory provided me with an overarching context within which to link postmodernism, feminist theory, and psychoanalytic self psychology. The combination made me realize that "empathic resonance was available in the world." It was clearly a twinship experience for me—it confirmed for me the feeling that I was, after all, "human among other human beings"—the hallmark of Kohut's (1984) idea of twinship. I had come to "see something about the world that was not visible to me before: that something existed which did not seem to exist in my experience before" (Gehrie, 2002, p. 19). This is, according to Kohut (in Gehrie, 2002, p. 17) part of the analytic cure and one of the results of an analyst's empathic understanding. I believe I managed to help Franco, whose case material follows, in this way. This disguised material illustrates many of the issues raised above.

As I started working on this chapter, I became increasingly aware of how Kohut's (1984) concept of twinship was enmeshed in both the therapy itself and the content of this chapter at a number of different levels. I had gently led Franco on a journey very similar to one I had taken so many years earlier—one in which he began to experience the presence of others essentially like himself and thus to feel that he was "human among other human beings" (Kohut, 1984). I believe that Franco's ride was much smoother than my own, and a significantly quicker one. I think this was partly because of the way in which I integrated intersubjectivity, feminist theory, and self theory with postmodern ideas, including the contemporary literature focusing on the notion of multiple selves and the multiple ways in which we inhabit these varied selves. But it was also because of the presence of an essential dimension of the twinship experience, only implicit in Kohut's (1984) idea and therefore needing much further theorizing, that the therapist "recognizes herself in the patient" (Togashi, 2006, p. 1) In this sense, using Togashi's (2006) additional dimension of Kohut's unfinished conceptualization, because I had traveled this path myself meant that there was an important and significant reciprocal, mutual dimension to this therapy.

CLINICAL MATERIAL

Franco's mother referred him to me. He was not at all sure about what therapy could offer. At the time, he was living with his mother, stepfather, and a younger half sister. When he entered therapy, he was extremely depressed and had been for a considerable time. He spent most of his days in bed, sleeping. At night, he watched television. A few months before I saw him, he had applied to a local college to study in the hospitality industry, partly, he said initially, in the hope of meeting other gay men. Acceptance was dependent on the quality of a complex project for which Franco had no energy and dreading doing.

On the up side, Franco occasionally went out with his half sister to raves. He loved trance music and told me later in the therapy that he sometimes dreamed of becoming a DJ at one of the local trance clubs. When he told me about this, he became unusually articulate and quite animated. This was in direct contrast to our many silent and tortuous sessions in which he said little. I had to work extremely hard with him initially because he was so insufferably self-conscious and shy. He hardly made any eye contact. He spoke with his face cast downward and eyes focused firmly on the floor. From time to time, he would raise his eyes and furtively look at me through his relatively short-cropped hair. He spoke in short, sharp, almost incoherent sentences peppered with the words "you know" and "like." While still communicating in this way, I discovered that he had had one, in his words, "horrible" sexual experience with a fellow waiter a year earlier. It had ended with a reluctant "outing" of Franco at the restaurant where they both worked. This had shamed Franco terribly partly because, at the time, he was not at all sure he was gay. Feeling betrayed, Franco left the restaurant immediately after this event and had not worked or hardly socialized since then. In spite of this experience, and inexplicably to me early on in the therapy, Franco had come to firmly believe he was, and wanted to be, gay.

At the time of entering therapy, Franco had only told his mother that he thought he was gay. He suspected that his mother had told his stepfather who remained silent on the subject. But, whenever a good-looking woman appeared on the television, Franco's stepfather would say something like, "Hey, Franco, how about her—do you fancy her?" This would infuriate Franco, who believed that, even though it was an act of self-betrayal, he had to say, "yes" because this effectively ended the conversation. Franco's mother, although clearly uncomfortable with his announcement about being gay, was extremely concerned for his happiness and prepared to accept that he was gay.

Much of our halted and tortuous discussions in early sessions revolved around the agony arising out of Franco's wish that his stepfather and his half sister would acknowledge him as a gay man. He was intensely fearful of the anticipated stigma that would follow. In this sense, just as Franco was "embarking upon what is in the best of circumstances, a difficult stage of early adult self-development," he had begun to struggle with the "traumatic loss of cultural selfobject support" (Abramowitz, 2001, p. 4).

Illustrating, at another theoretical level, Franco's struggle with his positioning within or outside of the discourse of "heterosexuality as the norm" and endorsing something of his lifelong struggle with his own sexuality, he told me how he had felt different from other boys for as long as he could remember. As a young boy, he went to a single-sex school and for the most part, at least from an objective standpoint, seems to have managed to fit in with his peers. He was good at sports and is a well-built, conventionally masculine-looking young man, so he could "pass" as heterosexual and hence become a member of what Abramowitz (2001, p. 11) refers to as a "model minority." From a subjective perspective however, the behavior required of him to gain acceptance as "one of the boys" cost him psychologically. From his description, it seemed that at worst, he felt utterly alienated from himself and at best, he felt like a fraud and completely inauthentic. Somewhere in between he felt like a total failure, socially.

Worse, however, than his experience at school, was what lay ahead for him. Franco's decision that he was gay "heightened his selfobject needs, as does any transitional life stage" (Abramowitz, 2001, p. 3) and put him at odds with wider cultural norms. He had decided he was gay at a developmental stage when "ordinarily, vital selfobject experiences of peer twinship and family mirroring are generally found in walking arm and arm with a date of the opposite sex at college or bringing home the right young person for the family to admire and accept" (Abramowitz, 2001, p. 4). In Franco's case, he could find nothing in his surroundings that admired or affirmed him as a homosexual. He certainly did not have the feeling that he was a "human among other human beings." He was unaware of any cultural institutions from which to derive the selfobject support he so badly needed. And, worse, having decided that he was gay, Franco found himself faced with a dilemma of how to *be* a gay man, socially.

Theoretically speaking, he was going to have to begin a process of shifting back and forth between contradictory discourses. Demonstrating his initial positioning, he spent many a session "educating" me with recurring stereotypic, but dominant ideas, about what gay men looked like, how they behaved and what discursive practices were therefore available to him. From his exposure to ideas at home, at school, in the books he had read, the television he had watched, and the movies he had seen, Franco believed that he would have to be either "camp and effeminate" or "butch and aggressive." He decided that the latter was impossible because, even though he was a conventionally masculine-looking man, he was far too shy to be an "aggressor." He reluctantly decided therefore that he would have to become "camp." He spent hours in his bedroom, looking at himself in the mirror as he tried out various movements with his hands, to see how he could cultivate the "limp wrist" required to indicate to others that he was gay. He had discovered that there was a gay language and he would try out some of the words and speak them with an acquired lisp.

When I asked him why he felt he had to acquire these behaviors, he described a fear that if he did not do so, he would never be noticed as a gay man and would therefore never find a partner, which he so badly wanted. His experience a year earlier, when he had spent time at gay clubs (which is where he had observed these different behaviors) had been agonizing, mainly because he was so excruciatingly shy and because of what his fellow waiter had done to him. In spite of this, demonstrating in part his vital need for Kohut's version of the twinship selfobject experience, that is, the need to experience the other as alike, he felt that he had to present himself in public "looking gay," so that others, at shopping malls or movies, would approach him and make the "first move." In this way, Togashi's dimension would be present, that is, the other finding himself in Franco. However, this was a double-edged sword because dressing and behaving in this way made it likely that his queerness would be "discovered" by other members of his family and old school friends. He knew this would fill him with shame and he dreaded the traumatic ridicule and stigma that he imagined would follow this discovery.

I could completely identify with Franco's dilemma and I could not bear what he was doing to himself. I could identify myself in this struggle very clearly. Twenty-six years earlier, long before I discovered psychotherapy, in a similarly depressed state, an ex-boyfriend of mine had put me in touch with a group of lesbians who, when I met them, dressed mostly in denim jeans, sneakers, and checked shirts. None of them wore makeup. Immediately on meeting them, they asked me to join what they called a "lesbian rap group" due to start some weeks ahead. That evening they invited me to a gay and lesbian nightclub. This was my first experience (and unfortunately, not my last) of such a club! A model scene evoked by that evening was the horror and confusion I felt when I met Jamie, an extremely butch-looking woman in denim jeans, boots, and a checked shirt. She wore no makeup and regaled us all with stories about her relationship with her partner, who was heavily made-up, wore a pink miniskirt, pink frilly top, and high-heeled pink shoes. The stories included expectations that cooked meals would be ready for Jamie at whatever time she returned home from work and other similar expectations including putting out of Jamie's slippers and running her a bath. I distinctly remember leaving the club that night feeling despair as to what my growing belief that I was a lesbian was going to mean in realistic terms. Was I going to have to be butch or femme? Which would I choose? At the time, I was an accountant with a multinational oil company. I power-dressed as this was expected of me in this position—I wore makeup, skirts, jewelry, etc. On the evenings that I was due to join the rap group I would rush home, remove all traces of makeup, and change into jeans, sneakers, and my newly acquired checked shirts! One evening I went to the theater with a group of nonlesbian friends. I was smartly dressed, I wore makeup, and I bumped into some of the members of the lesbian rap group. I was devastated, confused, and wished that the floor would open up beneath me to enable me to simply disappear. It took me a very long time to work with this issue, helped of course by the fact that discursive practices have changed in the last twenty-six years, resulting in my having found ample and appropriate twinship selfobject support in my shifting surroundings over time.

Kohut (1959) argued that in order to be truly empathic, the therapist has to find something in herself or her own experience that affectively resonates with what the patient describes. I believe that the experiences described enabled me to understand what Franco felt about having to mold himself into something that truly did not come easily for him and the psychological dangers involved in doing so. I felt that Franco's perhaps reluctant decision to affect a camp and effeminate persona would only lead him down a one-way street to alienation and misery. I felt it was my job to help Franco realize that he did not have to try to reinvent himself into a unitary, camp, and effeminate being in order to find empathic resonance in the world (see Gehrie, 2002). I knew theoretically and personally that for anyone, this would be restrictive, potentially alienating, and likely to be painful and psychologically damaging. It could only lead to the development of more of an alienated self with a greater loss of what I was beginning to see in Franco, as a delightfully idiosyncratic and potentially multifaceted self.

Intersubjectivity, postmodern theory, and feminist theory helped me to formulate the question which came to mind at this point in the therapy, which was, Whose pathology are we dealing with? Through the lenses of these theories it seemed clear to me that Franco's predominant struggle was with the belief systems and dominant discourses that existed in the context in which he lived. He was struggling with the effects of the dominant discourses to which he had been exposed all his life, each of which cemented the message that heterosexuality was the norm and that anything else was "different" and "other." Being different and other meant that it was deviant, something of which to be ashamed, and something which everyone found funny—funny because of the way in which gay men are depicted in movies such as *The Bird Cage*, which was a constant point of reference for Franco.

I felt frustrated and intolerant of these ideas. This led me to conceptualize the foreground of his struggle and his major source of distress and depression not so much as a consequence of his shyness and lack of confidence or self-disorder, but rather as a result of the belief systems or "pathology" to which Franco was accommodating. This included the beliefs imposed upon him by his long-standing and hitherto unquestioned positioning within the "heterosexual as the norm discourse" and the discourses that dictated the discursive practices of homosexuals. In recognizing this, I decided that, initially at least, I needed limited but clearly focused goals for this therapy, one of which involved the introduction of alternative discourses and discursive practices, or put differently, cultural "norms." I hoped that these discoveries would enable Franco to discover the kind of empathic resonance that he had not yet been able to find in his current context and ultimately to feel "human among humans" (Kohut, 1984).

I found myself having to bite my tongue whenever I was tempted to challenge the ideas Franco presented and I struggled to carry out my therapeutic goal. But, theoretically and personally, I knew there were other options open to him and I was determined to set about facilitating his discovery of these alternative options, which would enable him to realize that empathic resonance could be available to him (Gehrie, 2002). I wanted to encourage him to play with these alternatives so that he could find his own optimal positioning within these discourses.

In retrospect, and thinking about Togashi's (2006) additional dimension of twinship, it would seem that Franco probably felt something of my recognizing myself in him. However, at a conscious level he clearly had no idea that I was gay, nor did it occur to him, it seemed, that I might see or know other gay men or women. I think he saw a middle-aged, or even very old, straight, professional woman. I decided early on that it would be inappropriate for Franco to discover that I was gay or that I knew anything about homo-prejudice from a personal perspective. He was so completely confused and inarticulate about it all that I believed he would have to find his own voice and his own way through the maze that the whole issue of his sexuality presented to him. However, knowing the pain involved in this process, I felt that he, like I had twenty-six years earlier, needed some help. I also knew that this was not initially going to come from other confused gay men like his first sexual partner. This earlier experience had understandably left him mistrustful and fearful and had left him feeling completely isolated, dreadfully lonely, and confused.

Severed as he was from collective twinship selfobject support had also left Franco with unmet idealized selfobject support (see Abramowitz, 2001, p. 5). He felt this absence acutely. I was concerned that his current depression would intensify and that suicide was possible or that he would become vulnerable to another painful and exploitative relationship of the kind that had seemed to precipitate his depression. It felt important that he meet and experience the presence of others who, like myself, had "journeyed through cultural bigotry's rough terrain with intact and productive selves, or who had as they had proceeded along adulthood's developmental path, repaired and restored themselves from this relational wounding and thus developed to their full potentials" (Abramowitz, 2001, p. 1).

This occurrence, from a self psychological perspective, would act as a mirroring experience for him and hopefully provide him with a developmentally significant twinship (Kohut, 1984; Togashi, 2006) or kinship (Basch, 1992) selfobject experience. For this to occur, support was necessary for his attempts at studying with others whose interests were similar to his own and his wish to find a peer group with whom he could identify rather than from which he would feel alienated.

In this process, perhaps attuned to what appeared as "tendrils of psychological growth," the "forward edge" as described by Tolpin and Lachman (2006), I hoped that Franco could find a way to develop to his full potential. I wanted him to experience the exploration of the range of selves that seemed to be in his repertoire and to feel comfortable with their diversity and any contradictions. This included, for example, inhabiting and playing with his more camp self, who enjoyed cooking and presenting exotic meals and wearing jewelry, something I noticed him trying out increasingly as time went on. However, he also loved watching rugby and football and was quite capable of doing traditionally male odd jobs around the house, like painting and repair work. He often did this happily and companionably with his stepfather. I hoped he would be able to feel comfortable with all of this and to move in and out of these facets of himself, as his mood and perhaps his context changed.

One of my first interventions involved some "bibliotherapy." In retrospect, this catalyzed a shifting of the family dynamic into a cohesive selfobject support system for Franco's emerging identity. I gave Franco a revised and updated edition of a book that, in a similar space to Franco, I had bought in a department store in Cape Town twenty-six years earlier. At that time, I told the sales assistant that it was for a "friend of mine." Perversely perhaps, she put it into a see-through packet and I remember walking out of the store desperately trying to cover up the title before I caught a train home.

The book was entitled *Loving Someone Gay* (Clark, 1987). Franco took it home and glanced through it. He found it interesting. Being a particular kind of South African, he especially liked the way in which the author equated homo-prejudice to racism. However, he is not a great reader and he passed the book on to his mother to read. She devoured it and spoke enthusiastically with Franco about much of the content. He loved these discussions with her. Later, he believed that his mother must have shared aspects of the book with his stepfather and his half sister, because it became apparent that they had, as therapy continued, come to know and seemingly accept that he was gay. To his surprise, neither of them appeared horrified. His stepfather stopped the comments about good-looking women on television and his half sister became the source of his meeting a number of other gay people, both women and men, one of whom, Dave, was to become extremely significant to Franco toward the end of the therapy. And so Franco began to discover others close to him who "joyfully responded to him, became available to him as sources of idealized strength and calmness, (were) silently present but in essence like him, and, at any rate, able to grasp his inner life" (Kohut in Abramowitz, 2001, p. 3). He began to feel human among other humans.

Going beyond the family, with a view to helping Franco find affiliation with others in the same predicament, or who had found a solution to it (Blechner, 1996, p. 232), I told Franco about the Triangle Project that I said I had come across. It is a gay organization that has a library, voluntary HIV-AIDS workers, counseling programs, and so on, though, sadly, at that time no facilitated groups looking at gay issues such as coming out. I discovered this after Franco had phoned them to find out if there was such a group for him to join. He never explored any other possible activities, for example, volunteer work, reading in the library, or helping to catalog gay books donated to the organization.

The apathy with which Franco approached aspects of his life continued but, suggesting something of Tolpin's idea of a "forward edge," there was energy in the room whenever we talked about the hospitality industry and the project that had to accompany his application for the college course. In the process of these discussions, Franco completed the project and gained acceptance into college. This was hugely affirming for him.

While waiting for the course to begin, Franco began to look for a job as a waiter. He told me that he knew about "gay-friendly restaurants" and, since he assumed that I did not know, he explained to me what this meant. I sat attentively listening to him, fascinated that he truly seemed to believe that this was not self-evident. He said they were the only kind of restaurant he wanted to work in and from a personal perspective I could completely understand his wish to be with others like himself.

However, he seemed to be getting nowhere. He was only trying small restaurants and he remained painfully shy. This made it difficult for me to imagine him conducting any form of interview that would get him a job as a waiter. However, since I had no idea how he was outside of therapy and because of my experience of his animation when talking about the hospitality industry and being a DJ, I could not be sure that in other contexts he was necessarily the same as he was in therapy with me. It was perfectly possible that there were slices of his life and his behavior unseen by me. For these reasons I did not ask questions that might make him question this chosen path and look for other ways of earning money. Instead, I helped him pursue this idea.

I knew a gay man who was ordinary looking, relatively masculine, neither particularly camp nor particularly butch (in his professional life at least), and who owned a large restaurant. Moreover, I knew that this was on Cape Town's "pink map." I told Franco that I had come across the map somewhere, and that I had heard the restaurant was owned by a gay man and without having any contact with the owner, I suggested to Franco that he might perhaps try to find work there. I said I had been to the restaurant and liked it very much.

Franco approached the restaurant, which offered him a job following a brief training period. He met the owner in one of his interviews and began to see him on a beach that Franco frequented with a girl friend. He felt good about being able to nod "hello" to such a successful and quite ordinary-looking man who he knew was gay only because I had told him so. This was quite a surprise to Franco, who had never met a gay man who was, from appearances and behavior, neither camp and effeminate nor butch and aggressive and who was successful *and* out. A man who, in Abramowitz's (2002) terms, had apparently "journeyed through cultural bigotry's rough terrain with [an] intact and productive [self]" (p. 1).

By this time, Franco had begun to look at me when he spoke. He was looking forward to his college course and meeting his classmates, who he remained convinced would be predominantly gay. He had, through two "old" lesbians (who turned out to be twenty years my junior), met Dave, who I believe provided Franco with the kind of idealized selfobject experience he needed. Dave is gay, thirty-something, divorced with two sons. He is a successful professional man who is completely "out" in his professional and personal life. Franco described him as masculine-looking and he seemed to be an intact and productive self. For fun, Franco said he fixed cars and "dances topless on his toes at gay nightclubs." Franco loved him. Franco's family seemed to enjoy him and he became a regular visitor at their home. Quite soon after their first meeting, Franco moved in to share digs with him and the two of them began to go out frequently to dinner, gay clubs, and to the movies. Franco clearly felt wonderfully human and filled with energy. In Dave, the lesbian couple he had met, and in his family members, Franco had begun to have the kind of developmentally essential selfobject experiences of peer twinship and family mirroring, as described by Kohut (in Abramowitz, 2001, p. 3). Franco had discovered that there were others outside there who were like him, and that empathic resonance was after all available in this world. This according to Kohut (in Gehrie, 2002, p. 6) is the major constituent of a sense of security in adult life.

Kohut (in Abramowitz, 2001, p. 2) also argued that "when the adult experiences the self sustaining effects of a maturely chosen selfobject, the selfobject experiences of all the preceding stages of this life reverberate unconsciously." I believe that this is what happened with Franco and in this sense the therapy was, while unorthodox perhaps, transformational and certainly not directive and educational, as some might venture to suggest.

Because of what had occurred in the therapy up to this point, Franco was feeling increasingly confident in the world. This led to talk about terminating therapy, which we did after only six months. While I am aware that there was and is much more that can be done in therapy with Franco, which is always true of any therapy, it nevertheless seemed appropriate at the time to end the therapy for a number of reasons, some already mentioned above. In summary, this therapy was not about being a good object. It was not about steering Franco in a direction that might reduce his tension and conflict. I would argue that predominantly because of the twinship experiences, it was developmentally appropriate and transformational. Franco's discovery of the availability of empathic resonance and other cultural institutions from which he could derive collective selfobject support was crucial for him at this critical developmental stage. This enabled Franco to draw vital affirmation and admiration at a time when, feeling severed from collective selfobject support, he was seriously depressed and potentially suicidal (Abramowitz, 2001, p. 5). Finally, according to Kohut (in Gehrie, 2002, p. 17), "the essence of the psychoanalytic cure resides in a patient's newly acquired ability to identify and seek out appropriate selfobjects—both mirroring and idealizable—as they present themselves in his realistic surrounding and to be sustained by them."

I believe that Franco had learned to do this. In realistic surroundings he had found cultural and relational selfobject support and the relationship between himself and his selfobjects had changed significantly as a result. Franco had become more of a cohesive self and this increased cohesion had augmented his ability to use selfobjects for his own sustenance. This had helped facilitate a freedom within himself to choose (appropriate) selfobjects. He had found a comfortable way to come out and to play with his diversity. The diversity had enabled him to find rather than lose, as he had imagined, "certain representatives of his human surroundings . . . joyfully responding to him . . . available to him . . . sources of idealized strength and calmness . . . being silently present but in essence like him, and, at any rate, able to grasp his inner life" (Kohut in Abramowitz, 2001, p. 3). At this point, we agreed that he could and would return to therapy should he ever feel the need to do so in the future.

Only after I began to prepare the case material for this chapter did I consciously realize how similar Franco's "coming out" process was to my own twenty-six years earlier, and what effect this had on the way in which the therapy unfolded. This raises questions about the implications of therapists working with people from different cultures or whose organizations of experiences or presenting problems are not something with which we can affectively resonate, or without the theoretical tools with which to understand the complexities of the contextual problems with which our patients present.

This chapter focuses on me as a gay therapist. However, because I have foregrounded the importance of the social/cultural field as a vital context beyond the therapeutic dyad that shapes not only the therapy process but the subjectivity of each participant, it also speaks to the general problem of difference and otherness, both in ourselves and our clients. Since most, if not all of us live in a range of diverse discourses while not being completely at ease with any of them, this possibly enables us to do what Kohut (1959) said we needed to do in order to vicariously introspect, and hence be "truly" empathic, and to act appropriately in the therapy. However, to do this I believe that we need the selfobject support from others who can resonate with our particular brands of difference or with the effects of a marginalized status. This is what motivated this chapter; I wanted to fill the conspicuous gap I identified. We, as therapists, need much of what Franco needed in his context and developmental stage in life from our cultural/professional institutions. In our contexts, we need the affirming selfobject experiences, which accompany vital reciprocal exchanges with our fellow professionals (Abramowitz, 2001). I hope that this chapter will encourage others to come out and share similar experiences of diversity and difference, both from a theoretical perspective and with regard to our work in the room with "difference."

REFERENCES

Abramowitz, S. (2001). Adult homosexual development and the self. Paper presented in workshop entitled "The Self and Orientation: The Next Step" at the twenty-fourth annual International Conference on the Psychology of the Self, San Francisco.

Basch, M. F. (1992). *Practicing Psychotherapy: A Casebook.* New York: Basic Books.

Blechner, M. J. (1996). Psychoanalysis in and out of the closet. In B. Gerson (Ed.), *The therapist as a person* (pp. 223–239). Hillsdale, NJ: Analytic Press.

Brandchaft, B. (1985). Resistance and defense: An intersubjective view. In A. Goldberg (Ed.), *Progress in self psychology, vol. 1* (pp. 88–96). Hillsdale, NJ: Analytic Press.

Brandchaft, B. (2001). Obsessional disorders: A developmental systems perspective. *Psychoanalytic Inquiry, 21*(2), 253–288.

Clark, D. (1987). *Loving someone gay.* Berkeley, CA: Celestialarts.

Gehrie, M. J. (2002). Heinz Kohut memorial lecture: Reflective relativism and Kohut's self psychology. In A. Goldberg (Ed.), *Postmodern self psychology: Progress in self psychology, vol. 18* (pp. 15–30). Hillsdale, NJ: Analytic Press.

Hollway, W. (1984). Gender difference and the production of subjectivity. In J. Henriques, W. Hollway, C. Urwin, C. Venn, & V. Walkerdine (Eds.), *Changing the subject.* London: Metheun.

Kohut, H. (1959). Introspection, empathy and psychoanalysis. *J. Amer. Psychoanal. Assn., 7,* 459–483.

Kohut, H. (1984) *How does analysis cure?* Ed. A. Goldberg with P. E. Stepansky. Chicago: University of Chicago Press.

Kottler, A. E., & Swartz, S. (1995). Talking about wolf-whistles: Negotiating gender positions in conversation. *South African Journal of Psychology, 25*(3), 184–190.

Mitchell, S. A. (1993). *Hope and dread in psychoanalysis.* New York: Basic Books.

Togashi, K. (2006). A new dimension of twinship selfobject experience and transference. Paper presented at the twenty-ninth International Conference on the Psychology of the Self, Chicago, IL, October 26–29, 2006.

Tolpin, M., & Lachman, F. (2006). Forward & leading edge transference: Application to doing psychotherapy. Paper presented at the twenty-ninth International Conference on the Psychology of the Self, Chicago, IL, October 26–29, 2006.

NOTES

1. Obviously, in very similar (but also very different) ways, all that is said in this paper will apply to individuals whose site of marginalized difference is located in their race, their culture or religion, their marital status, their disability, etc.

2. I prefer this term to that of homophobia, a term which is misleading.

3. We could add to this the dominant discourses of "white as the norm" or "married as the norm." (Don't those women who have actually chosen to be single hate being asked if we are Miss or Mrs., especially as we get older and are forced to take on the stigmatized spinster status in the eyes of the bank clerk attending to us who refuses to hear our answer, "Ms."?)

13

Improvisational Moments in a Self Psychological Relational Psychoanalysis

Philip A. Ringstrom, PhD, PsyD

In an episode of the highly acclaimed NBC television series *The Office*, the notoriously narcissistic boss, Michael Scott (played by actor Steve Carell), attends an after-office hours improvisational acting class. Although, throughout the show's first two seasons fans of *The Office* have seen Michael recurrently the buffoon through his grandiosely self-inflated perceptions, including that he is a really great actor, it is in his improvisation class that they see most clearly why Michael recurrently fails in all relationships in work, in love, and now in play.

Eager to act in every scene, Michael is boorishly insistent and when his teacher yields to his pressure, Michael jumps on stage adopting the same character over and over. He instantly becomes some version of a pistol-brandishing law enforcement officer (e.g., cop, detective, or FBI agent), who within a matter of seconds responds to whatever his scene partner initiates by pointing his two-hand-clasped feigned finger gun, screaming, "Freeze! Detective Michael Scott!" And, no matter how his scene partners reply, he inevitably shoots to kill, sometimes getting carried away with shooting other sideline classmates who are not even in the scene. Responding to his instructor's withering plea for him to listen to his scene partners and to be open to other dramatic choices, Michael insists that the introduction of a gun in every scene is always dramatically commanding, far better, he mutters, than the "boring scenes" his classmates introduce.

Then something truly improvisational happens: his instructor steps forward commandingly and says, "Michael! No more guns! Gimme your guns! All of them!" Caught off guard, Michael begrudgingly starts to mime pulling out a huge array of imaginary pistols from imaginary shoulder, belt, and pocket holsters, one after another as his instructor correspondingly mimes taking each and every one placing them aside on an imaginary table. In that rare instance, Michael is induced to momentarily shift from the stereotypical behavior of his character. That is, he is induced into a moment of playing with the other, rather than compulsively dominating the other. This brief exchange captures an improvisational moment in which the complementarity of the dominance and submission of the "doer and done to" (Benjamin, 2004) is broken. In other words, there is a shift from subject-to-object relating to subject-to-subject relating (Benjamin, 2004), or from "I-it" relating to "I-thou" (Buber, 1923). Furthermore, their scene itself becomes a co-created "third" element to which neither can claim exclusive authorship (Ogden, 1994), but in which both actors' creative contribution is essential. This contrasts starkly with the previous scenes in which "negative thirdness" (Ringstrom, 2001a) stifles both parties by virtue of one's subjective worldview dominating the others. All of these terms will be elaborated upon momentarily, but for now they are suggestive of the moment-to-moment role of liberation that improvisation can hold for an analytic dyad floundering in stalemates, deadlocks, and impasses. Meanwhile, this brief vignette also captures something quintessential about how play (discussed in this chapter in terms of improvisational moments) can fail miserably as well as what needs to happen for it to succeed. In this nugget, we can potentially see much correspondence to the role of improvisational play in psychoanalysis.

What is captured in the above scene work is how character pathology often manifests in an invariant style. Such invariant organization has been discussed in many ways by a host of theoreticians (Stolorow, Brandchaft, & Atwood, 1987; Mitchell, 1988, 1993) all suggestive of ways in which personality organization imposes its constrictions across a very wide variety of relational contexts. What Michael does in play, he does in life, which is to always have to be the boss. In this vein, Michael is a quintessential unconscious bully, though since it is intolerable for him to see himself as such, he commonly masquerades with feigned collegiality, as though he imagines himself an ever playful fellow actor in all of life's dramatic moments.

Unlike Michael the bully, however, his fellow classmates actually do follow the cardinal rule of improvisational theater and that is to always accept the reality your scene partner presents to you, and work off of and with what has been creatively given to you as you may expect your fellow actors to do in return. Improvisational theater counts on this, and improvisational moments in psychoanalysis do too.

Nevertheless, following this cardinal rule each classmate falls dead upon being shot, each scene abruptly ending, to the instructor's dismay. In effect, under Michael's sway, the improvisation is over before it has even begun. What restores the realm of improvisation in the instructor's move to confiscate Michael's guns, however, is that rather than simply ordering Michael that he cannot introduce guns in any further scenes—which would have merely turned the tables of domination—he playfully accepts the "reality" of Michael's "guns." In so doing, he can playfully insist that Michael literally (through imaginary gesture) "hand them over." This move instantaneously co-creates a transitional space for playing with Michael's rigid personality organization rather than yielding to it. In short, it suggests that more than merely noting through empathy or interpretation Michael's (or any patient's for that matter) self-defeating personality style, the instructor/therapist gets "inside" the actor/patient's invariant organization, engaging it in its very "as-if-ness," but then doing something entirely unpredictable in response to it. This is the form and substance of improvisational moments (Ringstrom, 2007a, 2007b).

Study of the preceding scene then, not only demonstrates how improvisation works, it is also highly suggestive of the living experiential world of psychotherapy, as opposed to our scripted versions of psychotherapy enshrined in platitudes of traditional analytic technique. I have taken up this point in earlier publications (Ringstrom, 2001b, 2001c), distinguishing between metaphorical correspondences of classical theater and traditional psychoanalytic technique in contrast to improvisational theater and improvisational technique in psychoanalysis. Whereas the former attitude involves the position that what is "known" in any psychoanalytic theory lends itself to prescriptions of roles and scripts and delineations of the analytic setting, the latter, improvisational attitude plunges us into a bath of the unknown and the unpredictable.

Among the most glaring of platitudes from traditional psychoanalysis are the three ideals that both Mitchell (1997) and Hoffman (1998) have amply challenged along with the rest of scholars of the relational canon. These three ideals are anonymity, neutrality, and abstinence, all of which seek to cultivate a sense of therapeutic objectivity, which, Knoblauch (2004) noted, attempts to generate the myth of the uncontaminated interpretation. While interpretations have been the hallmark of the "talking cure"—as Knoblauch noted—the study of enactments has in recent years replaced verbal association and interpretation at the center of analytic attention. What is it then that we see from such scholarship that corresponds with the improvisational in the preceding scene?

First of all, improvisational acting often begins with an encounter of strangeness, that is, that either as actors/persons we haven't met before, or if we have, we are about to encounter something novel. That novelty may involve something exciting, or it may be something deeply conflictual and troubling requiring a solution, but whatever it is, it demands our attention. Note that this experience corresponds neatly with Bion's (1967) admonition that the analyst and analysand engage each session "without memory or desire," as if they are meeting for the very first time. How we approach such a "present moment" that is a "moment of opportunity," also known as "kairos," will call out something about each of us in a manner that is "sloppy, dynamic and highly unpredictable" (Stern, 2004). This means that the improvisational moment is ripe for moving "unformulated experience" (Stern, 1998) into a prospectively, playfully meaningful experience. Each actor, whether in the drama of the theater or the drama of the therapeutic encounter calls upon something in their character makeup, their prereflective unconscious, their organizing principles if you will (Stolorow & Atwood, 1994), that is often of the realm of nonconscious awareness (Stern, 2004) or an "unthought known" (Bollas, 1987). Needless, to say, that which thwarts improvisation in life, theater, and therapy is precisely the fear of revealing this, first to oneself, and then to another. The question then is how open will the parties be to allowing the unrehearsed, the unscripted, the "unthought known" to emerge?

Now whether or not things "move along" (Stern, 2004) in the treatment to cultivate these openings has to do with the relative openness or closedness in any local moment in the intersubjective field. This field is constituted according to Stern (2004) with a basic intersubjective motivation to know the other and to be known. This requires reading one another's intentions and feelings while defining, maintaining, or reestablishing one's own identity.

Improvisational moments in the intersubjective field reflect an ongoing quality of emergent mutual recognition. A good scene in either improvisational theater or therapy therefore reflects the experience of each party having a sense of "fit" or what Stern (2004) calls "fittedness." I believe in such moments, each person has the sense that "it feels right to be in my skin." Playfully, inducing Michael to relinquish his "guns" actually "fits" within his personality organization though it seeks to move him beyond its daunting constrictiveness. The sense of fittedness contrasts with many moments which do not have this quality and, sadly in some analyses, almost never have this quality. As Stern notes, "When we're not intersubjectively oriented, anxiety rises and coping or defense mechanisms mobilize." He refers to this state as intersubjective anxiety, and it is a state that can surely occupy patient and therapist alike.[1]

In fact, in states of intersubjective anxiety the parties are vulnerable to devolving into what Benjamin has described as states of split complementarity or the one-up, one-down positions. Rather than each partner's contribution to the intersubjective matrix stimulating openness and creativity in kind, split complementarity triggers a quality of paranoid engagement between and within each other. Guardedness ensues, with an often life-or-death vying over whose perspective on reality will be upheld. Often this erupts in what Benjamin has also called reversible complementarity, insofar as both parties are competing to get out of the one-down position and into the one-up. In real life split complementarity may be a consequence of the incoherence of a situation causing overwhelming anxiety in one or the other or both, lending to their vying for control of their "scene" in a life and death-like power struggle. This interactional gambit, while unfortunately common in human relationship systems, constitutes the opposite of an intersubjective context open to improvisation and change. In fact, it replicates the systemic madness of mutually assured destruction found in such conditions as the nuclear arms race, revenge slayings between inner-city gangs, mutually escalating systems of spousal abuse, and revenge killings throughout the Middle East.

Split complementarity is also evident in bad improvisational acting when one actor negates the other. Consider this dreadful scene: Actor A says to Actor B, "What kind of cab driver are you, you're driving slower than my grandmother?!" Actor B kills the improvisation when he retorts, "I'm not a cab driver, I'm a farmer 'driving' a tractor!" Actor B is unwilling to build upon Actor A's perspective. Instead, he negates it replacing it with his own. Actor A may try to salvage the scene by acting "mad" such as saying, "Oh silly me, I must have forgotten my meds this morning and I am hallucinating we're in a taxi!" However, note that in his attempt to save the scene, Actor A does what many people do for the sake of love and relationship, that is, to relinquish their own version of reality. As Davies (2003) notes, in intense relational impasses, "To feel sane I must forgo love and to feel loved, I must forgo my sanity." From the self psychological standpoint, this could be understood as the patient and analyst rupturing each other's selfobject needs, either placing their cohesion and worth in jeopardy, or to preserve the attachment, introducing deadening "pathological accommodation" (Brandchaft, 1993).

I want to now shift to a patient of my own, to flesh out a kind of improvisational encounter. D is a graduate student in his early twenties. Approximately a year before this writing, D was referred by a colleague from back East. D and I have worked steadily once a week, with breaks for vacations and his trips back home. He came to me for help with some social anxieties, specifically, manifesting in worries about meeting friends, both male and female.

During a particular session we had been discussing his vacation, his time with his family, his loss of his long-distance girlfriend, and assorted other topics. As happens over the course of most therapy sessions, these topics had each reached something of a temporary "conclusion." Intersubjective sequences have their own elapsed beginning, middle, and end, often very short in duration. This in fact is why psychotherapy sessions can be efficaciously examined as a succession of dramatic scenes. Such intersubjective moments can reveal salient aspects of life that otherwise unfold outside of or on the periphery of awareness. Stern (2004) notes such sequences come to a close when there is some signal in the dyad that we have for the moment fulfilled our intentions with this discussion or "we did not get there so let's drop it and go elsewhere."

So, all of a sudden, D said to me, "Is it all right if we change the subject, because there is something that I am curious about, and I am reminded of it right now." I said, "Shoot."

D asked, "Why is your face always so serious?" I asked him to explain, and he said, "I don't know, its just you have this expression that is so serious, and you know, it seems kind of fake." This is of course what the Boston Change Process Study Group would patently call a "now moment" that is a moment of opportunity or kairos. I would call this a delightful "holy shit" moment of improvisation.

One thing for sure is that in such moments, the patient has put the therapist on the spot, challenging him to "come on in here and play with me, don't just stand out there watching me." Now it could be very tempting to do something like what Lichtenberg, Lachmann, and Fosshage (1992, 1996) call wearing the attribution, which is in fact sometimes a very helpful technique for furthering exploration in a manner that suggests that the therapist is nondefensive about the attribution. Wearing the attribution might go something like, "So, D, how is it for you to be with a therapist who is fake?" In my own two analyses stretching over eighteen years I certainly heard this a lot from my analysts and found frequently that it was a good opening for my own reflection as a patient. Furthermore, as an analyst, I have worn the attribution innumerable times myself and even have written about its technical efficacy (Ringstrom, 1995).

The trouble is, to respond with technique to a technical question about one's manner of relating seems to potentially mask oneself and distance oneself from a highly unusual moment of engagement with D. I offer this point of view retrospectively about my work with D, because there really wasn't time to consider it then. Instead, I said, "You know that's really curious, I have no idea what my face looks like." Now D became very curious. I continued, "You know I have often found that one of the greatest paradoxes, maybe greatest cosmic hoaxes in life is that we are all clueless what our face looks like, and yet it's communicating something about us all the time."

Clearly, I was on something of a roll, fascinated with my own unfolding ideas, as this was apparently the "character" that I had become in this scene—which is not to suggest that it is anything less than an aspect of me, but also that it was nothing more either—more on the point of multiple versions of self shortly. So I proceeded, "In fact, I recently bought a couple of digital cameras. . . ." "Wait!" D said, "how come two?" So I went on. "Mine broke on my trip to Europe this summer and I was so pissed about it, that the first week I was home, Dell sent me an e-mail with a fabulous camera sale and I just up and bought two." Okay, it is quite possible that perfectly reasonable analysts might question what I have been telling D more than he needed to know about me. Perhaps, on the other hand, speaking improvisationally, you are either in the scene or outside of it, and if you are in it, you flow, and if you don't, well, you really can look fake.

D laughed, as I went on. "Anyway, one night I was fiddling with one of my cameras and I started taking a bunch of photos of my face. In fact, I started making all sorts of expressions that I thought resembled how my face might appear to others, for example, I began making expressions that I thought I might make relative to patients telling me something very emotional, you know something that was happy, or sad, or conflictual. To my utter amazement, many of them simply didn't look at all like I would have imagined, though on second thought, I never actually imagined what I look like, just not how I appeared on the camera."

D was intrigued, he added, "Well, you know, what the camera captures in a split second can look quite different than on videotape," a point to which I readily agreed. I then said, "But tell me more about my expression, what seems 'fake' about it?" He said, "Well, maybe 'fake' isn't the right word, it's more that you are staring so seriously at me, maybe, come to think of it, it's how you look when you are listening closely and concentrating." I noted that that could be the case, and then added that I was especially curious about what he was saying since, "I always thought of myself as a pretty interactive analyst."

I asked D, "Is my expression more serious than Dr. M's (the referring analyst)?" And, D burst out laughing and said, "Oh, God no! He was really serious!" I asked him if he had ever brought this up with Dr. M in his previous treatment and he said, "You know what, I don't think that I ever did. I guess I didn't feel comfortable enough." Then he continued, "You know, I just realized, your expression is when you are really listening closely to what I am talking about especially when I am anxious about something. Maybe this isn't about you at all, but about my anxiety." Now I submit that that was a pretty good bit of analysis of a projection of a defense. It gets played with in a manner that allows D to make his own illuminating interpretation without having to suffer a potentially shaming one from me. In fact, improvising instead of wearing the attribution momentarily made me a participant in curiosity about myself, rather than making myself the subject of curiosity in the manner that exercises in attribution wearing often does. My improvisation represents a momentary solo, to invoke a jazz concept, then inviting D to play with his own. Parenthetically, three sessions later, D asked me if we can start meeting twice a week.

Most importantly, improvisation actually enlarges the scope of intersubjectivity from one-way intersubjectivity, that is, an "I know what you feel" derived from the therapist's sustained introspective, empathic inquiry, to the two-way intersubjectivity of the relational canon found in the experience of "I know that you know that I know what you are feeling" and vice versa. Stern (2004) notes of "present moments" in therapy—and I would add this applies to improvisational ones—that:

> In each present moment [each improvisational moment—I would add] [each party] carries out the regulation [of the intersubjective field] by probing, testing, and correcting the reading of the other's mental state in light of [their] own. This dyadic process of parallel, simultaneous reading of the patient and therapist occurs largely nonconsciously. Present moments are thus devoted to intersubjective questions [and, these, I will remind you, are the structure of every improvisational moment] such as: "What is happening here and now between us?"; "What do I sense or know about how you experience me, now?"; [and] "What do you know about how I now experience you?" (p. 120)

And so on. Once again, from a self psychological standpoint, this intersubjective interpenetration alludes to how each is participating in the other's sense of cohesion and worth or fragmentation or depletion depending on how they convey their experiences of one another (Kohut, 1984).

The reason thinking improvisationally can be so beneficial to analysts is that it is a theatrical metaphor that applies not only to our enterprise, but also is powerfully descriptive of life. From the anti-Cartesian philosophical challenges of Stolorow, Atwood, and Orange (2002) to the neuroscientific study of mirror neurons (Stern, 2004), one powerful conclusion is that we do not have a homunculus watching over our experience. Indeed, from infancy forward, our sense of consciousness is entirely social in origin, we cannot develop a subjective sense of reality sans "audience members and fellow actors in" our life drama. Stern (2004) notes that "Reflective consciousness will not occur unless there is an 'other' present to witness our having a phenomenal experience, in other words, to play the role of the homunculus sitting in the theater of the mind" (p. 128).

One curious exception to this is when we have "versions of self" observing other "versions of self." This relates to the domain of experiencing that Bromberg (1998) tackles in his discussion of the problem of dissociation wherein aspects of self become "narcissistic islands" separated and made incommunicado by psychic chasms. It is in this "space" he argues that the therapist must stand by first making intersubjective connections to each version of the patient's self. It is through the therapist's dialogue with each version that dialogue between them begins to emerge. Can one think of a better way of doing this than to engage each with the fresh authenticity of the improvisational? In this manner, versions of self become the audience members of other versions—or as I suggest to my patients, "You have a 'committee of mind' which works well or not depending on the degree to which each version of self gets its needs heard in relation to all of the rest."

Pursuing this line mitigates against a psychic world partitioned by vertical and horizontal splits, generating one in which reflective symbolization and negotiation bridges the gaps between heretofore disparate parts of self as has been so brilliantly articulated by Pizer (1998).

In one of the concluding comments in Stern's book, which parallels my arguing on behalf of analysts cultivating an improvisational attitude, Stern (2004) writes that,

> "Now moments" also carry a double danger. If not responded to and redirected toward another purpose, they can quickly lead to greater and more disruptive acting in. Additionally, they may provoke anxiety in the therapist, who responds by hiding behind technique which prevents the now moment from bearing much fruit. Acceptance of the now moment [what I am calling the improvisational] as not only a normal event in therapy, but also is a rare creative opportunity, changes the therapist's threshold for this kind of anxiety. This permits him or her to tolerate the situation with enough freedom to be more authentic and find a response that is well-suited to the specific situation and carries the therapist's personal signature. (p. 226)

Correspondingly, each moment in analysis is prospectively a new present remembering context (Stern, 2004). This is incredibly important because it theoretically posits that every moment is indeed improvised, understanding that improvisation very much is working with something of the person's character, only selecting, reassembling, and re-creating a version of the past that in fact occupies the present. In effect, this is playing improvisationally with the person's composition, or character. Grasping that therapy is a prospective proliferation of present remembering (improvisational) contexts helps us readily grasp degrees of invariance in our patients revisitation of the past upon the present and along with this, what their personal composition imposes on each "present moment." It is because of the potentially dynamic fluid nature of present remembering in terms of its selection and assemblage of past facts that the structure of transference is potentially mutable. This makes possible newly assembled recollections and revisions of past interpretations, and this makes possible new encounters with the "past" in the present. Such recollections are especially powerful when they arise spontaneously in play, thereby playing with transference, that is, moving it out of a model of stasis and into one of ongoing, transformative process.

Comparatively, this is what is so daunting in the treatment of trauma. The trauma victim often involuntarily "rehearses" the trauma over and over in a manner that makes it become a fixture of narrative, that is, a version of personhood that remains invariant across a multitude of present remembering contexts holding everyone, including oneself, "hostage." In this manner, it can defy or ward off improvisational reselection and assembly of the past elements in the present. Improvisation with trauma victims can feel like a perilous venture to both parties, but nevertheless can be an important means for playfully introducing new possibilities.

Shifting focus, sometimes one of the best ways to study a subject is to study its opposite, or in this case, what improvisation is not. It is certainly not a slapdash, fly-by-the-seat-of-your-pants ramshackle affair. Upon my return from participating in a day-long seminar on improvisation in negotiation at the Harvard Business School, I was asked by my then thirteen-year-old daughter Lena, a pianist, what is meant by improvisation. I walked over to her piano and began randomly striking its keys. I turned to her and said, "It's not that!" I then began singing the standard happy birthday song to her but at a certain point broke off into a different harmonic scheme, also changing the rhythm and tone. I was showing her that improvisation is always playing off of some other composition, but changing it in a way that preserves something of a connection, even identity to the original, while dramatically changing it. That is what I think psychotherapy and psychoanalysis does.

Every time we meet with a patient, we instantly become something of a duet—pick your favorite metaphor—as musicians, dancers, boxers, etc. In all of these cases, each and every meeting between us is about informing each other about the old—that is, laying down our old scores, our old compositions, our old steps, our old punches—with the prospective of co-creating new ones that may well become tomorrow's new "old" composition, such as in classical analysts' admonition that Friday's breakthrough insight becomes Monday morning's first line of resistance.

Now if you are going to play with my metaphor, then you are going to have to ask yourself, Where did the music between us stop? Where did we stumble? How did I miss that jab? All of these questions ask this single question: Where did the free flow of our thinking, feeling, and expressing ourselves gum up and bog down? You have to look seriously at your participation in this, but hopefully now with a sense of excitement, because after all, all we're doing here is figuring out how to dance together, to sing together, to spar, and to think and feel and express our selves as freely as possible. And, at any moment, like in jazz, it can be perfectly appropriate for us to solo off of the harmonic structure we just wrote together, though to do so, we must also be tracking our roles in the leading and following of such riffs. When we are on track, we are best stationed to catch moments of split complementarity—for example, who is hogging the microphone, so to speak—which may be our signal of intersubjective anxiety (Stern, 2004) either in our patients, ourselves, or in both.

One more brief vignette may help show how improvisation plays with one kind of affectivity on a surface plane—often a defensive one—that through the play removes the necessity of the defense, at least for that moment, enabling the presentation of the defended against affect. Here is an example: "I think that I am angry with you over last week's session," my typically nonconfrontational forty-five-year-old Eastern European engineer patient "Sami" tells me. In his mannered style, compensating for his self-consciously thick accent he continues, "I think that I am angry that you were suggesting that I should have more feeling about my mother being hospitalized after her heart attack. I am wondering," he continues, "Who do you think you are to tell me how I should feel? Or, that I should feel anything when I don't!" "Who am I indeed?" I ponder aloud. Sami ignores my question and continues, "And, besides, what good is it for me to feel?! How is that supposed to solve my problems—the problem I came to you for, like my procrastination?" "I am not sure," I venture, "but tell me more about my telling you how you should feel?"[2] "It's not very good psychoanalysis, you know. It's not 'exploring my core issues.'" "So, it looks like I am being more 'Dr. Phil'[3] than Dr. Phil." "Or maybe it's because I am not as important to you as some of your other patients." "How come?" I inquire. "Because they are more successful than me, you care about them more. They are more important to you." "You mean like my rich Hollywood celebrities?" "Yeah, like 'George.'" "You mean George Clooney?" I ask wryly. "No, more like George Hamilton. You would only see B-actors whose careers are mostly over." We're now smiling at one another as if engaged in a wicked game of ping-pong. "Now is that because I practice in the Valley, instead of Beverly Hills?" "Maybe," he retorts, "Just the 'has-beens' live in the Valley." Then he stops abruptly and questions aloud, "Where is all of this coming from?!" as if he is channeling a demon heretofore never given voice. "Let's not worry about that now, just keep going," I encourage. Sami says, "Yeah, so no truly successful actor would come to see you! Actually, they wouldn't come to see anyone in L.A." "How come?" I wonder. "It's too nice here, the weather is too good, it's too sunny. You'd have to go to New York for a good psychoanalysis, where it's cold, and rainy, and dark, and gloomy, and depressing, where the analysts would all be depressed and understand you." Then Sami's expression shifts markedly to one of sadness. "I feel like crying. I won't, not here, but for the first time, I feel like maybe I could, maybe someday, maybe here too."

Several points about this improvisational form of relational psychoanalysis bear repeating. First, improvisation is more than just about being spontaneous. It is ensemble work that plays off and with patterns emergent in the personalities of both parties. These patterns illuminate something about the unconscious of each, thus improvisational moments constitute configurations of a co-creative, relational unconscious, a kind of thirdness, in which both parties are distinctive authors, yet neither can lay exclusive claim to being the sole author of their improvised moment, a moment from which blossom things heretofore unimagined or unarticulated.

In our improvisational moment, here was Sami's and my challenge, though one that was only knowable in retrospect. To access Sami's complicated grief over a mother for whom he has had a very tormented and bitter relationship, a grief that remains unformulated and unarticulated—an unthought known—Sami and I had to first engage in a kind of sadomasochistic play, a kind of playing with his aggressive defensives against recognizing these obscure thoughts and feelings. To do so, we discovered ourselves engaging in an improvisational scene in which we both had to be able to encounter themes of our respective feelings of inadequacy. Sami had to be free to spontaneously enunciate his need to see me as profoundly lacking, and I had to be able to sincerely play along with his challenge. To do so we had to both accept the stereotypical charges of our respective second-class citizenships. He had to face feeling like an "eminently ignorable immigrant," and I, a "comparatively inferior psychoanalyst." And, for this play to be experienced as real there had to be some part of each of us that could feel our second-class status without it puncturing either of us. What enables the analyst and analysand to engage in such a manner that inoculates their respective narcissistic injuries? I submit that it is the cultivation of a play space, similar to the one that children naturally convene, and that is one in which "bang, bang, you're dead" can be taken deadly seriously without anyone really dying.

Improvisational moments, however, are not the only unpredictable moments, so too are their results. Sometimes their impact can be extraordinary, as in the notion of positraums I have described in far greater detail (Ringstrom, 2007a, 2007b) wherein an event can occur, almost always in an unpremeditated fashion that has the effect of dramatically altering a patient's entrenched emotional conviction. The Pizers (2004) independently wrote about this phenomenon as "positive traumas." What the Pizers and I are positing is that when something dramatically positive happens that cannot be assimilated within the patient's intransigently negative belief system, that positive event forces the accommodation of a new organizing principle, that is, a new emotional conviction.

The impact of improvisational moments is also about slow accretions of change, tiny moments of chipping away at seemingly invariant organization, a notable example being Michael Scott's resistance as exemplified at the beginning of this chapter. The writers of *The Office* clearly understood this when they made it clear that Michael's character, though visibly impacted by his instructor's improvisation, was only minimally impacted. In a later scene in the same episode, played with an Asian classmate-actor, we witness that in the midst of their scene Michael quickly leans over and whispers something into his scene partner's ear. Suddenly, the Asian actor throws his hands over his head in the position of someone being arrested.

The flabbergasted class instructor abruptly stops the scene and queries the actor about what he is doing, to which he replies, "Michael whispered that he has another hidden gun!"

REFERENCES

Bacal, H., & Thompson, P. (1996). The psychoanalyst's selfobject needs and the effect of their frustration on the treatment: A new view of countertransference. In A. Goldberg (Ed.), *Progress in self psychology, volume 12*. Hillsdale, NJ: Analytic Press.

Benjamin, J. (2004). Beyond doer and done to: Recognition and the intersubjective third. *Psychoanal. Quar., 73*(1), 5–46.

Bion, W. (1967). Notes on memory and desire. *Psychoanalytic Forum, 2*, 272–273.

Bollas, C. (1987). *The shadow of the object: Psychoanalysis of the unthought known*. New York: Columbia University Press.

Boston Change Process Study Group: Bruschweiler-Stern, N., Harrison, A., Nahum, J., Sander, L., Stern, D., & Tronick, E. (2002). Explicating the implicit: The local level and the microprocess of change in the analytic situation. *Int. J. Psychoanal., 83*, 1051–1062.

Brandchaft, B. (1993). To free the spirit from its cell. In R. Stolorow, G. Atwood, & B. Brandchaft (Eds.), *The intersubjective perspective*. Northvale, NJ: Jason Aronson.

Bromberg, P. (1998). *Standing in spaces: Essays on dissociation, trauma and clinical process*. Hillsdale, NJ: Analytic Press.

Buber, M. (1923). *I and thou*. New York: Scribners, 1970.

Davies, J. (1998). Multiple perspectives on multiplicity. *Psychoanal. Dial, 8*(2), 195–206.

Davies, J. (2004). Whose bad objects are these anyway?: Repetition and our elusive love affair with evil. *Psychoanal. Dial., 14*(6), 711–732.

Davies, J. (2005). Transformations of desire and despair, termination and a dissociative model of mind. Paper presented at the IARPP Conference in Rome, Italy, June 26, 2005.

Hoffman, I. (1998). *Ritual and spontaneity in the psychoanalytic process: A dialectical constructivist view*. Hillsdale, NJ: Analytic Press.

Kohut, H., (1984). *How does analysis cure?* Ed. A. Goldberg. Chicago: University of Chicago Press.

Knoblauch, S. (2000). *The musical edge of therapeutic dialogue*. Hillsdale, NJ: The Analytic Press.

Knoblauch, S. (2001). High risk, high gain: Commentary on paper by Philip A. Ringstrom. *Psychoanal. Dial, 11*(5), 785–795.

Knoblauch, S. (2004). Body rhythms and improvisation: Playing with the music behind the lyrics in psychoanalysis. Paper presented at the twenty-seventh Annual International Conference on the Psychology of the Self.

Lichtenberg, J. D., Lachmann, F. L., & Fosshage, J. L. (1992). *Self and motivational systems: Towards a theory of psychoanalytic technique, vol. 13*. Hillsdale, NJ: Analytic Press.

Lichtenberg, J. D., Lachmann, F. L., & Fosshage, J. L. (1996). *The clinical exchange: Techniques derived from self and motivational systems*. Hillsdale, NJ: Analytic Press.

Mitchell, S. (1993). *Hope and dread in psychoanalysis.* New York: Basic Books.
Mitchell, S. (1997). *Influence and autonomy.* Hillsdale, NJ: Analytic Press.
Ogden, T. (1994). *Subjects of analysis.* Northvale, NJ: Jason Aronson, Inc.
Orange, D., Atwood, G., & Stolorow, R. (1997). *Working intersubjectively: Contextualism in psychoanalytic practice.* Hillsdale, NJ: Analytic Press.
Pizer, S. (1998). *Building bridges: The negotiation of paradox in psychoanalysis.* Hillsdale, NJ: Analytic Press.
Pizer, B. (2003). When the crunch is a (k)not: A crimp in relational dialogue. *Psychoanal. Dial., 13*(2), 193–204.
Pizer, B. (2005a). The heart of the matter in matters of the heart: Power and intimacy in analytic and couples relationships. Paper presented at the sixteenth Annual Conference for the Psychotherapies Training Institute, Behind Closed Doors: The Power of Intimacy in the Personal and Analytic Relationship, New York, February 5, 2005.
Pizer, S. (2005b). The shock of recognition: What my grandfather taught me about psychoanalytic process. Paper presented at the sixteenth Annual Conference for the Psychotherapies Training Institute, Behind Closed Doors: The Power of Intimacy in the Personal and Analytic Relationship, New York, February 5, 2005.
Ringstrom, P. (1995). Exploring the model scene: Finding the focus in an intersubjective approach to brief psychotherapy. *Psychoanalytic Inquiry, 15*(4), 493–513.
Ringstrom, P. (2001a). The noxious third: The crimes and misdemeanors in the treatment of Tony Soprano and Dr. Jennifer Melfi. Paper presented at the twenty-first Annual Spring Meeting of Division of Psychoanalysis, Santa Fe, NM.
Ringstrom, P. (2001b). Cultivating the improvisational in psychoanalytic treatment. *Psychoanal. Dial., 11*(5), 727–754.
Ringstrom, P. (2001c). "Yes, and. . . ."—How improvisation is the essence of good psychoanalytic dialogue: Reply to commentaries. *Psychoanal. Dial., 11*(5), 797–806.
Ringstrom, P. (2003). "Crunches," "(k)nots," and double binds—When what isn't happening is the most important thing: Commentary on paper by Barbara Pizer. *Psychoanal. Dial., 13*(2), 193–204.
Ringstrom, P. (2007a). Scenes that write themselves: Improvisational moments in relational psychoanalysis. *Psychoanal. Dial., 17*(1).
Ringstrom, P. (2007b). Reply to Stern's comments on "Scenes that write themselves: Improvisational moments in relational psychoanalysis." *Psychoanal. Dial., 17*(1).
Stern, D. N. (2004). *The present moment in psychotherapy and everyday life.* New York: W. W. Norton.
Stolorow, R., Brandchaft, B., & Atwood, G. (1987). *Psychoanalytic treatment: An intersubjective approach.* New Jersey: Analytic Press.
Stolorow, R., & Atwood, G. (1994). *The intersubjective perspective.* Northvale, NJ: Jason Aronson.
Stolorow, R., Atwood, G., & Orange, D. (2002). *Worlds of experience: Interweaving philosophical and clinical dimensions in psychoanalysis.* New York: Basic Books.

NOTES

1. Noting from Bacal and Thompson (1996) that the analyst also has selfobject needs, an important self psychological contribution is that this fittedness in the improvisational moment pertains to the meeting of both the patient's and analyst's selfobject needs. Fundamental to the improvisational moment is the instantiation of each one's sense of cohesion, continuity, and worth. Such intersubjectively intertwined selfobject configurations are the substance of connectedness between the two parties. One can picture this in terms of a kind of Venn diagram in which aspects of each one's sense of self overlaps with the other's (Kohut, et al., 1984). This mutual looping becomes part of the relational unconscious script that emerges between them.

2. So far as I recall I never told Sami anything about how he should feel. This raises an interesting question, one Steve Mitchell often introduced, which is what might have been unwittingly revealed nonverbally about a range of feelings I was wondering that Sami might have, or could have, or might have difficulty experiencing, and how might that be insinuated in my facial expression as an implied directive?

3. Dr. Phil is a television celebrity psychotherapist who, after minimal exploration of his guest-patient's issue du jour, instantaneously dispenses the pabulum of daily advice sandwiched between commercial breaks and the show's end credits.

Index

About the Contributors

Peter Buirski is Dean of the Graduate School of Professional Psychology at the University of Denver. Dr. Buirski holds Diplomates in both Clinical Psychology and Psychoanalysis from the American Board of Professional Psychology. He is a clinical professor in the Psychiatry Department of the University of Colorado Health Sciences Center and he is on the faculty of the Denver Institute for Psychoanalysis. Dr. Buirski is a member of the International Council of the International Association of Psychoanalytic Self Psychology. He is the coauthor with Pamela Haglund of *Making Sense Together: The Intersubjective Approach to Psychotherapy* and is the author of *Practicing Intersubjectively*. He sees adults and couples in private practice in Denver, Colorado.

William J. Coburn is editor-in-chief of the *International Journal of Psychoanalytic Self Psychology* and is an editorial board member of *Psychoanalytic Inquiry*. He is a faculty member and training and supervising analyst at the Institute of Contemporary Psychoanalysis in Los Angeles and at the Northwestern Center for Psychoanalysis in Portland, Oregon. He is a council member of the International Association for Psychoanalytic Self Psychology and an advisory board member of the International Association for Relational Psychoanalysis and Psychotherapy. He has researched and written extensively in the areas of intersubjectivity, complexity, countertransference, and supervision.

Shelley R. Doctors, clinical psychologist and psychoanalyst, is a faculty member and supervising analyst at the Institute for the Psychoanalytic Study of Subjectivity (New York City) and the Institute for Contemporary

Psychoanalysis and Psychotherapy (Washington, D.C.). A member of the International Council for Psychoanalytic Self Psychology and the advisory board of the International Association for Relational Psychoanalysis and Psychotherapy, she has recently completed twelve years as secretary of the International Society for Adolescent Psychiatry and Psychology. Her many articles and chapters appear in psychoanalytic and adolescent journals and texts and often draw on developmental themes. "Interpretation as a Relational Process," will appear in a forthcoming issue of the *International Journal of Psychoanalytic Self Psychology*.

Jacqueline Gotthold is a supervisor, faculty member, and coordinator of admissions at the Institute for the Psychoanalytic Study of Subjectivity (IPSS). She is also a faculty member and supervisor at the National Institute for the Psychotherapies' (NIP) Child and Adolescent training program and the National Training Program. She is the author and coauthor of several articles and presentations on the explicit and implicit dimensions of psychoanalytic treatment, as well as, on the child and adolescent psychoanalytic treatment process. She is in private practice treating children, adolescents, and adults.

Arthur A. Gray is a psychoanalyst in private practice in New York City. He teaches and supervises at the Jewish Board for Family and Children's Services, Postgraduate Center for Mental Health, and the Training Institute for Mental Health. His latest publication is "Effective and Efficient Supervision: Doing it in Group" appearing in *Power Games: Influence, Persuasion, and Indoctrination in Psychotherapy Training*. He has other publications on individual and group psychoanalysis, and supervision.

Amy Joelson is faculty and supervisor at the National Institute for the Psychotherapies (NIP), recipient of the 2005 Educators Award from NIP, and member of the Institute for the Psychoanalytic Study of Subjectivity. She has a private practice in New York City in adult, child, and adolescent psychotherapy and psychoanalysis.

Rosalind Chaplin Kindler is a child and adolescent psychotherapist in private practice in Toronto. She is director of the Toronto Child Psychoanalytic Program where she also serves as faculty member and supervisor. She is past president of the Canadian Association of Psychoanalytic Child Therapists. Ros is a registered drama therapist with a background in theatre and drama. She has presented and published in the field of adult and child psychoanalytic psychotherapy and has a special interest in bridging the gap between the worlds of child and adult psychoanalytic practice.

Amanda Kottler is a council member of the International Association for Psychoanalytic Self Psychology, an international editor (South Africa) of the *International Journal of Psychoanalytic Self Psychology*, and a founding member of the Cape Town Psychoanalytic Self Psychology Group. Previously a faculty member at the University of Cape Town, she is now in full-time private practice and is actively involved in teaching and supervising in the areas of Self Psychology and Intersubjectivity. She is a coeditor of *Culture, Power & Difference: Discourse Analysis in South Africa* and has written about the dilemmas facing progressive psychologists working within the multiple and contradictory discourses of race, gender and identity in South Africa.

Carla Leone is on the faculty of the Institute of Clinical Social Work in Chicago and is the director of a group private practice in Skokie, Illinois specializing in the treatment of children, adolescents, adults, couples, and families. She is the author of two articles on the application of self psychology to couples and family therapy and has been a regular presenter at the annual International Conference on the Psychology of the Self.

Andrew P. Morrison is associate clinical professor of psychiatry, Harvard Medical School; supervising analyst at the Massachusetts Institute for Psychoanalysis; faculty, Boston Psychoanalytic Society and Institute. He is author or editor of three books on shame, including *Shame, the Underside of Narcissism*, and many papers in psychoanalysis and psychotherapy. His clinical practice is in Cambridge, Massachusetts.

Donna Orange is a training and supervising analyst and faculty member at ISIPSe (*Istituto di Specializzazione in Psicologia Psicoanalitica del Se e Psicoanalisi Relazionale, Roma* [Institute for Specialization in the Psychoanalytic Psychology of the Self and Relational Psychoanalysis]); faculty and supervising analyst, Institute for the Psychoanalytic Study of Subjectivity, New York. She is author of *Emotional Understanding: Studies in Psychoanalytic Psychology*, and with George Atwood and Robert Stolorow, of *Working Intersubjectively: Contextualism in Psychoanalytic Practice.*

Philip A. Ringstrom is a senior training and supervising analyst and faculty member at the Institute of Contemporary Psychoanalysis in Los Angeles, where he is in full time private practice. He is on the editorial boards both of *Psychoanalytic Dialogues: International Journal of Relational Perspectives* and *International Journal of Psychoanalytic Self Psychology.* He is a member of the *International Council of Self-Psychologists* and on the board of directors of IARPP—the *International Association of Relational Psychoanalysis and Psychotherapy.*

Ellen Shumsky is faculty and supervisor at the Institute for Contemporary Psychotherapy, the Psychoanalytic Psychotherapy Study Center, and the Training and Research Institute for Self Psychology, all in New York City. She has co-authored numerous articles extending fundamental theoretical ideas from relational self psychology and intersubjective systems theory. Her ongoing interest is in how these expanded ideas both shape and find expression in micromoments of clinical process.

Dorienne Sorter is cochair, faculty member and supervisor at the Institute for the Psychoanalytic Study of Subjectivity and faculty of the Psychoanalytic Psychotherapy Study Center in New York. She is coauthor of *Forms of Intersubjectivity in Infant Research and Adult Treatment*. She has also published several articles and made numerous presentations on the application of infant research to adult psychoanalytic treatment.

Maxwell S. Sucharov is a founding board member of the Western Canada Psychoanalytic Psychotherapy Association. He is an active member of the self psychology/intersubjectivity community and has contributed numerous articles and chapters to psychoanalytic publications including *The Intersubjective Perspective, Progress in Self Psychology,* and *Psychoanalytic Inquiry*. He lives and practices in Vancouver, Canada.

Judith Teicholz is a supervising analyst and faculty member at the Massachusetts Institute for Psychoanalysis. She is author of *Kohut, Loewald and the Postmoderns* and editor (with Dan Kriegman) of *Trauma, Repetition, and Affect Regulation*. She is on the editorial board of the *International Journal of Psychoanalytic Self Psychology* and from 1978 to 1999 was on the Harvard Medical School Faculty in Psychiatry and Psychology at Massachusetts General Hosptial.

www.ingramcontent.com/pod-product-compliance
Ingram Content Group UK Ltd.
Pitfield, Milton Keynes, MK11 3LW, UK
UKHW012034150926
475560UK00001B/8

9 780765 704351